Inventions

a children's encyclopedia

Inventions

a children's encyclopedia

DK London
Senior Editor Carron Brown
Senior Art Editor Rachael Grady
Editorial team Ann Baggaley, Ashwin Khurana, Camilla Hallinan, Jessica Cawthra, Sarah Edwards
Art Editors Chrissy Barnard, Louise Dick
Jacket Designer Surabhi Wadhwa-Gandhi
Jacket Editor Claire Gell
Jacket Design Development Manager Sophia MTT
Producer, Pre-production Gillian Reid
Senior Producer Angela Graef
Managing Editor Francesca Baines
Managing Art Editor Philip Letsu
Publisher Andrew Macintyre
Associate Publishing Director Liz Wheeler
Art Director Karen Self
Design Director Phil Ormerod
Publishing Director Jonathan Metcalf

DK Delhi
Senior Editor Sreshtha Bhattacharya
Senior Art Editor Ira Sharma
Project Editor Priyanka Kharbanda
Editorial team Ankona Das, Neha Ruth Samuel, Rupa Rao, Vatsal Verma
Art Editors Heena Sharma, Mansi Agrawal, Sachin Singh, Shailee Khurana
Jacket Designer Juhi Sheth
Jackets Editorial Coordinator Priyanka Sharma
Senior DTP Designer Harish Aggarwal
DTP Designers Sachin Gupta, Mohd Rizwan, Vikram Singh, Bimlesh Tiwary
Picture Researchers Nishwan Rasool, Deepak Negi
Managing Jackets Editor Saloni Singh
Picture Research Manager Taiyaba Khatoon
Pre-production Manager Balwant Singh
Production Manager Pankaj Sharma
Managing Editor Kingshuk Ghoshal
Managing Art Editor Govind Mittal

Written by John Farndon, Jacob Field, Joe Fullman, Giles Sparrow, and Andrew Humphreys
Consultant: Roger Bridgman

First published in Great Britain in 2018 by
Dorling Kindersley Limited
80 Strand, London, WC2R 0RL

Copyright © 2018 Dorling Kindersley Limited
A Penguin Random House Company
10 9 8 7 6 5 4 3 2 1
001–308121–July/2018

A CIP catalogue record for this book is available from the British Library.
ISBN: 978-0-2413-1782-2

Printed and bound in China

A WORLD OF IDEAS:
SEE ALL THERE IS TO KNOW

www.dk.com

Contents

EARLY
BREAKTHROUGHS

Simple stone tools were probably the first things invented by our ancestors. Other great ideas such as the wheel changed our lives for ever.

Early tools

Our earliest human ancestors appeared in Africa more than two million years ago. Scientists gave them the Latin name *Homo habilis*, which means "handy man", because they are believed to have made and used stone tools – the very first invention. As humans evolved, they developed increasingly complex tools for a variety of tasks.

Flint arrowhead, c.4000 BCE

STONE TOOLS

Early people made tools by striking round pieces of stone, such as flint or quartz, with another hard stone. This shaped the stones into hand-held tools that had a wide range of uses, including chopping, scraping, and engraving. The best-known early tool was the hand axe, which could be used to dig, kill prey, carve meat, and chop wood.

Axe was shaped by chipping flakes off a stone

HUNTING FROM A DISTANCE

Humans needed weapons for hunting. Among the first weapons invented were wooden spears tipped with sharp stones, developed more than 400,000 years ago. These allowed hunters to attack prey from a distance, which was safer than getting up close to large and dangerous animals. Around 60,000–70,000 years ago, the first bow and arrow weapons were invented, which had an even longer range.

Harpoon made of deer antler, c.6500–4000 BCE

Hand axe from around 1.5 million years ago

MAKING FIRE

Fire was vital for cooking food as well as providing warmth and light. More than 6,000 years ago, probably in Egypt, prehistoric people invented the bow drill for lighting fires. The device was rotated to cause friction, which produced enough heat to burn small particles.

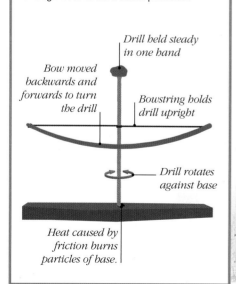

Drill held steady in one hand

Bow moved backwards and forwards to turn the drill

Bowstring holds drill upright

Drill rotates against base

Heat caused by friction burns particles of base.

Egyptian copperworkers

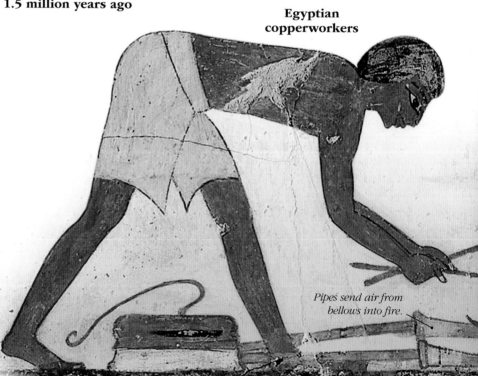

Pipes send air from bellows into fire.

METAL TOOLS

By around 3500 BCE, people in Europe, Asia, and Africa were using metal. This was a far better material than stone because it was easier to shape and work with and kept a sharper edge. At first, metalworkers used copper and bronze, but from 1200 BCE they started to use iron. Metal could be used to make many things, including weapons, armour, agricultural equipment, jewellery, nails, and cooking pots.

Copper blade bound to a wooden shaft with leather strings

Prehistoric copper axe

Bronze cutting edge

Bronze Age sickle

Iron Age sickle

This sickle would have been attached to a wooden handle.

WOW!

The earliest stone tools, known as the "Oldowan toolkit", are 2.6 million years old. They were found in the Olduvai Gorge in Africa.

▶ **FARMING TOOLS**
While sickles were commonly used for harvesting cereal crops, axes were used to clear forested areas for farming. These three examples show copper, bronze, and iron tools.

MELTING AND MIXING

Before metals can be made into anything, they have to be "smelted". In this process, metal ores (rocks that naturally contain metal) are heated over a very hot fire to remove unwanted substances. Once people had found out how to extract metals, they went on to discover that mixed metals could create a stronger material, called an alloy. The first alloy invented was bronze, which was made by adding tin to copper.

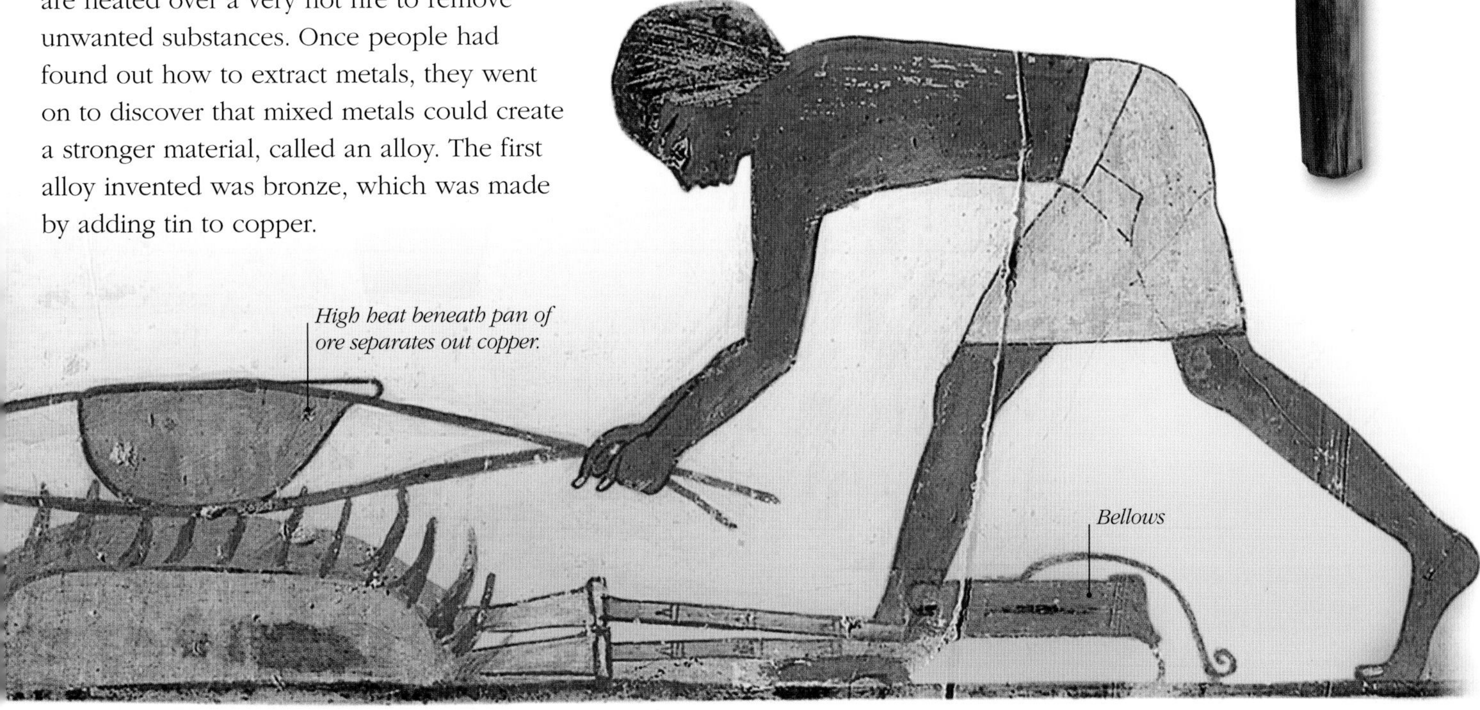

High heat beneath pan of ore separates out copper.

Bellows

Farming

For thousands of years, our ancestors were hunter-gatherers, constantly roaming the land to hunt animals and collect wild plants for food. Around 12,000 years ago, people in the Middle East began to live in settled farming communities. This settling-down process was known as the "Agricultural Revolution", and it gave people a more certain supply of food. By 500 BCE, agriculture had spread across most of the world.

BETTER CROPS

Ancient farmers found out that by planting only the largest and best wild species they could gradually improve their crops, a system known as domestication. In the Middle East, people grew wheat or barley developed from wild grasses. In the Americas, the most important crop was maize (corn), which was domesticated by 7000 BCE.

◄ PRIMITIVE TO MODERN

The primitive type of corn (left) was developed to become the much bigger modern corn (right).

THE FERTILE CRESCENT

The first farmers lived in the region of Mesopotamia, in modern-day southern Iraq. This was located between two rivers – the Tigris and the Euphrates – where crops grew well in the rich soil and domesticated animals thrived. By 9000 BCE, farming had spread across the Middle East in a crescent-shaped area that reached into Egypt.

Map labels:
MESOPOTAMIA
Mediterranean Sea
Euphrates
Tigris
Western Desert
Syrian Desert
Nile
Red Sea
EGYPT
ARABIAN PENINSULA
INDIAN OCEAN
■ Fertile Crescent

HARROW

One of the first important farming inventions was the harrow. This rake-like tool was used after ploughing to break up the soil and smooth out the surface. It made planting crops easier. The first harrows were made of wood, but later, iron was used.

Pulled by animals, often in pairs, the plough could quickly slice through hard soil.

Model of a Sumerian plough

PLOUGH

The plough was developed in East Asia by 5000 BCE. It was a blade attached to a wooden frame that prepared soil by cutting through the top layer, which brought nutrients to the surface. Ploughing created trenches, called furrows, where seeds were planted.

PERSIAN *QANAT*

Water is essential to farming. In dry regions, some kind of system is needed to bring water to agricultural areas. In the early first millennium, the Persians did this by building underground canals. Called *qanats*, these canals sloped gently, helping gravity move the water. A *qanat* was usually around 5 km (3 miles) long, but some measured more than 65 km (40 miles).

Shaft is used for maintenance.

Watered area

Qanat *carries water for distribution.*

This well is the main source of water.

Qanat outlet

▼ SOIL PREPARATION
Farm implements, including the harrow, were usually hitched to oxen, like this one, or horses. Such animals were domesticated to help with farmwork and were used for food.

Clay model of a granary, China, c.150 BCE

Storing grain above ground level helps to keep it dry and at the right temperature.

Second level could be reached by a staircase.

GRANARY

In around 9000 BCE, the first grain stores, or granaries, were built in what is now modern-day Jordan. These buildings were designed to store dry grain and other crops, such as rice, so they wouldn't spoil. People needed places to store crops that they didn't want to eat or sell right away.

Inventing the wheel

The wheel is one of the most important things ever invented, although no one knows who first thought of it. Originally, wheels helped potters to make perfectly round pots. Then, around 3500 BCE, someone had the idea of using them to move people and materials around on land. The wheel completely changed everyday life, making it easier for people to travel, trade, and work.

Wooden peg keeps the axle in place.

Crosspiece holds the planks together.

ROLLER AND SLEDGE

Before the wheel, heavy objects were sometimes transported using the "roller and sledge" method. The sledge was a platform placed on top of a number of round logs. As people dragged the sledge along, others continually moved the last roller to the front. It was hard work, but the load shifted.

Rolling creates less friction (force created when two surfaces touch) than sliding.

Ancient Egyptian workers moving a load to build pyramids

POTTER'S WHEEL

The Mesopotamians, who lived in the region known today as Iraq, are believed to be the first people to make wheels, possibly as early as 5000 BCE. These wheels were discs of stone or clay used in pottery making. Wet clay was placed on the wheel, which was then turned by hand while the potter shaped the clay into pots or other vessels.

Wheel

Ancient Egyptian model of a potter

DISC WHEEL

The earliest wheels to be used for transportation were solid discs made from wooden planks. They were attached to simple carts, wagons, and chariots that were pulled by horses or oxen. Travel on these vehicles would have been rough and bumpy.

Handle used for pushing or pulling cart

Chinese wheelbarrow

WHEELBARROW

The wheelbarrow may have been invented either in ancient Greece between the 6th–4th centuries BCE or in China during the 2nd century CE. While the Greek wheelbarrow had a wheel towards the front, as many barrows do today, the Chinese placed the wheel in the middle.

PRAYER WHEELS

Prayer wheels are an important part of Buddhism, one of the world's major religions. These wheels are hollow metal cylinders containing a scroll printed with a mantra (a holy verse or phrase). Buddhists believe that spinning the wheel, or letting it turn in the wind, is the same as saying a prayer out loud.

Model of wheel shaped from three wooden planks, c.2000 BCE

WHEEL AND AXLE

In most vehicles today, the wheels driven by the engine are attached to cylindrical shafts, or axles. When the vehicle moves, the shafts and wheels rotate together. The axles of the other wheels are fixed to the vehicle and move with it. On the earliest vehicles, all the axles were fixed to the wheels.

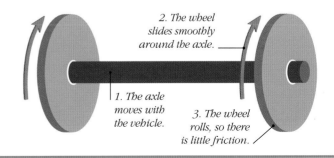

2. The wheel slides smoothly around the axle.

1. The axle moves with the vehicle.

3. The wheel rolls, so there is little friction.

Travelling by road

The use of wheeled vehicles for movement on land began more than 5,000 years ago. These vehicles were usually pulled by animals (although sometimes people did the hauling themselves). There were various types of early carts and wagons, some of which carried passengers and goods while others were designed for use in warfare.

War wagon

- **What?** Sumerian battle chariot
- **Who?** Unknown
- **Where and when?** Mesopotamia, c.2500 BCE

The Sumerians, people whose homeland is now modern-day Iraq, invented a war wagon with four solid wooden disc wheels. It was pulled by onagers (Asian asses) and used to carry important leaders into battle. The wagon also provided a platform on which soldiers armed with javelins could stand.

Early wheeled cart

- **What?** Two-wheeled vehicle
- **Who?** Unknown
- **Where and when?** Mesopotamia, c.3000 BCE

Among the earliest land vehicles were simple two-wheeled carts that were pulled by one or two large domesticated animals such as oxen or horses. They were developed in several different places, especially Mesopotamia (now mainly in Iraq), the Caucasus (a region between Europe and Asia), and Eastern Europe, at around the same time. Later, the use of wheeled carts spread further, reaching Africa and Asia.

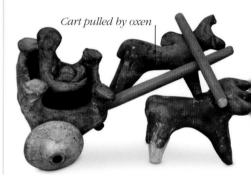

Cart pulled by oxen

Terracotta figurine from an ancient site in the Indus Valley (in Pakistan), c.2400 BCE

War wagon depicted on a decorated box from the ancient Mesopotamian city of Ur, c.2500 BCE

Trade wagon

- **What?** Covered wagon
- **Who?** Unknown
- **Where and when?** Eurasia, c.2500 BCE

Four-wheeled wagons were common across Europe and Asia by 2500 BCE. Hitched to teams of powerful animals, they could transport very heavy loads. Such wagons had a protective cover and were ideal for use by people trading goods or riding as passengers.

The cover protected the goods or passengers.

Model of a covered wagon, c.2400–2300 BCE

Egyptian chariot

- **What?** Two-wheeled chariot
- **Who?** Unknown
- **Where and when?** Egypt, c.1600 BCE

Chariots were the racing cars of the ancient world. These small, two-wheeled, horse-drawn vehicles usually carried just two people. The Mesopotamians were the first to develop chariots, but the Egyptians made improvements by using spoked wheels instead of solid wooden ones.

This reduced the vehicle's weight and made it swifter and easier to drive.

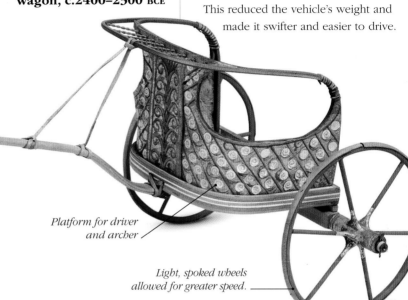

Yoke pulled by two horses

▲ LIGHTWEIGHT WAR CHARIOT
War chariots, built to be fast and highly steerable, provided a mobile platform that carried archers rapidly around the battlefield.

Platform for driver and archer

Light, spoked wheels allowed for greater speed.

Carriage

- **What?** *Raeda*
- **Who?** Unknown
- **Where and when?** Rome, 2nd century BCE

The Romans built a road network across their empire. For travelling, they used the *raeda*, a four-wheeled vehicle pulled by up to 10 horses or mules. This could carry several passengers and their luggage, taking loads of around 350 kg (750 lb) and covering up to 25 km (15 miles) a day.

Coach services

- **What?** Stagecoach
- **Who?** Unknown
- **Where and when?** Europe, 17th century CE

The stagecoach, which first appeared in Britain, provided regular services over set routes between stops like a modern-day bus. With their shock-absorbing springs, and travelling on improved roads, coaches offered a less bumpy ride than earlier vehicles. Stagecoaches remained an important form of transport until the mid-19th century, when they were replaced by the railways.

A closed coach carries passengers or goods inside.

Team of four horses

Engraving of a stagecoach, 19th century

Sailing the seas

People first started travelling by water more than 10,000 years ago. To begin with, their boats were simple canoes and rafts propelled with oars or poles. Over time, vessels became bigger and more complicated, fitted with sails of fabric or animal skin to capture the power of the wind. This made longer voyages possible, so people had to invent devices that told them where they were and in which direction they were heading.

The three ranks of rowers were positioned so their oars did not strike each other.

THE TRIREME

A ship mainly powered by three rows of oars, the trireme also had one or two sails. It was developed by either the Greeks or Phoenicians in around 700 BCE, and it enabled both civilizations to travel and trade across the Mediterranean Sea.

At the top, a mirror reflected sunlight by day, while at night a fire was lit.

GUIDING LIGHT

Lighthouses warn ships of dangers lying ahead and help guide them to safety. The first known was built on Pharos, a small island near the Egyptian city of Alexandria, in 280 BCE. Called the "Pharos of Alexandria", it stood around 110 m (360 ft) high and was one of the seven wonders of the ancient world.

Model of the Pharos of Alexandria

POLYNESIAN STICK CHART

The Polynesian peoples navigated across the vast expanse of the South Pacific, sailing between islands that were hundreds of kilometres apart. They mapped the position of islands, atolls (rings of coral), and ocean currents using charts made of strips of dried coconut leaf, wood, and shell.

IN THE RIGHT DIRECTION

The compass was invented in China in the 3rd century BCE. Modern instruments have a magnetized needle at the centre that works with Earth's magnetic field, so it always points to the north. Early compasses pointed south. From the 11th century CE, sailors began to use the compass at sea.

The compass's needle works only if it can spin freely.

Chinese compass, mid-19th century

The device is held by this ring.

NAVIGATING SEAS

Early mariners calculated their position at sea with a device called an astrolabe that measured the angle between objects in the sky, such as the Moon, and the horizon. Ancient Greeks may have designed early astrolabes around 200 BCE and they were definitely in use by the 7th century CE. The astrolabe was then improved by Muslim astronomers who used it to find the direction of Mecca, their holiest city.

Scale to measure the altitude of stars or planets above the horizon

▼ **MARINER'S ASTROLABE**
Invented in the 16th century CE, this device gave accurate readings on board ships at sea.

Rotating pointer fixed to the centre

Viewing hole through which the stars were observed

Heavy bottom to keep the device stable

Chinese junk

- ■ **What?** Chinese sailing ship
- ■ **Who?** Unknown
- ■ **Where and when?** China, c.2nd century CE

Early sailing boats, including junks, were designed in China and are used across Asia even today. They had square sails, held in place by pieces of wood called "battens", which allowed each sail to be pulled open or closed easily and quickly.

Modern Chinese junk

Longship

- ■ **What?** Viking ship
- ■ **Who?** Unknown
- ■ **Where and when?** Norway, c.9th century CE

The Norse people, also called the Vikings, of Scandinavia developed the longship. Vessels of this type were narrow and light enough to navigate up rivers but strong enough for the open sea. They could also navigate shallow waters. A longship had one large central sail and wooden oars for when there was little wind to power the boat.

The mast supports a big, square sail, which is made from wool or linen.

Model of a Viking longship

Sailing ships

The first wooden sailing ships were built in Egypt around 5,000 years ago, but across the world, other civilizations produced similar vessels. Until the 19th century, ships on sea voyages were mainly powered by wind captured in cloth sails. The vessels were used for trade, exploration, and war.

Sails were usually made of woven textiles.

Round ship

- **What?** Cog
- **Who?** Unknown
- **Where and when?** Northern Europe, c.10th century CE

One of the most common sea vessels in medieval Europe was the "round ship". A common round ship was the cog. This vessel had a design described as "clinker-built", meaning that the planks that made up the hull overlapped one another. Cogs were mostly used for trading because they were sturdy, easy to build, and had lots of space for cargo.

Model of a cog

Some cogs were converted into warships and had platforms added to their fore where sailors stood to fire arrows and cannon at enemies.

Treasure ship

Sails were made of strips of bamboo.

Model of Chinese explorer Zheng He's treasure boat

- **What?** Chinese treasure ship
- **Who?** Unknown
- **Where and when?** China, 15th century CE

From 1405 to 1433, the Chinese admiral Zheng He led seven "treasure voyages" across Asia and East Africa. His fleet was made up of dozens of "treasure ships". They had many sails and may have been around twice the size of European ships in use at the same time. These huge vessels carried treasures that displayed China's wealth and clever technology.

Completely armoured ship

- **What?** Korean turtle ship
- **Who?** Unknown
- **Where and when?** Korea, 15th century CE

The Koreans were the first to cover a ship's deck with armour plates to protect it from enemy missiles. Their so-called turtle ships were armed with many cannons. Some were mounted with a dragon's head at the prow that belched out a foggy gas to hide the ship's movements.

Upper deck, covered in spiky iron plates

Dragon's head may have hidden a cannon.

Model of a Korean turtle ship

Long-distance European ship

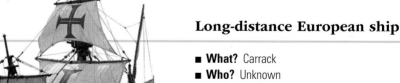

Replica of a medieval carrack

- **What?** Carrack
- **Who?** Unknown
- **Where and when?** Europe, 15th century CE

By the 15th century, the most common type of ship in Europe was the carrack. It was a large vessel that could sail on rough seas and carry enough provisions for a long journey. The Italian explorer Christopher Columbus used a carrack in 1492 for his voyage to America.

Archimedes

One of the greatest ancient inventors, Archimedes was also a brilliant mathematician and physicist. Born in the Greek city of Syracuse in Sicily in 287 BCE, it is believed he was sent to Egypt to be educated. Archimedes invented many important mechanical devices, including a pulley system that could lift enormous weights. His scientific writings are still useful to scholars today.

FIGHTING THE ROMANS

When Rome attacked Syracuse in 214 BCE, it is believed that two of Archimedes's inventions were used to defend his home city. The first used mirrors to focus the Sun's rays on the Roman ships and set fire to them. The second, called the "iron hand" (below), was a crane with a giant grappling-hook that could grab the ships and capsize them.

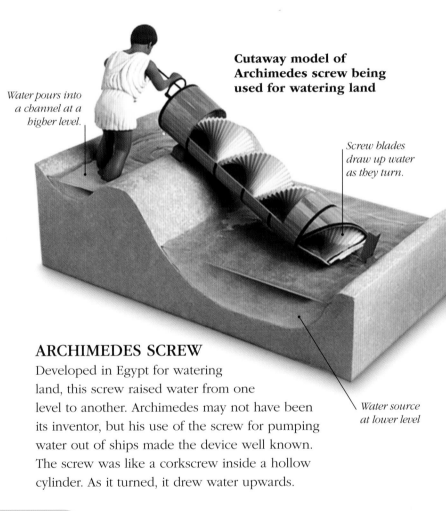

Cutaway model of Archimedes screw being used for watering land

Water pours into a channel at a higher level.

Screw blades draw up water as they turn.

Water source at lower level

Italian painting showing Archimedes's grappling-hook as a huge hand, 1600

ARCHIMEDES SCREW

Developed in Egypt for watering land, this screw raised water from one level to another. Archimedes may not have been its inventor, but his use of the screw for pumping water out of ships made the device well known. The screw was like a corkscrew inside a hollow cylinder. As it turned, it drew water upwards.

LIFE STORY

287 BCE	c.250 BCE	c.225 BCE	218 BCE
Archimedes is born in Syracuse, Sicily, at the time a Greek city-state. His father was an astronomer and mathematician.	He is believed to go to Egypt to study. Archimedes writes a paper on geometry called *On the Measurement of a Circle*, and another about fluids called *On Floating Bodies*.	He writes two other important works: *On Spirals* and *On the Sphere and the Cylinder*.	Second Punic War begins between Carthage and Rome. Archimedes's home, Syracuse, allies with Carthage.

TESTING GOLD FOR A KING

The king of Syracuse suspected his new crown was not pure gold and
wanted it tested. Archimedes put the crown into a tub of water, noting
that it displaced a greater volume of water than a piece of gold of the
same weight. This showed the crown contained other, less dense metals.

▲ EUREKA – I'VE GOT IT!
*Archimedes was the first to discover
that when an object is submerged, it
loses weight equal to the amount of
fluid it displaces. This insight is said
to have come to him in his bath.*

214 BCE	C.212 BCE		75 BCE
Roman forces begin to lay siege to Syracuse.	The Romans capture and destroy Syracuse. They kill Archimedes, although they had been ordered not to harm him.	**A Roman attacks Archimedes**	While visiting Sicily, the famous Roman writer Cicero finds that Archimedes's elaborate tomb has fallen into disrepair, and he has it restored.

The beginnings of industry

The invention of mechanical devices that took over much of the work of people or animals was an early step towards industrialization. The first machines were powered by water, wind, or the force of gravity, and did not need many people to operate them. Major industries would not develop until the opening of factories employing large workforces in the late 18th century.

WOW!

Treadmills turned by people or animals powered some early machines. Working on a treadmill could be used as a punishment for criminals.

▶ **LARGEST IN THE WORLD**
The most famous noria were located in Hama, Syria. Seventeen can still be found there, including one that is 22 m (72 ft) in diameter, the largest in the world.

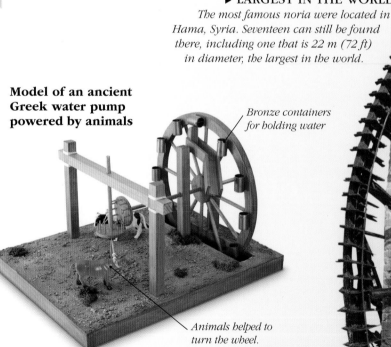

Model of an ancient Greek water pump powered by animals

Bronze containers for holding water

Animals helped to turn the wheel.

EARLY MACHINES

From the 4th century BCE, large wheels were invented to do work such as pumping water or driving machinery. It is uncertain where this first happened, but India, Greece, or Egypt are all possible. Some versions were powered by humans or animals. However, it was more efficient to turn the wheel using flowing water from a river or stream. These waterwheels were the first machines to turn a natural force into mechanical energy.

TRIP HAMMER

By the 1st century BCE, the ancient Chinese were using massive pieces of equipment called trip hammers to process food, crush bamboo to make paper, or shape red-hot metal. Too heavy to be lifted by a single person, a trip hammer has to be raised by mechanical means. The earliest of these devices were powered by waterwheels.

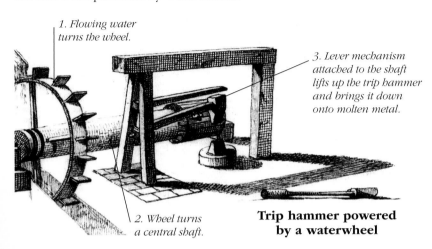

1. Flowing water turns the wheel.

3. Lever mechanism attached to the shaft lifts up the trip hammer and brings it down onto molten metal.

2. Wheel turns a central shaft.

Trip hammer powered by a waterwheel

NORIA

During the Middle Ages, Arab engineers invented a type of waterwheel known as the noria. A noria raised water from streams or lakes so that it could be carried into homes for drinking or washing, or to farmland for watering crops. As the wheel turned, hollow chambers around the rim scooped up the water and emptied it into a trough to be piped elsewhere.

POWERING MILLS

An important use of waterwheels was in the making of cloth. The power of the turning wheel drove machinery that could spin thread and weave and finish materials. Before the invention of coal-powered engines in the 18th century, cloth mills had to be located near running water.

HOW WATERWHEELS WORK

Blades or buckets are positioned around the rim of a waterwheel. As falling or flowing water strikes them, it turns the wheel. The rotation turns an axle at the centre of the wheel that is linked to machinery.

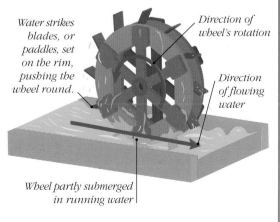

Water strikes blades, or paddles, set on the rim, pushing the wheel round.

Direction of wheel's rotation

Direction of flowing water

Wheel partly submerged in running water

23

Early mechanical devices

Once people had settled down in permanent towns and villages, they began to invent and build devices to help them with their everyday tasks, such as processing food. Many of the most important early devices were for producing materials that could be made into clothes. People mostly used them in their own homes or in small workshops.

A woman in India turns a spinning wheel to produce thread

First handloom

- **What?** Weaving loom
- **Who?** Ancient Egyptians
- **Where and when?** Egypt, c.5000 BCE

Cloth is made by intertwining lengths of thread placed at right angles to each other. The handloom was invented to make this process easier and quicker. Early looms were simple frames that held vertical threads (called the warp) firmly in position, while horizontal threads (called the weft) were woven through them.

Model of a handloom used by early European people, 800–600 BCE

Rotary quern

- **What?** Hand mill for grinding grains
- **Who?** Unknown
- **Where and when?** Southern Europe, c.600 BCE

Quern-stones grind cereal grains such as wheat into flour. The rotary quern consists of two circular stones, one placed on top of the other. The bottom one, called the "quern", does not move. The top part, or "handstone", has a handle attached so it can be rotated. As the quern turns, it crushes the grain that is fed in through a hole in the centre.

First drawloom

- **What?** Pattern weaving loom
- **Who?** Ancient Chinese
- **Where and when?** China, c.400 BCE

The drawloom, which allowed greater control over the threads than the handloom, was invented to weave highly patterned cloth, mainly silk. The key part was an arrangement called the "figure harness" that lifted individual warp threads. Drawlooms were large devices, often 4 m (13 ft) long, and required two people to operate them.

Figure harness

Rotary querns are still used in some parts of the world

Wooden handle to turn handstone

Hole for grain

First spinning wheel

- **What?** Hand-turned spinning wheel
- **Who?** Unknown
- **Where and when?** Probably India, c.600 CE

Before materials such as cotton or wool can be woven they need to be spun into threads. Early people used to do this by pulling out and twisting the fibres of the raw material between their fingers. This time-consuming task was greatly speeded up by the invention of the spinning wheel. The hand-turned wheel twists fibres into thread, which it winds around a stick called a "spindle".

Vertical-axis mill

- **What?** Post mill
- **Who?** Unknown
- **Where and when?** Northern Europe, c.1200 CE

The most common use of windmills was to grind grain into flour, but they were also used for other purposes, such as pumping water. As the sails of a windmill turn in the wind, gears inside the mill use the rotational force to move mechanical parts. A post, or vertical-axis, mill had a large central shaft that allowed the sails to be moved to face the wind.

Treadle wheel

- **What?** Foot-powered spinning wheel
- **Who?** Unknown
- **Where and when?** Germany, c.1533 CE

As the spinning wheel developed, a foot-operated board called the "treadle" was added. Pressed up and down by the operator's feet, the treadle's rocking motion drove the spinning wheel round. The raw fibres were held on a rod attached to the treadle wheel, leaving the operator's hands free to guide the thread.

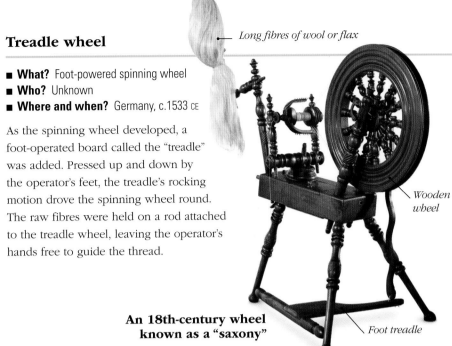

Long fibres of wool or flax

Wooden wheel

An 18th-century wheel known as a "saxony"

Foot treadle

▼ WIND POWER
These types of windmill could not be used for industry because they did not produce as much energy as coal-powered engines.

Sail

Central shaft is connected to a gear system.

Body of mill could be turned to face sails into the wind.

DESIGNING THE FUTURE

The Italian artist Leonardo da Vinci (1452–1519) is famous
not only for his paintings, but also for his numerous
inventions. His many designs include a helicopter, a
parachute, and an armoured tank. Pictured here are his
sketches and notes on the workings of water pumps,
water wheels, and gears.

The power of gunpowder

During the 9th century CE, scientists in China produced gunpowder – the first explosive material. Their invention must have come as a surprise because they were trying to make something quite different. However, the powerful force that they created was rapidly put to use for launching weapons, blowing things up, and creating spectacular displays with noise and colour.

Modern Chinese firecrackers

THE INVENTION OF GUNPOWDER

Medieval Chinese scientists invented gunpowder by accident, when they were mixing chemicals together in the hope of finding a life-lengthening potion. The ingredients of the mixture were saltpetre, charcoal, and sulfur. Within a few decades of its discovery, gunpowder was being used in weapons of war.

Painting of Chinese families enjoying a celebration with fireworks

FIREWORKS

The first fireworks came from China. People simply threw gunpowder into a fire to enjoy bright sparks and loud bangs. The next step was to stuff gunpowder into a hollowed-out bamboo stick and light an attached fuse. When the burning fuse ignited the gunpowder, the tube shot into the air and exploded in the sky, just like firework rockets do today.

FIRE-LANCES

In around 950 CE, people began to understand the destructive power of gunpowder. One of the first weapons propelled by gunpowder was the fire-lance, which was an explosive charge attached to a pole. The charge was created by filling a bamboo cylinder with gunpowder. When lit with a fuse, the cylinder would explode in the direction of the enemy, sending flames shooting out.

Sometimes bits of metal or pottery were added to the explosive charge.

Fire-lances used in warfare, China, c.1000 CE

WOW!

Adding metals to the gunpowder in fireworks makes sparks of different colours: copper for blue, barium for green, calcium for orange.

HAND CANNON

The earliest version of the handgun was invented in China in the 13th century. Known as a hand cannon, it was loaded by dropping stone or iron balls down its barrel. Gunpowder was packed into a chamber at the back of the hand cannon, where there was a small hole to place a lit fuse. When the gunpowder was ignited, it exploded, blasting out the ammunition.

Chinese bronze hand cannon, 1424

GREEK FIRE

The Chinese led the medieval world with explosive weapons, but they were not the first to use chemicals in warfare. The Byzantine Empire (centred on the area now in modern-day Turkey and Greece) invented a substance called Greek Fire in around 672 CE. It was a thick flammable liquid that burned even on water, making it deadly in sea battles. Its secret recipe probably included oil, sulfur, and saltpetre.

A 12th-century manuscript showing Byzantine sailors using Greek Fire

Gunpowder weapons

By the 13th century, knowledge of how to make gunpowder had spread beyond China to the rest of Asia and into Europe. People soon saw how this deadly invention could be used as a weapon. As armed forces began to use gunpowder in increasingly powerful and accurate firearms, warfare changed rapidly.

Earliest known picture of a fireball from a 10th-century Chinese wall painting

First fireball

- ■ **What?** Grenade
- ■ **Who?** Medieval Chinese
- ■ **Where and when?** China, 11th century

A fireball, or grenade, is a small bomb that can be thrown by hand. Early fireballs, first developed in China, were hollow clay or metal vessels filled with gunpowder. Attached to the fireball was a paper fuse, which was lit and left to burn down until it ignited the gunpowder, causing the weapon to explode.

Fire chariot

- ■ **What?** Rocket launcher
- ■ **Who?** Chinese
- ■ **Where and when?** China, 14th century

Although the Chinese were the first to invent simple rocket launchers, the Koreans developed a more powerful weapon called the *hwacha*, or fire chariot – a two-wheeled cart on which was mounted a rectangular wooden frame. This frame was loaded with *singijeon*, or fire arrows, each carrying a gunpowder charge timed to explode when an arrow struck its target. The largest *hwacha* could launch 200 fire arrows all at once, at a range of 100–450 m (330–1,475 ft).

Hwacha

Arquebus

- ■ **What?** Hook gun
- ■ **Who?** Unknown
- ■ **Where and when?** Northern Europe, 15th century

Serpentine was attached here.

German arquebus, c.1500

The arquebus was the first gun to be fired from the chest or shoulder. It consists of a metal tube fitted to a wooden stock, or handle. Its name comes from an Old French word meaning "hook gun", because many models had a hook on the barrel to hold the weapon steady against a support. The gun was fired with an S-shaped lever called a "serpentine" that lowered a lit match into a pan of gunpowder, creating a flash.

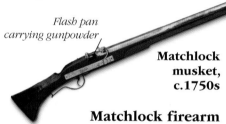

Flash pan carrying gunpowder

Matchlock musket, c.1750s

Matchlock firearm

- ■ **What?** Arquebus with matchlock mechanism
- ■ **Who?** Unknown
- ■ **Where and when?** Northern Europe, c.1475

The matchlock made firing weapons quicker. It was a trigger-controlled device that used a spring to move a lit match towards a gunpowder charge placed at the rear of the weapon. This set off a small explosion, which produced high-pressure gas that shot down the barrel, forcing out the ammunition.

WOW!

Reloading early firearms such as the musket took a long time: even the best-trained soldiers could fire no more than five times a minute.

A piece of a mineral called pyrite created the sparks that fired the gun.

▼ HOW IT WORKS
A wheel lock works by rotating a steel wheel against a sparking material, causing friction and sparks that ignite the gunpowder.

Handgun

- **What?** Pistol
- **Who?** Unknown
- **Where and when?** Europe, 16th century

During the early 16th century, smaller firearms were developed. Although not as accurate or powerful as longer-barrelled weapons, their smaller size made them easier to shoot with. Once loaded, handguns could be fired with one hand and also used while on horseback, but early models could fire only a single shot before they had to be reloaded.

German wheel lock handgun, 1590

Long barrel

Flintlock firearm

- **What?** Musket with flintlock mechanism
- **Who?** Unknown
- **Where and when?** Northern Europe, c.1550

The flintlock mechanism was used in a type of gun called a musket. When the trigger was pulled, it struck a flint against a piece of steel, creating a spark that ignited the gunpowder. Some muskets were "rifled", which meant that grooves were marked on the inside of the barrel to make the bullet spin and travel towards its target with greater accuracy.

Flint

Sling, which could be used to steady the aim

Baker rifle, a type of flintlock gun, 1802–1837

Percussion cap

- **What?** Firearm with percussion cap
- **Who?** Unknown
- **Where and when?** USA/northern Europe, c.1820

The percussion cap was a small metal cup filled with an explosive mixture of chemicals called "fulminate" and sealed with foil. When the trigger of the gun was pulled, it moved a part called the "hammer" that struck the percussion cap, sparking off the gunpowder charge and firing the ammunition.

▼ FIRING AWAY
Dressed as soldiers in the American Civil War of the 1860s, these riflemen are firing percussion-cap weapons.

Percussion-cap mechanism

The printing revolution

The invention of printing was one of the biggest leaps forward in human history. Before, when people made records, or spread information and ideas, they had to write out every copy of a text by hand. Printing did the job much faster and produced a lot of copies more cheaply and accurately. The earliest known printing dates back to 3rd-century China. However, the first printing system using mass-produced type appeared in Europe in 1439.

Lever tightens wooden plates together, bringing inked type into contact with paper.

Wooden frame holds paper ready for printing.

METAL MOVABLE TYPE

Movable type is a system where moulds of separate letters (or characters) are used to print text. The first-ever movable type was made in China in the 11th century CE, using clay or wooden character moulds. Later, people found that metal was the best material for making type.

Metal type

In movable type, separate characters are moved around to make up the text that the person operating the press wants to reproduce.

Jikji, the oldest surviving book printed using metal movable type, Korea, 1377

GUTENBERG PRESS

The German Johannes Gutenberg set up the first European printing press in 1439. His most successful invention was a method of rapidly casting metal type moulds in large quantities. Gutenberg could print 250 pages per hour. The first book he produced was a Bible. Printing spread across Europe, and books became cheaper to make and buy.

INTAGLIO PRINTING

In 15th-century Germany a new type of printing called intaglio was invented. This process uses images cut into a metal plate often made of copper or zinc and covered in ink. The plate is pressed into paper, creating sunken areas that hold the ink.

Copperplate printing press

◄ HAND PRESS
Gutenberg set up his press with metal type that could be arranged to print any page, and used a specially developed thick, sticky ink.

CHIAROSCURO WOODCUT

In this technique, invented in Germany around 1509, an image's outline is carved into a wood block, and then further blocks are carved with additional details. The blocks are pressed in turn onto paper, each block overprinting the image made by the one before. The result is a picture with contrasting areas of light and shape that make an image look three-dimensional. *Chiaroscuro* is an Italian word meaning "light-dark".

Chiaroscuro print of a ceiling design with three angels

A solid wood framework held the press steady during printing.

When the image is printed, it appears in reverse on the paper.

Lithography printing in a workshop

LITHOGRAPHY

Invented by the German Alois Senefelder in the 1790s, lithography is based on the fact that oil and water do not mix. A greasy substance is used to draw an image onto limestone, which is then dampened with water. When ink is spread on the stone it sticks only to the grease, and the image is pressed onto paper.

Writing and printing

Ancient peoples first invented writing to record information and thoughts through signs, symbols, or letters. Records could be kept, and people could communicate without meeting. The later invention of printing meant that multiple copies of a document with words and pictures could be reproduced much faster and more accurately.

The first writing

- **What?** Cuneiform
- **Who?** Sumerians
- **Where and when?** Mesopotamia, 3100 BCE

Early cuneiform

The ancient Sumerians were among the first people to live in organized towns, and soon needed a system to keep track of the goods they traded, the animals they kept, and the taxes they paid. They invented a style of writing that used wedge-shaped marks made on clay tablets with a stylus. Today, this is known as cuneiform. Within 400 years, signs representing words were in use across Mesopotamia.

Papyrus

- **What?** Writing surface
- **Who?** Ancient Egyptians
- **Where and when?** Egypt, 3000 BCE

Ancient Egyptians used a pictorial script, called hieroglyphs.

The ancient Egyptians developed a newer writing surface than clay. This was made from the inner stem of the papyrus plant. The plant was cut into strips, which were laid together to form sheets, moistened, and dried. They were written on with a reed pen and ink.

Script on turtleshell

Oracle bone script

- **What?** Earliest known Chinese writing
- **Who?** Ancient Chinese
- **Where and when?** China, 1200 BCE

In ancient China, people tried to foretell the future by carving questions onto animal bones (usually ox) or turtleshell. These bones were heated until they cracked, and the patterns of the cracks were read as answers to the questions. The characters used on oracle bones represented words, not speech sounds, and are the first known example of Chinese writing.

The first phonetic alphabet

- **What?** Written alphabet
- **Who?** Phoenicians
- **Where and when?** Mediterranean, c.1500 BCE

The Phoenicians were traders of the ancient Mediterranean. They invented an alphabet – a writing system simpler than cuneiform or Egyptian hieroglyphs. The Phoenician alphabet had 22 characters, which were the first written symbols to record speech sounds rather than words.

Phoenician inscription on a cylindrical base, c.600–500 BCE

Paper making

- **What?** First paper
- **Who?** Probably Ts'ai Lun
- **Where and when?** China, 105 CE

Before paper, people mainly wrote on materials such as wood, animal skins, or fabric. A Chinese court official called Ts'ai Lun is thought to have been the first to make paper. Using mashed plant fibres that were pressed and dried, he created a cheaper and lighter writing surface.

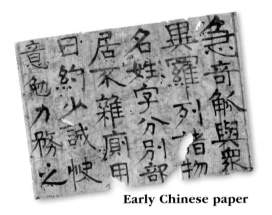

Early Chinese paper

Quill pen

- **What?** Writing tool
- **Who?** Unknown
- **Where and when?** Europe, c.500 CE

The feathers of large birds such as the goose and the swan were used as writing implements for hundreds of years, right up to the early 20th century. They were light to hold, and the trimmed and sharpened quill tip made writing easy. The hollow feather shaft held the ink.

Most writers stripped away the lower part of the feather to make it easy to hold.

Sharpened point

Block printing

- **What?** First printing
- **Who?** Unknown
- **Where and when?** China, 600 CE

In block printing, the mirror images of the text and pictures are carved into a piece of wood. The wood is inked and pressed onto paper, which prints the page the right way round. This technique was first mainly used to print Buddhist texts, and eventually entire books were made this way.

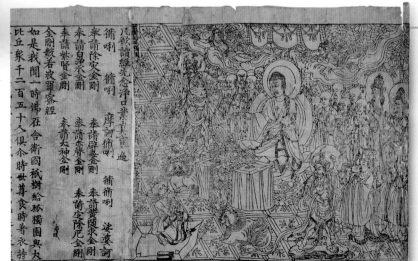

Part of the *Diamond Sutra*, the earliest surviving printed book, produced in China in 868 CE

Zhang Heng

One of the greatest scientists in Chinese history, Zhang Heng combined being an inventor with a career as a government official. He rose to become China's chief astronomer, as well as an important advisor to the Emperor. As if this was not enough, Zhang was also a famed map-maker, poet, and artist.

▼ EARTHQUAKE INDICATOR
The most famous of Zhang's inventions was his seismoscope, or "earthquake weathervane", which could tell the direction in which an earthquake had occurred.

Each dragon head faces a different direction.

WATER-POWERED ARMILLARY SPHERE

An armillary sphere is a framework of rings that was used to understand how planets and stars move through the sky. Zhang's big idea was to use a waterwheel to power the sphere's machinery so that it turned automatically, making one rotation a year.

Rings were positioned to mirror the movement of objects in space.

Replica of Zhang Heng's armillary sphere, 1439

Bronze urn

Pendulum inside drops a ball through the dragon's head facing the direction of the quake.

NAVIGATIONAL CHARIOT

Zhang may have also invented a device to indicate direction. This was a "chariot" with a figure on top that could be positioned to point in any direction. A complicated system of gears meant that no matter what path the chariot followed it continued to point in the same direction, similar to the way a compass does.

Figure always points to set direction.

Model of a navigational chariot from China, 2700–1100 BCE

LIFE STORY

78 CE	95 CE	108 CE	112 CE
Zhang Heng is born near Nanyang, a city in central China. His father died when Zhang was just 10 years old.	He leaves home to go to Luoyang, China's capital at the time, to study at the Imperial Academy.	While working as a local official, he begins to publish papers about astronomy and mathematics.	Zhang Heng is summoned by the Emperor to work as an official at the imperial court in Luoyang.

MAN OF LEARNING

Zhang Heng's work on mechanical devices was much admired by many Chinese scholars and inventors who followed him in later centuries. Zhang was also highly thought of for his astronomical studies and observations. He made a catalogue of 2,500 stars and more than 120 constellations. Zhang is pictured here with his earthquake indicator.

120 CE	125 CE	132 CE	138 CE
He publishes *The Spiritual Constitution of the Universe*. This includes his theory that Earth is at the centre of the Universe.	He describes his armillary sphere and helps to make a mechanical cart with an odometer, an instrument for calculating distances travelled.	Zhang Heng introduces one of his most famous inventions to the imperial court: the earthquake indicator.	He retires from official duties and returns home to Nanyang for a short time. Zhang Heng is recalled by the Emperor to the capital, where he dies in 139 CE.

MAKING THE MODERN WORLD

MAKING THE MODERN WORLD

Ever since the Industrial Revolution, technology has progressed at a rapid pace. From the steam engine to robots, these inventions have changed how we live, work, and play.

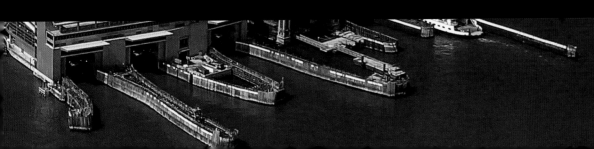

Tools

The onset of the Industrial Revolution in the 1760s required a new set of tools beyond the basic hammers and chisels of old. The scale and volume of production, using new materials including metals, now required more power, more speed, and more precision than a human alone could achieve.

SCREW-CUTTING LATHE

A lathe spins metal against a tool to give it a circular shape or cut a screw thread. This could be done by hand but, in the 1790s, the Englishman Henry Maudslay and American David Wilkinson invented lathes separately, in which the tool was driven by a screw geared to the lathe.

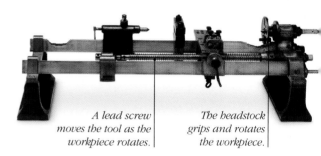

A lead screw moves the tool as the workpiece rotates.

The headstock grips and rotates the workpiece.

CIRCULAR SAW

Traditionally, logs were sawn by hand using a pit saw, with an up-down motion. This was slow and inefficient. In 1813, Tabitha Babbit, a member of a Shaker community in the USA, introduced the first circular saw in a saw mill, which was powered by water.

Timber is pushed through a circular saw that requires more power to operate than a hand saw, but cuts much faster.

STEAM HAMMER

When English engineer Isambard Kingdom Brunel started work on his ship SS *Great Britain*, he discovered that hammering out the giant shafts for its paddlewheels was beyond human ability. Scottish engineer James Nasmyth came up with the idea of a giant steam-driven hammer. He made the first in 1840 and patented it in 1842.

Workers feed a red-hot piece of iron into a steam hammer, which pounds the metal into shape.

SPANNER FORCES

When someone rotates a spanner, they apply a twisting force called torque. If force is applied further from the point of rotation, torque is greater and the spanner is easier to turn.

Force is applied to the end of the spanner.

The further from the nut the force is applied, the greater the torque.

The jaw is adjusted by a rotating screw just under it.

ADJUSTABLE SPANNER

An adjustable spanner has a movable jaw, which allows it to be used with different-sized nuts and bolts. The English agricultural engineer Richard Clyburn is credited with its invention in 1842, while he was working at an iron works in Gloucester, UK.

The metals are melted so they can be bonded together on cooling.

ARC WELDING

Since ancient times, blacksmiths have used concentrated heat to bond metals together. In 1881, French inventor Auguste de Méritens invented a way of using electricity to create enough heat to melt metals that would then be joined when cooled, in a process known as arc welding.

SPIRIT LEVEL

A bubble in a liquid always rises to the highest point. In an upward-curved level tube it will settle at the centre. This was recognized by the French scientist Melchisédech Thévenot, who invented the first spirit level in 1661. Spirit levels have been used by builders ever since to ensure their work is perfectly horizontal or vertical.

A yellow-coloured liquid is used for easy reading.

Modern spirit level giving vertical, horizontal, and angle readings

Tools workshop

The 19th and 20th centuries saw the development of a wide variety of tools that help us work more quickly, accurately, and efficiently. These tools have revolutionized home improvements, allowing people to measure things precisely and fasten them together securely. In industry, the use of computer control and lasers paved the way for new and improved cutting tools.

Pocket tape measure

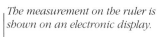

The measurement on the ruler is shown on an electronic display.

Digital caliper

Tape measure

- **What?** Retractable pocket tape measure
- **Who?** William H Bangs
- **Where and when?** USA, 1864

Retractable tape measures can fit into a pocket or toolkit, but contain enough tape to measure distances of several metres.

Typical tape measures have 7.6 m (25 ft) of tape. A locking button allows a length of tape to be held in position out of its case. Sliding the button makes a spring pull the tape back into its case and wind it around a coil so it can be stored conveniently.

Electric cordless hand drill

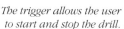

The drill bit rotates to cut a hole in a surface.

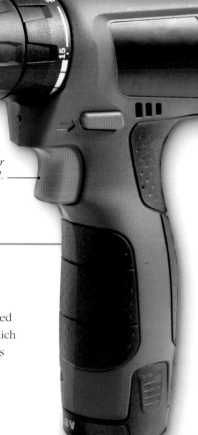

The trigger allows the user to start and stop the drill.

Micrometer

- **What?** Micrometer screw gauge
- **Who?** Jean Palmier
- **Where and when?** France, 1848

A caliper measures the distance between opposite sides of an object. In 1848, Jean Palmier received a patent for the micrometer screw gauge, a type of caliper that uses a screw to accurately measure very small objects. The object is placed between a fixed frame and a screw. Measuring the rotation of the screw as it moves towards the object shows how far it has moved forward much more precisely. Modern-day calipers show distances on a digital display.

Electric drill

- **What?** Drill driven by an electric motor
- **Who?** Arthur James Arnot and William Blanch Brain
- **Where and when?** Australia, 1889

Arthur James Arnot and William Blanch Brain invented the first drill to be powered by an electric motor, which was faster and more efficient than existing drills. This first electric drill wasn't portable, but the portable handheld drill was invented just six years later, in 1895, by German brothers Wilhelm and Carl Fein.

Allen key

Allen keys in different sizes

- **What?** Hexagonal socket key
- **Who?** William G Allen
- **Where and when?** USA, 1910

Created by the Allen Manufacturing Company in 1910, the Allen key is used to drive bolts and screws with hexagonal sockets in their heads. It is also known as a hex socket key. Allen keys drive screws right into the surface that they are fastening, keeping the surface smooth.

Phillips screwdriver

- **What?** Cross-headed screwdriver
- **Who?** Henry F Phillips and Thomas M Fitzpatrick
- **Where and when?** USA, 1936

In the 1930s, Henry F Phillips and Thomas M Fitzpatrick invented cross-headed screws and screwdrivers. Cross-headed screws were particularly useful on automated car assembly lines, as they could take greater turning force and provided tighter fastening. With their cross-shaped tips, Phillips screwdrivers fit securely into screw heads.

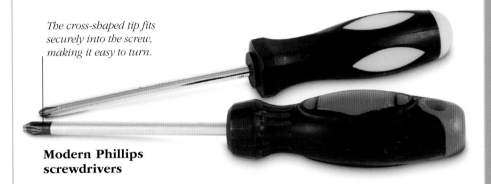

The cross-shaped tip fits securely into the screw, making it easy to turn.

Modern Phillips screwdrivers

Water-cooled CNC milling cutter

CNC milling machine

- **What?** Computer-controlled cutting machine
- **Who?** John T Parsons
- **Where and when?** USA, 1940s

Milling is a process that uses a circular rotating cutter to cut into materials in several different directions, creating a variety of shapes. Milling machines have existed since the early 19th century, but in the 1940s, engineer John T Parsons was the first person to consider using the earliest computers to control the milling process. CNC (computer numerical controlled) milling machines cut more precisely than manual machines.

Laser cutter

- **What?** Carbon dioxide laser
- **Who?** Kumar Patel
- **Where and when?** USA, 1964

The laser, which produces a narrow, highly concentrated beam of light, was invented in the early 1960s. In 1964, engineer Kumar Patel discovered that carbon dioxide gas could create a laser beam that was intense and hot enough to cut through metal. Carbon dioxide lasers are still widely used today in cutting and welding, and for delicate surgical procedures such as eye surgery.

Metal laser-cutter

Laser level

- **What?** Laser level
- **Who?** Robert Genho
- **Where and when?** USA, 1975

A laser level projects horizontal and vertical beams of light which can then be compared with a work surface. Laser levels are used in the construction industry so that builders can make sure they are working on perfectly horizontal surfaces or along straight lines.

Laser level on a building site

Feeding the world

Every invention made, from hunting tools to computers, would be useless if we were not able to keep ourselves healthy enough to use them. Food is essential for survival, and as Earth's population has grown, it has become even more vital that humans find effective ways of producing ever-greater quantities of nourishing food.

TINNED FOOD

The ancient Romans preserved food in containers lined with rust-resistant tin. In 1810, the Frenchman Nicolas Appert developed tinned cans to preserve food for Napoleon's army. In 1823, the tin can above, which contained roast veal, was made for a British voyage.

THE SEED DRILL

Growing crops used to be very hard work, with farmers laboriously scattering seeds in the field by hand. In 1701, Englishman Jethro Tull changed all that with his invention of the seed drill. Pulled along by a horse, this machine carved out neat furrows, then dropped seeds into them, which proved to be a very efficient way of growing crops.

Many farmers came to witness the Jethro seed drill in action.

This worker carefully transplants seedlings into empty pots, at this modern-day hydroponic farm.

A helicopter sprays potatoes with pesticide in the UK

PEST CONTROL

In 1939, Swiss chemist Paul Müller discovered that a chlorine-based chemical, commonly called DDT, killed insects but had little effect on warm-blooded animals. DDT was used widely in agriculture for years, but today it has been replaced by more effective and safer pesticides.

HYDROPONICS

In 1929, the American researcher William Gericke grew tomato vines 7.6 m (25 ft) long using just high-nutrition minerals mixed with water. This way of growing plants without soil became known as hydroponics. In the 1930s, vegetables were grown this way on soilless Wake Island, in the Pacific Ocean, to supply refuelling passenger airliners. Today, NASA is experimenting with hydroponics for potential plant cultivation on Mars.

WOW!

Nearly 30 per cent of the global population works in agriculture, making it the single largest industry in the world.

FERTILIZERS

In 1909, the German chemist Fritz Haber succeeded in capturing nitrogen from air to form ammonia, which could be made into plant fertilizers. Another German chemist, Carl Bosch, developed this method for large-scale ammonia production in massive factories (above). Since then, this breakthrough has led to a huge increase in food production globally.

GM CROPS

In 1969, American biochemists discovered how to alter living things (to add more flavour, for example) by splicing the genes of one organism into another. The first genetically modified (GM) food approved for sale was the Flavr Savr tomato (above), produced by the US company Calgene in 1994.

Working the land

People have always been looking to come up with inventions that would make farming more efficient. If the greatest game-changer was the plough, then the second most significant innovation was the motor engine, which offered far more power than horses, and drove tractors, combine harvesters, and all manner of heavy farming machinery.

Threshing machine

- **What?** Steam-driven thresher
- **Who?** Andrew Meikle
- **Where and when?** UK, 1788

Farm labourers used to thresh wheat by hand, beating the harvested corn with sticks to separate the grain from the stalks and its outer covering, known as chaff. In 1788, the Scottish millwright Andrew Meikle invented a machine that could do this quicker. It was powered by a separate steam engine.

McCormick's reaper at work

Mechanical reaping machine

- **What?** Horse-powered reaper
- **Who?** Patrick Bell
- **Where and when?** UK, 1827

Without mechanical help, harvesting requires many people. The Scottish farmer Patrick Bell invented a machine that could be pulled behind a horse to cut and gather crops in 1826. A few years later, in the USA, Cyrus McCormick came up with a similar machine, which he patented in 1834 and sold in the thousands.

1860 thresher

Steam-powered tractor

- **What?** Mobile steam engine
- **Who?** Charles Burrell
- **Where and when?** UK, 1856

In the 1790s, stationary steam engines were used on farms to power threshing machines A self-moving steam engine was exhibited in 1842, but Englishman Charles Burrell built the first practical steam-powered tractor that could cope with rough farm terrain, in 1856.

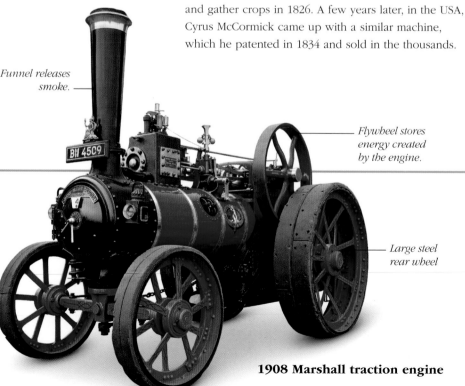

Funnel releases smoke.

Flywheel stores energy created by the engine.

BW 4509

Large steel rear wheel

1908 Marshall traction engine

Cattle-proof fencing

- **What?** Barbed wire
- **Who?** Joseph Glidden
- **Where and when?** USA, 1874

Barbed wire made large-scale cattle farming more practical by reducing the cost of enclosing land, as it was much cheaper and easier to erect than wooden fences. The American Michael Kelly invented the basic design for barbed wire in 1868, but Joseph Glidden improved upon the idea, and patented it in 1874. He helped turn America's Great Plains into profitable farming country.

Sharp barbs keep cattle at bay.

Gasoline-powered tractor

- **What?** Froelich tractor
- **Who?** John Froelich
- **Where and when?** USA, 1892

In 1892, John Froelich invented a gasoline-powered farm vehicle. It was not a success, but his 1914 model was better received. Seeing its potential, the John Deere company bought Froelich's business.

Froelich's 1892 machine

Lightweight tractor

- **What?** The Ivel
- **Who?** Dan Albone
- **Where and when?** UK, 1903

The Ivel was created by the English manufacturer and inventor Dan Albone, and is widely considered to be the first successful tractor designed to replace horses. It was described as a lightweight, petrol-powered agricultural motor for general purpose.

THE IVEL

Self-tie baler

- **What?** New Holland baler
- **Who?** Edwin Nolt
- **Where and when?** USA, 1937

Early machines compacted hay, but farmhands had to bind the bales manually. In 1937, the American farmer Edwin Nolt built a self-tying hay baler. The idea was picked up by the New Holland Machine Company and put into production.

Combine harvester

- **What?** Self-propelled harvester
- **Who?** Holt Manufacturing
- **Where and when?** USA, 1911

In 1836, in the USA, Hiram Moore built and patented the first combine harvester – pulled by horses – capable of reaping, threshing, and winnowing grain. In 1911, the first self-propelled harvester was produced by the Holt Manfacturing Company in California, USA.

Modern combine harvester

A tractor tows a modern baler

Crop-spraying drone

- **What?** Agras MG-1
- **Who?** DJI
- **Where and when?** China, 2015

Farmers have long used aircraft for spraying crops with pesticides, but it is expensive. "Dusting" by drone, however, is cheap and efficient. In 2015, Chinese drone company DJI exhibited a crop-spraying drone, called the Agras MG-1, which can fly for 12 minutes at a time, before needing to be refuelled.

Crop-spraying drone in China, 2017

Construction

For most of human history, construction was largely about piling things on top of each other, whether brick or stone, to create a building. Wood was commonly used for roofing. New materials in the 19th century – first iron, then steel, concrete, and sheet glass – made new kinds of structures possible. Engineers were able to build lighter and more versatile buildings more quickly. Most significantly, they could build much, much higher.

IRON BRIDGE

In 1779, the Englishman Abraham Darby built the world's first iron bridge (above), to the design of English architect Thomas Pritchard. Iron was a material previously too expensive to use on a large scale, but new methods of production brought prices down. The bridge's 30.5-m (100-ft) arch spans the River Severn in Shropshire, England. It is still used today.

Steel provides a much stronger framework than stone or brick, which allows for taller buildings.

WOW!

Rising to a massive 828 m (2,717 ft), the world's tallest building is the 160-storey Burj Khalifa in Dubai, UAE.

High-rise construction workers bolt together steel girders to form the supporting structure of the skyscraper.

STEEL STRUCTURES

Steel is mostly iron combined with a little carbon – and is much stronger than pure iron. China and India had steel industries in ancient times, but this material took off in 1856 when the Englishman Henry Bessemer invented a process to produce large amounts of it cheaply. This method was used to make ships, buildings, and armour up until the 1960s.

SAFETY LIFT

The American Elisha Otis demonstrated the first passenger safety lift in the 1850s in New York City, USA. This invention removed one of the major drawbacks of building high – too many stairs.

GOING UP!

The first escalator, invented by the American engineer Jesse Reno, was just a sloping, moving walkway, but George Wheeler added folding steps. It was marketed by the Otis Elevator Company and, by 1901, was appearing in some stores, as seen here in Boston, USA.

THE CURTAIN WALL

Early steel-frame buildings still supported heavy stone or brick walls. In 1918, however, walls made of lightweight steel and glass that hung from the frame were introduced – these were called curtain walls.

The Bauhaus building in Dessau, Germany, uses curtain walls

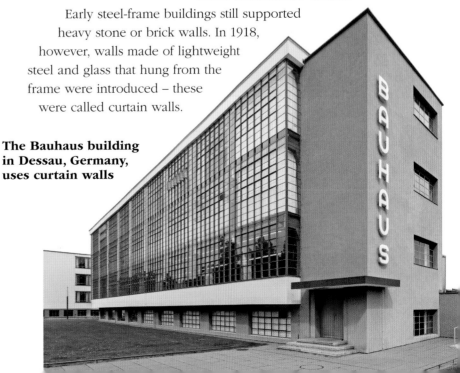

▲ **SCRAPING THE SKY**

The New York City skyline continues to rise, as workers put the finishing touches on the Empire State Building. This 102-storey steel-frame skyscraper opened in 1931. It was much bigger than the world's first steel skyscraper, a 10-storey building in Chicago, USA, completed in 1885.

Alfred Nobel

A Swedish chemist and engineer, Alfred Nobel is best known as the inventor of dynamite, as well as other more powerful and destructive explosives. To this day, his inventions have helped to blast open mines, and build canals, railways, and roads. His name lives on in the prestigious Nobel Prize, awarded annually in a number of categories, including peace.

MAKING DYNAMITE

In 1867, Nobel patented dynamite. Originally called "Nobel's Safety Powder", it was easier and safer to handle than previous explosives. One of the world's major dynamite-producing factories was in Ardrossan, Scotland (above).

EXPLOSIVE INTENTIONS

This painting shows Nobel testing dynamite by blowing up a ship. In 1875, Nobel invented another explosive called gelignite, which was more powerful than dynamite. In 1887, he also patented ballistite, which is still used today as a rocket propellant.

MAN OF PEACE

In 1888, a newspaper wrongly reported Nobel had died – it was actually one of his brothers. The obituary called him "the merchant of death" because of his dangerous inventions. Upset that he might be remembered in this way, he made a will that set aside a large fortune to establish the Nobel Prize.

LASTING LEGACY

The Nobel Prize is awarded annually for achievements in physics, chemistry, and medicine, all reflecting Nobel's scientific background. A fourth prize is for literature, and a fifth award is for a person or society that contributes to international peace.

LIFE STORY

1833	1850	1864	1867
Alfred Nobel is born in Stockholm, Sweden. He is one of eight children, although only four of them – all boys – survive into adulthood.	He goes to work in Paris, France, where he meets the inventor of nitroglycerin, a highly unstable explosive. He is determined to improve it.	Tragically, five people, including Alfred's younger brother Emil, are killed in an accident in a shed used for the preparation of nitroglycerin.	Nobel continues with his experiments and, eventually, manufactures dynamite. He patents this invention in the USA and UK.

AT HIS DESK
Posing next to the tools of his trade, Nobel was both a chemist and an industrialist. After inventing dynamite, he amassed a great fortune from the manufacture and sale of explosives.

Dynamite sticks with long fuses to light them

1875	1888	1896
Nobel invents gelignite, a mouldable explosive that is safer to handle and store than dynamite. It is also more powerful than dynamite.	Ludvig, another one of Alfred's brothers, dies. Newspapers mistakenly run an obituary of Alfred, calling him "the merchant of death".	Aged 63, Nobel dies in San Remo, Italy, from heart failure. He leaves his vast wealth to fund awards that would become known as the Nobel Prize.

51

Industrialization

Between about 1750 and 1850, Britain transformed itself from an agricultural nation into the world's top industrial power. Cloth making was its most profitable enterprise. At this time, many workers moved from farms into the new factories, where new machines were powered by steam – a period known as the Industrial Revolution.

WOW!

Not everyone welcomed the Industrial Revolution: Luddites were workers who destroyed machinery to protest change.

THE STEAM ENGINE

Steam was the world's first great power source. The English engineer Thomas Newcomen built the first steam engine in 1711 (see p.56), which was based on an earlier steam pump by Thomas Savery. Newcomen's machine, however, was inefficient, and it was not until the Scotsman James Watt made improvements and patented his own engine in 1769 (right) that steam engines were made to power machinery.

Piston rod

Steam in the cylinder pushes up the piston connected to the end of the beam by the piston rod.

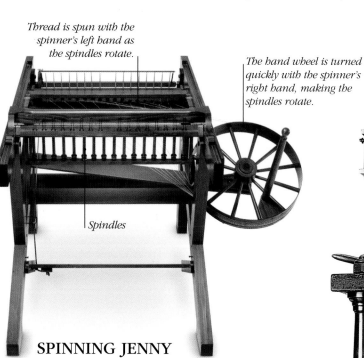

Thread is spun with the spinner's left hand as the spindles rotate.

The hand wheel is turned quickly with the spinner's right hand, making the spindles rotate.

Spindles

SPINNING JENNY

Traditionally, workers operated spinning wheels, which could spin only one thread at a time. James Hargreaves's Spinning Jenny of 1764 could spin several threads at once. Along with the steam engine, it helped to kick-start the Industrial Revolution in Britain.

POWER LOOM

The designer of the first power loom, Edmund Cartwright, was an English clergyman. He realized that the process of cloth making could be transformed using powered spinning machines. His first loom, built in 1785, was very crude but, by 1787, he had improved it enough to start a weaving factory in Doncaster, UK. This engraving shows a busy factory in the 1830s.

A steam-powered belt drives the loom.

The finished cloth is wound onto a roller.

The beam transfers the motion of the piston to the flywheel.

The flywheel stores energy so the engine can run smoothly.

HYDRAULIC PRESS

Joseph Bramah was an inventor who made locks and enhanced the design of the toilet, before turning his attention to improving the manufacturing process. His hydraulic press of 1795 operates by transferring pressure through liquids. It remains one of the most useful factory tools to this day, from making metal sheets to moulding tablets for medical use.

Hand-powered hydraulic press

BOTTLE-MAKING MACHINERY

American Michael Owens left school at 10 to became a glassblower. In 1903, he founded his own company to develop a bottle-making machine. His machines enabled standardized bottles to be mass-produced for the first time, supplying companies like Coca Cola.

Modern bottle-making factory

53

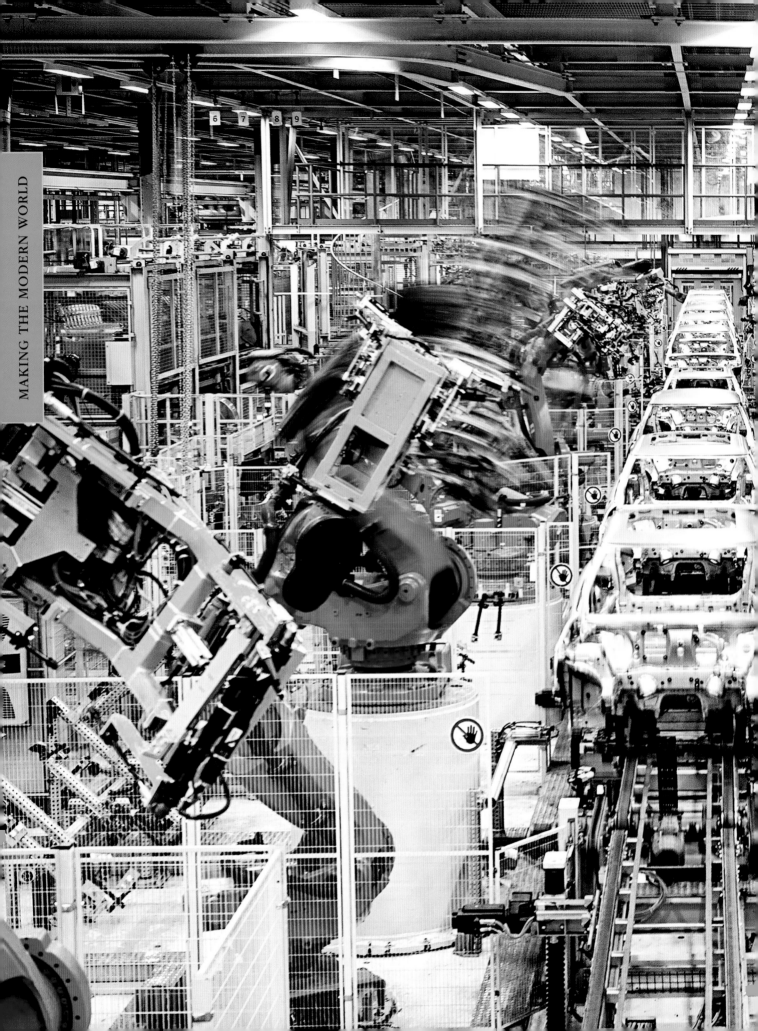

SMART PRODUCTION LINE

Some industrial plants, such as this Mini car factory in Cowley, UK, use intelligent robots that can run unsupervised for weeks at a time. Welding together the chassis and other car body parts was once done by humans. Today, machines do this work, communicating with each other and regulating their own workflow.

Powering up

Since the Industrial Revolution, engineers and industrialists have tried to generate power using different materials and machines. In turn, steam, gas, oil, and electricity have paved the way for many inventions. Indeed, breakthroughs in transport, lighting, heat, and construction would have been impossible without these sources of power.

Model of Newcomen's engine

Steam condenses in the cylinder and air pressure pushes the piston down.

Water is heated in the boiler and steam pushes a piston up.

STEAM ENGINE

It is unlikely that English engineer Thomas Newcomen knew how important the steam engine would be when he invented it in 1710. His device was used for pumping water out of mines, and was then later modified by James Watt (see pp.52–53), which led to steam locomotives. Steam powered the Industrial Revolution and changed the world.

GAS POWER

The Scottish engineer William Murdoch worked in the mining area of Cornwall, UK, servicing steam engines. A by-product of heating coal is gas, and Murdoch worked out a way of capturing this gas in a tank (above) and igniting it. In 1792, Murdoch became the first person to light up a house (his own) using gas.

CRUDE OIL

Ancient peoples burnt oil to generate light, but it was not until the mid-19th century that several individuals discovered how to extract oil from deep underground. Polish inventor Ignacy Łukasiewicz pioneered the oil industry as we know it when, in 1856, he created the world's first industrial oil refinery.

The blue beam is attached to a red, curved end that looks a bit like a donkey's head.

▼ DRILLING FOR OIL

This oil-pumping unit is called a "nodding donkey" because of the way its driving beam swings up and down. It is in an oil field in Kazakhstan, Central Asia.

PUBLIC ELECTRICITY SUPPLY

In 1882, the American inventor Thomas Edison launched the first steam-powered electricity-generating station in London, UK. He supplied the surrounding streets and businesses with electric light for a period of three months. Later that year, he opened the Pearl Street Power Station in New York City, USA.

New York City, 1882

Workers test electric cables before laying them in the ground.

GENERATING ELECTRICITY

Early power stations were powered by vast amounts of coal. Lumps of this fuel were fed into huge furnaces to produce the heat required to turn water into steam, which drove the turbines. In turn, this generated electricity. Later, oil replaced coal as this was less polluting.

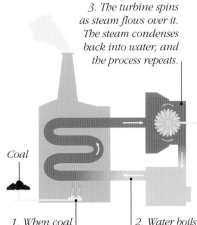

3. The turbine spins as steam flows over it. The steam condenses back into water, and the process repeats.

5. Electricity is carried away by wires and pylons, ending up in homes and businesses.

Coal

4. The generator turns the turbine's rotational energy into electricity.

1. When coal burns, it releases heat.

2. Water boils due to the heat, creating steam that flows around the furnace.

Deptford Power Station, 1890

POWER STATION

Sebastian de Ferranti was a British engineer and a pioneer in the field of electricity. In 1887, he was hired by the newly formed London Electric Supply Corporation for whom he designed the world's first modern power station, in Deptford, London, UK.

The plunger moves inside the well and brings oil to the surface.

Brokdorf Nuclear Power Plant, Germany

NUCLEAR POWER

In 1923, scientists discovered that "splitting" atoms unleashed tremendous power. In 1951, in the USA, a nuclear reactor was used for the first time to generate electricity. In 1954, in Russia, a nuclear power plant became the first to generate electricity for a power grid.

Renewable energy

Fossil fuels such as oil and gas power our world, but these resources are not unlimited. Their continued use also comes with serious environmental problems, including air pollution. As a result, we are increasingly turning to wind, water, and the Sun in search of more sustainable and less destructive sources of energy.

Modern solar-powered streetlight

Solar power

- ■ **What?** Solar-powered electricity
- ■ **Who?** Augustin Mouchot
- ■ **Where and when?** France, 1869

Maths teacher Augustin Mouchot was convinced that coal would eventually run out. In 1860, he began experimenting with capturing the heat from the Sun. In 1869, he displayed a "solar steam engine" in Paris. Unfortunately, coal remained cheap and plentiful and Mouchot's work was ignored.

Water power

- ■ **What?** Hydroelectricity
- ■ **Who?** William Armstrong
- ■ **Where and when?** UK, 1878

While fishing in the UK, William Armstrong was watching a waterwheel and it occurred to him that it harnessed only a small amount of power from the water. Armstrong dammed a nearby river to create a lake, making his house the first in the world to be powered by a hydroelectric generator.

Hoover Dam, USA, built in 1936, is a source of hydroelectric power

Geothermal plant, Iceland

Wind power

- ■ **What?** Wind-powered electric generator
- ■ **Who?** James Blyth
- ■ **Where and when?** Scotland, 1887

After constructing a windmill, James Blyth attached to it an electric motor to light his cottage. He offered to light his village's main street, but locals thought the strange light was the work of the devil. He did, however, build a larger wind generator to provide electricity for a hospital in a nearby town.

Electricity from hot springs

- ■ **What?** Geothermal electric generator
- ■ **Who?** Piero Ginori Conti
- ■ **Where and when?** Italy, 1904

The Romans used hot springs to heat their buildings, as people have in Boise, Idaho, USA, since 1892. Piero Ginori Conti was the first person to demonstrate a geothermal power generator, in 1904 in Larderello, Italy. The first commercial geothermal power station was built there in 1911.

Blyth's windmill had horizontal sails rather than vertical.

Blyth's electricity-generating windmill

Wind farm

- **What?** Electricity-generating wind farm
- **Who?** US Windpower
- **Where and when?** USA, 1980

Since 1927, the Jacobs company in the USA has been creating wind turbines for generating electricity. However, these were individual units used on remote farms. It was not until 1980 that US Windpower installed 20 wind turbines on a site at Crotched Mountain, New Hampshire, making it the world's first wind farm.

Modern-day wind farm

When put underwater, the massive blades on this turbine will rotate to generate electricity.

AK1000 turbine unveiling, Scotland

Tidal energy

- **What?** Tidal power station
- **Who?** Électricité de France
- **Where and when?** France, 1966

Tide mills have existed since medieval times. Barriers let the rising tide through, then close when the tide starts going down. The captured water is then let out to power a tidal turbine. In 1996, the world's first large-scale tidal power station went into operation in France. It uses a 750 m (2,461 ft) barrage across the Rance River.

Zero-carbon city

- **What?** Masdar City
- **Who?** Abu Dhabi government
- **Where and when?** UAE, 2030

Currently under construction just outside Abu Dhabi in the United Arab Emirates (UAE), Masdar City is planned to be the first city in the world to use only renewable energy. It will be car-free, with driverless electric shuttles to move people between buildings that incorporate the latest in smart, sustainable technologies. The project began in 2006 and is expected to continue until 2030.

▲ DEEP IN THOUGHT
Seen here in his laboratory, Tesla was clearly a man of science. However, he also claimed that he could speak eight languages.

LIFE STORY

1856	1882	1884	1887
Nikola Tesla is born in the village of Smiljan, in what is now the country of Croatia. He claimed a lightning storm was raging as he was born.	While living in Paris, France, Tesla works for the Continental Edison Company, set up by famed American inventor Thomas Edison.	Tesla emigrates to the USA, arriving with just four cents in his pocket, some of his favourite poems, and calculations for a flying machine.	He develops the AC induction motor as an alternative to DC. It would soon become the most widely used type of electric motor.

Nikola Tesla

The gifted inventor Nikola Tesla produced the first motor that ran efficiently on an alternating current, experimented with X-rays, and demonstrated a radio-controlled boat. During his life, he held about 300 patents, but ended up virtually penniless.

UNLUCKY GENIUS

Tesla claimed he had a photographic memory and that many of his ideas came to him fully formed. However, he was not a canny businessman. After moving to New York City, USA, Thomas Edison hired the young Tesla, and offered to pay him $50,000 for an improved design of a motor. When Tesla presented a solution and asked for the money, Edison replied that he was only joking.

INDUCTION MOTOR

In 1887, Tesla developed an induction motor (below) that ran on alternating current (AC) – a power system that performed better than the existing direct current (DC) in long-distance, high-voltage transmission. This device led to the adoption of AC as the standard for electricity supplies.

Rotor

Stator generates a rotating magnetic field that turns the rotor.

LIGHTING UP

Tesla and his financial backer Westinghouse were in a "war of currents" with Thomas Edison to promote their rival systems. In 1893, Tesla won the bid to light that year's World's Columbian Exhibition (left). His success was key to proving the reliability of AC electrical power.

1891	1898	1943
He invents the Tesla coil, which would be widely used in radio technology.  **Tesla coil, 1895**	At New York's Madison Square Garden, Tesla gives a public demonstration of a boat guided by remote control that uses radio signals.	Tesla dies in New York City, aged 86. The AC system that he developed remains the global standard for power transmission.

Plastics

The first plastic, made in 1856 by the British inventor Alexander Parkes, was formed using a plant-based material called Parkesine, later named cellulose. In the 1920s, chemists developed plastics from substances in oil. This led to the creation of a variety of plastics, such as polythene. Unfortunately, plastics can take hundreds of years to decompose, resulting in huge waste in landfills and in oceans.

CELLULOID

In the 1860s, a cellulose-based plastic called celluloid was developed by Alexander Parkes. Clear, flexible, and very easy to mould, it was used for many things, from photographic film to kitchen utensils. However, it proved to be extremely flammable and caused many accidents, so it is rarely used today.

The first purpose of celluloid was to make pool balls, however they are made from a different, safer type of plastic today.

BAKELITE

In 1907, Leo Baekeland – a Belgian-born chemist working in the USA – made a plastic from chemicals found in coal tar. His plastic, which he called Bakelite, was different from earlier plastics because heat made it set hard, rather than melt.

Bakelite-made rotary dial telephone, 1940s

WALLACE CAROTHERS

The American chemist Wallace Carothers produced a plastic called nylon in 1934. This revolutionary new material could be woven into a fine cloth or twined to create rope as strong as steel cable. Thin and durable, nylon is used to create many items, from stockings to guitar strings.

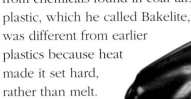

POLYSTYRENE

Although the history of polystyrene goes back to the 1830s, it was first developed for commerical use in the 1930s. It comes in two forms: hard, and a lightweight foam, called expanded polystyrene or styrofoam. The hard form is used for items like yogurt cartons; the lightweight type makes good packaging, especially egg boxes (left).

PLASTIC BOTTLES

In 1947, plastic bottles were first used commercially. However, they remained uncommon until developments in plastics in the 1960s reduced costs. Soon after, plastic bottles became popular due to their light weight and the fact that, unlike glass, they don't break.

▶ **PRACTICAL PLASTIC**
Today's plastic bottles come in all shapes and sizes, and can carry anything from water to fizzy drinks.

SQUEEZABLE KETCHUP BOTTLE

This handy bottle for ketchup was created by Stanley Mason, a prolific American inventor who also holds patents on such essentials of modern life as disposable nappies and dental-floss dispensers. In 1983, his bottle was first manufactured for home use by the food company Heinz.

Man-made materials

Since ancient times, we have made items – used for hunting or cooking, for example – from natural materials such as stone, clay, and wood. In the modern era, advances in chemistry and engineering have enabled us to produce man-made, or synthetic, materials, including rayon, fibreglass, and kevlar. In turn, these materials have led to inventions that benefit from a material's unique quality, from strength to elasticity.

Synthetic fibres

- **What?** Viscose rayon
- **Who?** Charles Cross, Edward Bevan, and Clayton Beadle
- **Where and when?** UK, 1892

Using their experience in soap- and paper-making, three British scientists – Charles Cross, Edward Bevan, and Clayton Beadle – invented the viscose process. This took cellulose (an organic compound from green plants) and, through chemical treatments, turned it into a synthetic fibre that resembled silk but cost less to produce.

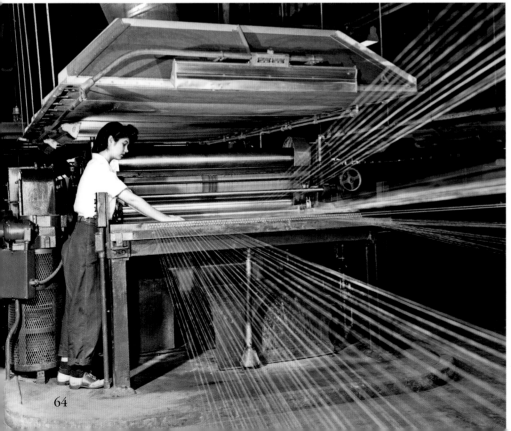

Rayon production, USA, 1950s

Kitchen tiles

Hardy floor covering

- **What?** Linoleum
- **Who?** Frederick Walton
- **Where and when?** UK, 1860s

Linoleum was invented by the British rubber manufacturer Frederick Walton as a smooth, resilient floor covering. He made it originally by coating cloth with layers of a substance containing linseed oil and other ingredients. This slowly reacted with air to form a thick, tough coating. Linoleum was plain until the 1930s, when decorative designs were added.

Making laminated, shatter-proof car windscreens

Laminated glass

- **What?** Triplex
- **Who?** Édouard Bénédictus
- **Where and when?** France, 1903

In his lab, French chemist and artist Édouard Bénédictus knocked a glass flask to the floor. It shattered but, to his surprise, the glass hung together in the same rough shape. He discovered that some cellulose nitrate (liquid plastic) in the flask had left a thin film, and this was holding the glass together. Further experiments led him to invent the world's first piece of safety glass.

Glass-based insulator

- **What?** Fibreglass
- **Who?** Games Slayter
- **Where and when?** USA, 1932

At the Owens-Illinois glass company, Games Slayter discovered a way of mass-producing glass wool, known today as fibreglass. The material traps air, making it ideal for insulation. In 1936, glass wool was combined with a plastic resin to create a strong, lightweight material, useful in the construction industry.

Fibreglass-coated canoe

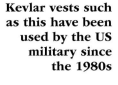

Kevlar vests such as this have been used by the US military since the 1980s

Kevlar bulletproof vests are very strong and light.

Elastic sportswear

- **What?** Spandex
- **Who?** Joseph Shivers
- **Where and when?** USA, 1958

While working at the DuPont company, the American chemist Joseph Shivers was looking for a light, synthetic material to use in women's clothing. In the 1950s, he found it – an elastic-like fibre that was named spandex, an anagram of "expands". It was patented in 1958 and marketed as Lycra.

Elastic attire made from spandex is ideal for flexible gymnasts.

Tough, protective plastic

- **What?** Kevlar
- **Who?** Stephanie Kwolek and Paul Morgan
- **Where and when?** USA, 1965

Kevlar is a plastic that is five times stronger than steel. It was developed by chemists working for DuPont in the USA. It is related to another man-made material called nylon, but with an extra chemical to add strength and stiffness. It was first used in racing tyres, and is also used in golf clubs and flame-proof clothing.

Flexible electronics

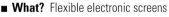

- **What?** Flexible electronic screens
- **Who?** Plastic Logic
- **Where and when?** Germany, 2004

German scientists have discovered a way to make light, thin, and flexible screens that can carry digital information. At present, this technology is used in signage, wristwatches, and other wearable devices, but we might soon have flexible computer screens (left).

FAST FACTS

- Man-made materials are typically much more durable than their natural counterparts. Once an advantage, this is now seen as an environmental problem, as they do not degrade.
- Chinese material scientists have created the world's lightest material, called graphene aerogel, which is almost entirely made out of air.

Buying and selling

The world's economy relies upon people buying and selling goods and services. Countless inventions have made it easier for us to do this, from cash registers to trolleys. In the digital age, shopping continues to change dramatically, and we can now shop with just the click of a mouse or the tap of a smartphone.

EARLY CALCULATING MACHINE
French insurance agent Thomas de Colmar created the first practical adding machine, or "arithmometer", in 1820. It could add, subtract, divide, and multiply.

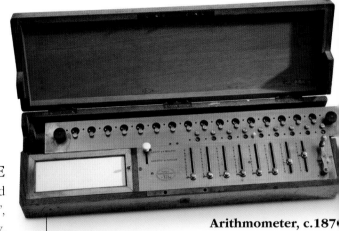

Arithmometer, c.187◦

A strong wooden case protects the machine.

Late 19th-century cash register from Germany

CASH REGISTER
The first cash register was patented by the American tavern keeper James Ritty, in 1879. It recorded sales and helped stopped workers from pocketing money. In 1884, coal merchant John Patterson improved upon the idea and marketed it.

Ornate metal casing

Modern-day shopping trolley invented by the American Orla Watson in 1946

SUPERMARKET TROLLEY
In 1936, the American shop-owner Sylvan Goldman saw that shoppers bought only as much as they could carry. So, he welded baskets to a folding chair and added wheels – the supermarket trolley was born.

WOW!
The first true e-commerce transaction was on 11 August 1994, when an album by the musician Sting was ordered and paid for online.

CASH MACHINE
In 1966, a Japanese bank launched its Computer Loan Machine, an automatic cash dispenser that advanced money on a credit card. Barclays Bank installed the world's first automated teller machine, or ATM, in London, UK, on 27 June 1967.

Crowds flock to the first ATM

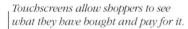
Barcode scanner

The barcode gives a number that the checkout computer uses to bring up details about the product.

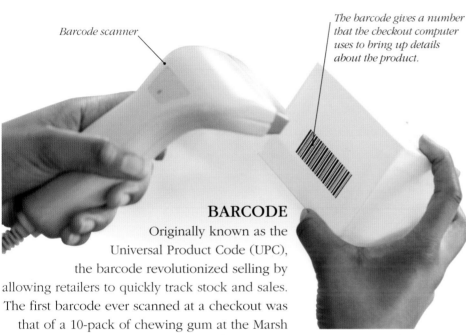

BARCODE
Originally known as the Universal Product Code (UPC), the barcode revolutionized selling by allowing retailers to quickly track stock and sales. The first barcode ever scanned at a checkout was that of a 10-pack of chewing gum at the Marsh supermarket in Troy, Ohio, USA, on 26 June 1974.

Scanning an item

BITCOIN
Operating since 2009, Bitcoin is a digital currency – it does not exist in cash form. It is not stored in, or controlled by, a financial institution such as a bank, and transactions take place directly between users.

Touchscreens allow shoppers to see what they have bought and pay for it.

SELF-SERVICE CHECKOUT
Inspired by a long wait to pay at a store in Florida, USA, David R Humble came up with a solution – in 1984, he launched the self-checkout machine. From the 1990s onwards, they have been adopted in supermarkets around the world. In fact, using one of these machines is no quicker than human cashiers, but retailers like self-service checkouts because they are cheaper than employing staff.

This shopper is paying using her credit card, but most machines will take cash, too

Money

People have been recording the exchange of goods since 30,000 BCE. Gold and silver coins were circulating in 600 BCE, while paper money emerged in China in the 11th century CE. In the modern era, new types of money and innovative methods of payment have been developed, from credit cards to contactless technology.

US dollar

- **What?** Dollar
- **Who?** Bank of North America
- **Where and when?** USA, 1785

In the period that followed American independence in 1776, the USA had no one single currency. In 1785, delegates from the 13 colonies authorized the issue of a new currency called the "dollar". In 1792, the US Congress confirmed the US dollar as the country's standard unit of money. The word "dollar" comes from the German *thaler*, which was a silver coin used throughout Europe for almost 400 years.

Traveller's cheque

- **What?** American Express traveller's cheque
- **Who?** Marcellus Flemming Berry
- **Where and when?** USA, 1891

A traveller's cheque is a bank-issued paper currency that allows the user to buy goods and services in a foreign country. In 1891, the president of American Express Marcellus Flemming Berry launched the first system of international traveller's cheques. Traveller's cheques were popular for a century, but there has been a steady decline in their use due to the widespread adoption of credit cards, ATMs, and online payments.

Traveller's cheque for use in Europe, 1990s

Credit card

- **What?** BankAmericard
- **Who?** Bank of America
- **Where and when?** USA, 1958

Diners Club issued the first charge card in 1950 in New York City, USA, but it could only be used at a small number of restaurants. In the USA in September 1958, Bank of America sent 60,000 Fresno residents what it called the BankAmericard, marking the launch of the world's first successful general-purpose credit card. In 1966, a rival group of banks launched MasterCharge, which would later become MasterCard.

Modern credit card

Plastic banknotes

- **What?** Australian dollar notes
- **Who?** Reserve Bank of Australia
- **Where and when?** Australia, 1988

Traditionally, banknotes have been made of a cotton-paper mix. In the 1980s, a group of institutions in Australia began looking at alternatives and, in 1988, the country's national bank issued the first plastic banknotes. They are highly durable, and are also much harder to forge.

Australian 100 dollar plastic banknotes

Internet banking

- **What?** Banking online
- **Who?** Stanford Federal Credit Union
- **Where and when?** USA, 1994

In 1981, the earliest versions of what would become online banking began in New York City, USA, when four banks (Citibank, Chase Manhattan, Chemical Bank, and Manufacturers Hanover) made home-banking available to their customers. People had

to use videotex – an early and not very user-friendly system combining televisions, keyboards, and modems. In 1994, with the spread of the Internet, Stanford Federal Credit Union became the first institution to offer online banking to all of its customers.

Contactless card

- **What?** UPass
- **Who?** Seoul Bus Transport Association
- **Where and when?** South Korea, 1995

In 1983, the American engineer Charles Watson patented the radio frequency identification device (RFID), which was like an electronic identity chip. This technology opened the door to contactless payment. In South Korea in 1995, the Seoul Bus Transport Association implemented the first large-scale use of contactless cards for the city's commuters. Now, many banks have adopted this payment system.

Smartphone payment

- **What?** ApplePay
- **Who?** Apple
- **Where and when?** USA, 2014

To add to the convenience of credit and debit cards and online banking, we can now increasingly pay for goods and services using smartphone apps. Wallets and purses may soon be a thing of the past. Sweden is a leader in this technology, and is very close to being a cashless society – in 2016, only one per cent of the value of all payments made there used coins or banknotes.

▼ COFFEE TO GO
Fast "smart" payments are useful for smaller purchases.

69

ONLINE SUPERSTORE

In 1995, the American Jeff Bezos launched Amazon as a book-selling website, but he always wanted his business to sell more than just books. Today, it has truly become an "Everything Store". With massive warehouses located globally, it is the world's biggest online retailer, selling and delivering nearly anything shoppers can think of. The warehouse shown here is in Peterborough, UK.

At the office

Modern offices run with help from large inventions such as photocopiers and computers, but are also full of smaller inventions that people rarely think about. From handy erasers to number-crunching calculators, office workers depend on these clever gadgets.

Sharpening pencils

- **What?** Pencil sharpener
- **Who?** Thierry Des Estivaux
- **Where and when?** France, 1847

Although the lead pencil dates back to the 16th century, it took two more centuries for a practical sharpener. Bernard Lassimone from France invented the first sharpener in 1828, but it was not until 1847 when Frenchman Thierry des Estivaux patented his design of the classic sharpener still recognizable today.

Desk-mounted sharpener

Handle is rotated to sharpen pencil.

Rubbing out mistakes

- **What?** Pencil eraser
- **Who?** Joseph Priestley
- **Where and when?** UK,1770

In 1770, the philosopher, theologian, and chemist Joseph Priestly discovered that rubber wiped the pencil marks from paper. However, it was English engineer Edward Nairne who developed the idea and marketed the first rubber eraser in Europe.

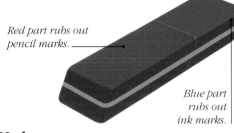

Red part rubs out pencil marks.

Blue part rubs out ink marks.

Modern eraser

Stapling paper

- **What?** Stapler
- **Who?** George McGill
- **Where and when?** USA, 1866

The first stapler was made in the 18th century for France's King Louis XV. In 1866, however, American George McGill patented what we would today recognize as a stapler. A few years later, patents were made by other inventors in the USA and UK.

Stapler, 1898

Securing documents

- **What?** Paperclip
- **Who?** Gem Manufacturing Company
- **Where and when?** UK, 1890s

Living in Germany, the Norwegian Johan Vaaler was an inventor who, in 1899, received the first patent for a paperclip. However, the improved paperclip we know and use today was created by the Gem Manufacturing Company.

Container to hold tape, 1930

Sticking objects together

- **What?** Clear adhesive tape
- **Who?** Richard Drew
- **Where and when?** USA, 1930

In 1930, American inventor Richard Drew – an employee of the 3M Company – created a clear, sticky tape to help make straight lines when painting cars. Five years later, it was marketed as an all-purpose adhesive tape.

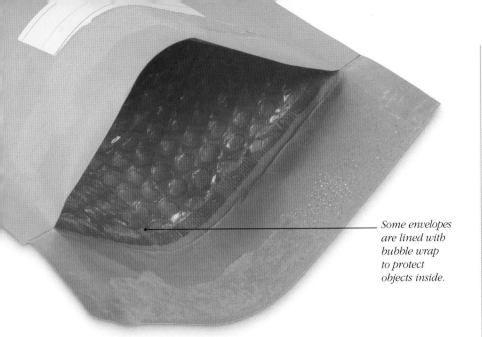

Some envelopes are lined with bubble wrap to protect objects inside.

Protecting fragile items

- **What?** Bubble wrap
- **Who?** Alfred Fielding and Marc Chavannes
- **Where and when?** USA, 1957

In 1957, two American engineers, Alfred Fielding and Marc Chavannes, sealed two shower curtains together, trapping air bubbles between the layers. They tried to sell it as "3-D wallpaper", but that venture soon failed. In 1960, they realized this material was perfect for packing fragile items, and bubble wrap was born.

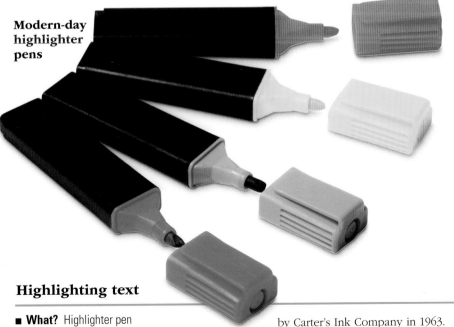

Modern-day highlighter pens

Highlighting text

- **What?** Highlighter pen
- **Who?** Carter's Ink Company
- **Where and when?** USA, 1963

Marker pens have been around since the early 20th century, but a felt-tip pen with translucent colour that made text stand out without obscuring it was first produced by Carter's Ink Company in 1963. It was sold under the name Hi-Liter. Although today many colours are available, 85 per cent of all bought highlighters are in fluorescent yellow and pink.

Calculating on the move

- **What?** Electronic calculator
- **Who?** Jack Kilby, Jerry Merryman, James van Tassel, and Clive Sinclair
- **Where and when?** USA, 1967

Engineers at the American company Texas Instruments developed the first handheld calculator in 1967. Other companies improved the technology and, by the 1970s, the calculator had become pocket-sized and affordable for everyone.

Canon Pocketronic, 1970

Re-using handwritten notes

- **What?** Post-it notes
- **Who?** Arthur Fry and Spencer Silver
- **Where and when?** USA, 1974

After making a unique adhesive by accident, Arthur Fry and Spencer Sullivan came up with sticky, re-usable pieces of paper. It was first marketed as Press 'n Peel in 1977.

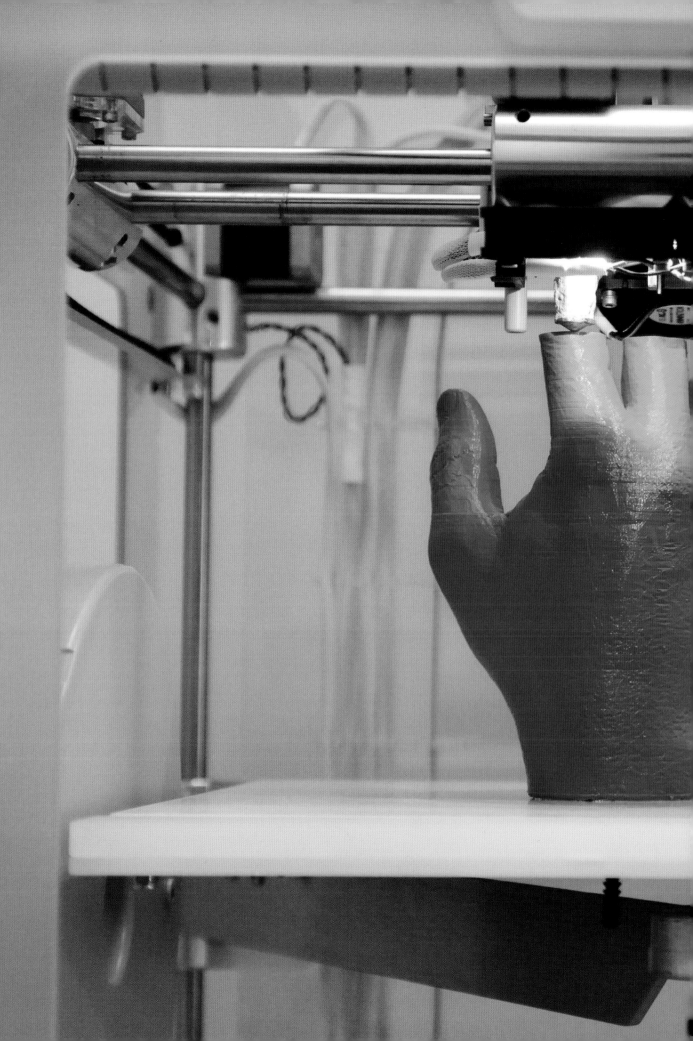

3-D PRINTING

We have barely begun to discover what 3-D printing can do. The process of feeding a digital 3-D design into a computer, which then instructs a machine to create the object with plastic, is limited only by our imaginations. Today, some hospitals print replacement body parts, engineers print houses, and the US luge team at the 2018 Winter Olympics rode 3D-printed sledges. Who knows what will come next?

Robots

When people first imagined robots, they thought of mechanical humans, with slow, jerky movements and slow thought. In fact, the first effective robots did repetitive, mindless work on factory production lines. However, with the introduction of AI (artificial intelligence), robots have shown that they can outsmart us. Who knows where robotic technology might take us?

WOW!

The term "robot" was invented by Czech author Karel Capek, from his 1920 play R.U.R. (*Rossum's Universal Robots*).

TORTOISE ROBOTS

The first autonomous (self-controlling) robots were Elmer and Elsie, created by the American-born neuroscientist William Grey Walter of the Burden Neurological Institute, UK, in 1948–1949. These robots could find their way to a recharging point when low on power.

Shell sensed when robot bumped into objects so it could move around them

Tortoise robot, c.1950

INDUSTRIAL ROBOTS

Americans George Devol and Joe Engelberger designed and marketed the first programmable robot arm, called Unimate, and sold it to General Motors in 1960. It was used to lift hot pieces of metal from a die-casting machine and stack them. From then, robotics quickly transformed the automotive industry.

Baxter, created by Rethink Robotics, 2012 – the first robot to work alongside humans on a production line

Baxter can do a variety of tasks, such as packing boxes.

WABOT-1

In 1972, scientists at Waseda University, Japan, unveiled Wabot-1, the world's first full-scale humanoid intelligent robot. It was the first android – a robot that resembled humans in some ways. It was able to walk, communicate with a person using its artificial mouth, measure distances and directions to objects, and grip and transport objects with its hands.

Wabot-1 was the first robot to walk on two legs like a human.

MILITARY ROBOTS

In the USA, Boston-based Denning Mobile Electronics designed the Sentry robot (right), in 1985, as a security guard that can patrol for up to 14 hours and radio in alerts to human security guards if it senses anything out of the ordinary. Today, South Korea uses Samsung armed military robots to guard the border with North Korea.

ROBOTS VS HUMANS

In 1997, IBM's Deep Blue robot beat the world chess champion Garry Kasparov in a match. In 2011, IBM's Watson robot defeated human panellists in the TV quiz show *Jeopardy!* Machines have also beaten humans at board games Scrabble and Go.

IBM's Watson robot competing against human contestants

LIFE-LIKE ROBOTS

Some of the latest robots are able to talk like humans, walk like humans, and express a wide range of emotions. In 2016, the Chinese presented Jia Jia, an AI (artifical intelligence) humanoid (right), which claimed to be the most human-like robot ever made.

Helpful robots

In 1920, the Czech writer Karel Capek staged a play that introduced the world to the word "robot". The story ends with the robots taking over from the humans. Since then, there have been continued fears about where artificial intelligence might lead us. In reality, however, robots are mostly developed to help us in almost every area of our lives.

The camera takes pictures where it is too dangerous for humans to go.

Search robots

- **What?** PackBot
- **Who?** iRobot
- **Where and when?** USA, 1998

The PackBot is a series of military robots. They have a robotic arm and camera and are mainly used for exploration – checking buildings for explosives, for example. They were used in Japan to measure radiation at the Fukushima Daiichi Nuclear Power Plant after it was destroyed in an earthquake in 2011, and to search the World Trade Center in New York City, USA, after the 2001 terrorist attacks.

Robo-pets

- **What?** AIBO
- **Who?** Sony
- **Where and when?** Japan, 1999

AIBO was a series of robotic pets made by Sony in 1999. With four legs and a tail, they looked like dogs. Sony stopped making them in 2005, but resumed with a new model in 2018, which is even more dog-like, using artificial intelligence, motion sensors, cameras, and cloud computing to interact with its owner and surroundings.

The robotic paws can "sense" objects like balls, and play with them, just like a real dog.

Robo-astronauts

- **What?** Robonaut 2 (R2)
- **Who?** NASA
- **Where and when?** USA, 2010

NASA developed Robonaut to work alongside astronauts on manned space missions. The latest version, R2, is designed to have tasks programmed and then carry them out without any human supervision. In February 2011, R2 was sent to work on the International Space Station.

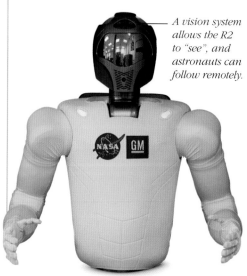

A vision system allows the R2 to "see", and astronauts can follow remotely.

Disaster-relief robots

- **What?** Chimp
- **Who?** Carnegie Mellon University
- **Where and when?** USA, 2012

Chimp was one of many robots designed to compete in a US Defense Agency challenge in 2015. The competition promoted the development of robots to work in emergency-response scenarios. The robots had to drive, clamber over rubble, open doors, climb ladders, and use tools.

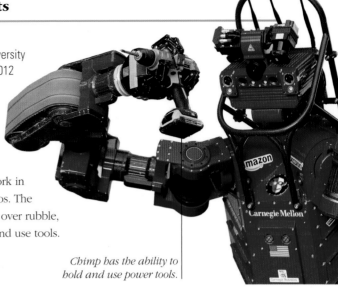

Chimp has the ability to hold and use power tools.

Educational robots

- **What?** NAO
- **Who?** SoftBank Group
- **Where and when?** France, 2004

NAO (pronounced "now") began life as a footballer, as the robot used in the RoboCup – an annual international robot football competition. It still plays in this competition, but increasingly this little robot is used for research and educational purposes in numerous academic institutions worldwide. Today, more than 10,000 NAO robots are in use in more than 50 countries. In a UK school, this robot was used to teach autistic children, as they can be a calming, positive influence on those with special educational needs.

The six-wheeled delivery bot can travel up to 6.5 km/h (4 mph).

Self-driving delivery bots

- **What?** Self-driving delivery robot
- **Who?** Starship Technologies
- **Where and when?** USA, 2015

In some cities, pedestrians are getting used to sharing pavement space with small robot vehicles taking fast food orders to customers. On arrival, the person receiving the delivery keys a code into their smartphone to access their food. San Francisco and Washington, DC, in the USA, as well as Tallinn in Estonia, are already using this technology, and many more countries are now testing it.

Warrior robots

- **What?** Spot
- **Who?** Boston Dynamics
- **Where and when?** USA, 2015

Boston Dynamics developed the first robots to run and manoeuvre like dogs. One of them, BigDog, was designed as a robotic packhorse to carry equipment over rough terrain into battle for the US Army. However, it proved to be too noisy and so the company developed smaller, quieter versions called Spot (right), then SpotMini.

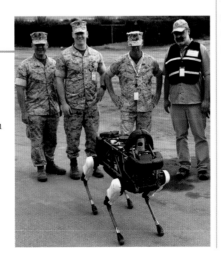

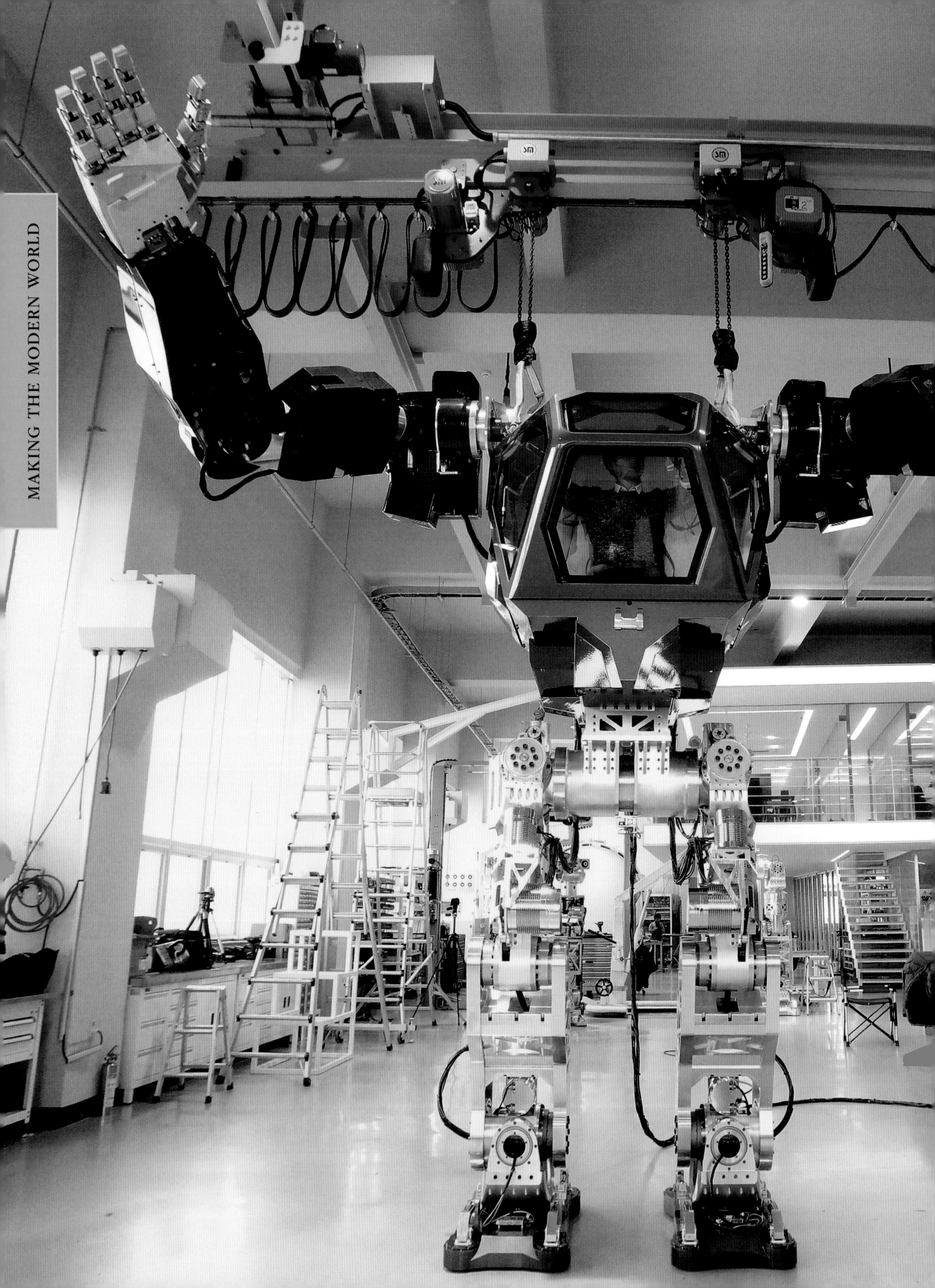

먼 저 치

THE ROBOTS ARE COMING!

For decades, film-makers have been designing awesome robots for movies, and at last it seems real life is catching up. In Korea, engineers are testing Future Technology's Method-2, a robotic, bipedal giant controlled by a human pilot sitting in its chest. If the pilot lifts an arm, Method-2 lifts an arm, only this arm is about 3 m (10 ft) long!

GET MOVING

More than two centuries ago, people travelled mainly on foot or horseback. Now we can whizz along motorways in cars, take a trip on a cruise ship, and jet between continents.

Bicycle

In the 1870s, riding a bicycle was for the brave few, with the rider perched on a giant wheel. The perils of this design led to the development of "safety" bicycles, which had a lightweight tube frame and two equal-sized wheels – a steerable front wheel and a chain-driven back wheel. The designs of bicycles today and the materials used to build them continue to be improved, while new technologies make cycling easier.

John Dunlop's son riding a bicycle with inflatable tyres, c.1888

Chain attached to pedals drives the rear wheel.

Rear and front wheels are the same size.

ROVER SAFETY BICYCLE

The safety bicycle was designed by the English inventor John Kemp Starley in 1885. With wheels no taller than a leg and a low, sprung saddle, the Rover Safety Bicycle was safer than other early bicycles, and more comfortable.

INFLATABLE TYRE

Until 1888, people often rode bicycles with tyres made of leather or solid rubber, resulting in a bumpy ride. Although the first inflatable rubber tyre had been invented by the Scottish engineer Robert Thomson in 1845, it didn't really catch on until the Scottish inventor John Boyd Dunlop made the first practical, air-filled tyre in 1887. He developed these tyres after experimenting with rubber tubing – made from garden hose – on the wheels of his son's tricycle.

WOW!

In 2017, more than 430 million people owned bicycles in China.

Some helmets have streamlined tails to reduce air resistance.

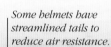

BICYCLE BELL

About the same time as Starley invented the Rover Safety Bicycle, the English inventor John Dedicoat is said to have invented the bicycle bell. It quickly became vital in those early days, when walkers had no experience of traffic, except for noisy horses. Its basic design – a small, thumb-operated lever inside a round metal case – has remained popular.

LED bulbs function as turning signals, and are controlled by buttons on the bicycle's handlebars.

HEADGEAR

Helmets provide vital protection for a cyclist's head in case of accidents. The first modern helmet, made of light, tough plastic foam, was introduced in the 1970s. Helmets have come a long way since then – the Lumos (left) is a smart helmet with its own signals and brake lights, just like a car.

Chin strap

SMART BIKES

Since the late 1990s, cyclists have been able to attach mini-computers to their bicycles to make them "smart". These can do anything from telling cyclists their exact position, speed, and route using Global Positioning System (GPS) satellites to changing gear automatically in response to conditions.

Display provides details of the course taken.

REFLECTIVE JACKETS

In traffic, a cyclist's life depends on being seen. They are often advised to wear reflective or high-visibility jackets, which glow in low light. Fluorescent jackets glow in bright colours by converting invisible UV light into visible light. After dark, retro-reflective strips reflect light from car headlamps.

▶ RACING BIKES

Olympic track bikes are made with thick carbon-fibre frames. These frames are specially designed to handle the force with which the Olympic cyclists pedal.

Handlebars

CARBON-FIBRE BIKES

Originally developed for the space industry, carbon-fibre composites are superlight, superstrong materials. In 1996, the American company Kestrel made a streamlined bicycle frame from carbon. Although carbon-fibre frames are expensive, carbon fibre is now used for making the frames – as well as the wheels – of all track racing bikes, and also for many road bikes.

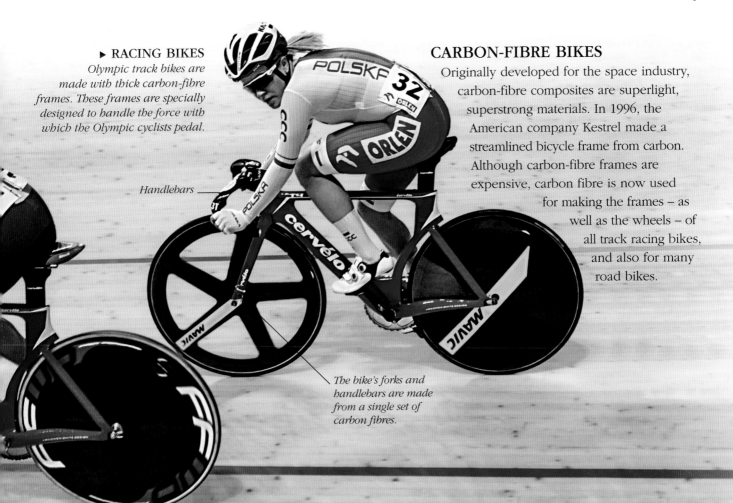

The bike's forks and handlebars are made from a single set of carbon fibres.

Two wheels

The idea of bicycles dates back to about 1817, when the German inventor Baron Karl von Drais linked two wheels together on a wooden frame. Drais's bicycle – the "draisine" – had no pedals, and the rider walked along when not freewheeling. People laughingly called it a dandy horse, but the idea caught on.

Michaux velocipede, 1869

Pedals on the front axle

Pedal power

- **What?** Velocipede with pedals
- **Who?** Pierre Lallemont and Pierre Michaux
- **Where and when?** France, 1863

The addition of pedals to bicycles led to the "velocipede". Cyclists pushed on these pedals, making the bicycles as fast as a horse. The velocipede was created in Pierre Michaux's workshop, but the idea may have come from his employee Pierre Lallemont. Riding a velocipede was so bumpy that it was also called a "boneshaker".

Electric bicycle (e-bike)

- **What?** Electric bicycle
- **Who?** Hosea Libbey
- **Where and when?** USA, 1897

The American inventor Hosea Libbey attached a battery-powered electric motor to a bicycle. However, electric bicycles (e-bikes) only really took off another century later. Today, pedelecs (bicycles in which the rider pedals to help the electric motor) are becoming very popular.

Battery

eZee Sprint, electric bicycle, 2016

Campagnolo Gran Sport 10-speed gear, 1963

Cable-change gears

- **What?** Campagnolo Gran Sport Cambio Corsa
- **Who?** Tullio Campagnolo
- **Where and when?** Italy, 1948

Until the 1940s, racing cyclists who needed to change gear for a hill had to get off the bike and change it by hand. The Italian rider Tullio Campagnolo got so fed up when he lost a race after stopping to change gears in freezing conditions that he invented a cable-operated gear lever system.

Schwinn Sting-Ray Apple Krate, 1973

BMX (Bicycle motocross)

- **What?** Schwinn Sting-Ray
- **Who?** Al Fritz
- **Where and when?** USA, 1963

In the 1960s, kids got the idea that bicycles weren't just for riding sedately along roads. They could be used for flinging about on dirt tracks like motocross bikes, and doing "wheelies". It started with the Schwinn Sting-Ray in the mid-1960s, and soon developed into the rugged, fun BMX bicycles.

WOW!
In 1995, Fred Rompelberg of the Netherlands set a world record with a cycling speed of 268.83 km/h (166.9 mph).

Folding bicycle

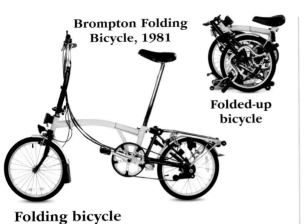

Brompton Folding Bicycle, 1981

Folded-up bicycle

- **What?** Graziella
- **Who?** Rinaldo Donzelli
- **Where and when?** Italy, 1964

People have been making folding bicycles for as long as there have been bicycles. Although the first fold-up design dates back to the 1860s, it was the Graziella that made these bicycles popular. In 1976, the British Brompton Folding Bicycle hit the road, and became world-famous. Light and speedy, it could be folded in less than 20 seconds to make a compact package.

Modern recumbent bicycle

- **What?** Avatar 2000
- **Who?** David Gordon Wilson
- **Where and when?** USA, early 1980s

On "recumbent" (reclining) bicycles, the rider lies right back, with the pedals out in front. This is not only comfortable, but it cuts down the body area presented to the wind, so is great for speed records, although the restricted view makes it less practical for city use.

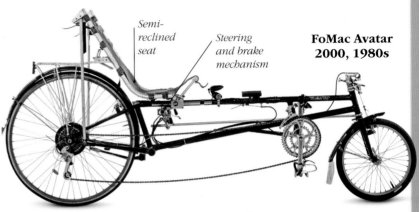

Semi-reclined seat

Steering and brake mechanism

FoMac Avatar 2000, 1980s

Mountain bicycle

- **What?** Specialized Stumpjumper
- **Who?** Tom Ritchey, Gary Fisher, Charles Kelly
- **Where and when?** USA, 1981

BMX bicycles were thought of mainly as bicycles for kids. Then, in 1981, the "Stumpjumper" was introduced. This was the first mountain bicycle. Today, mountain bikes are hugely popular with all ages – not just for those who want to ride off-road, but also those who want a rugged bicycle for bumpy city streets.

Raised knobs, or "lugs", on the wheels provide a firm grip on the rough terrain.

Strong, compact frame

Short, straight handlebars for easy handling

FAST FACTS

- In 1986, Kestrel made the first streamlined bicycle frame from carbon composites.
- In 2013, Shimano introduced an electronic system for changing the gears almost instantly.
- In 2016–2017, the American cyclist Amanda Coker cycled 160,930 km (100,000 miles) in just 423 days, averaging more than 380 km (236 miles) a day.

SKATING ON AIR

It is not known who thought of fixing rollerskate wheels to a board, but skateboarding first appeared in California, USA, around the 1950s. Skaters use streets for their sport, showing off stunts, such as an "ollie" or a "kickflip", or go to specially designed skateparks. In the 2020 Olympic Games in Tokyo, Japan, skateboarding will be included as an event for the first time.

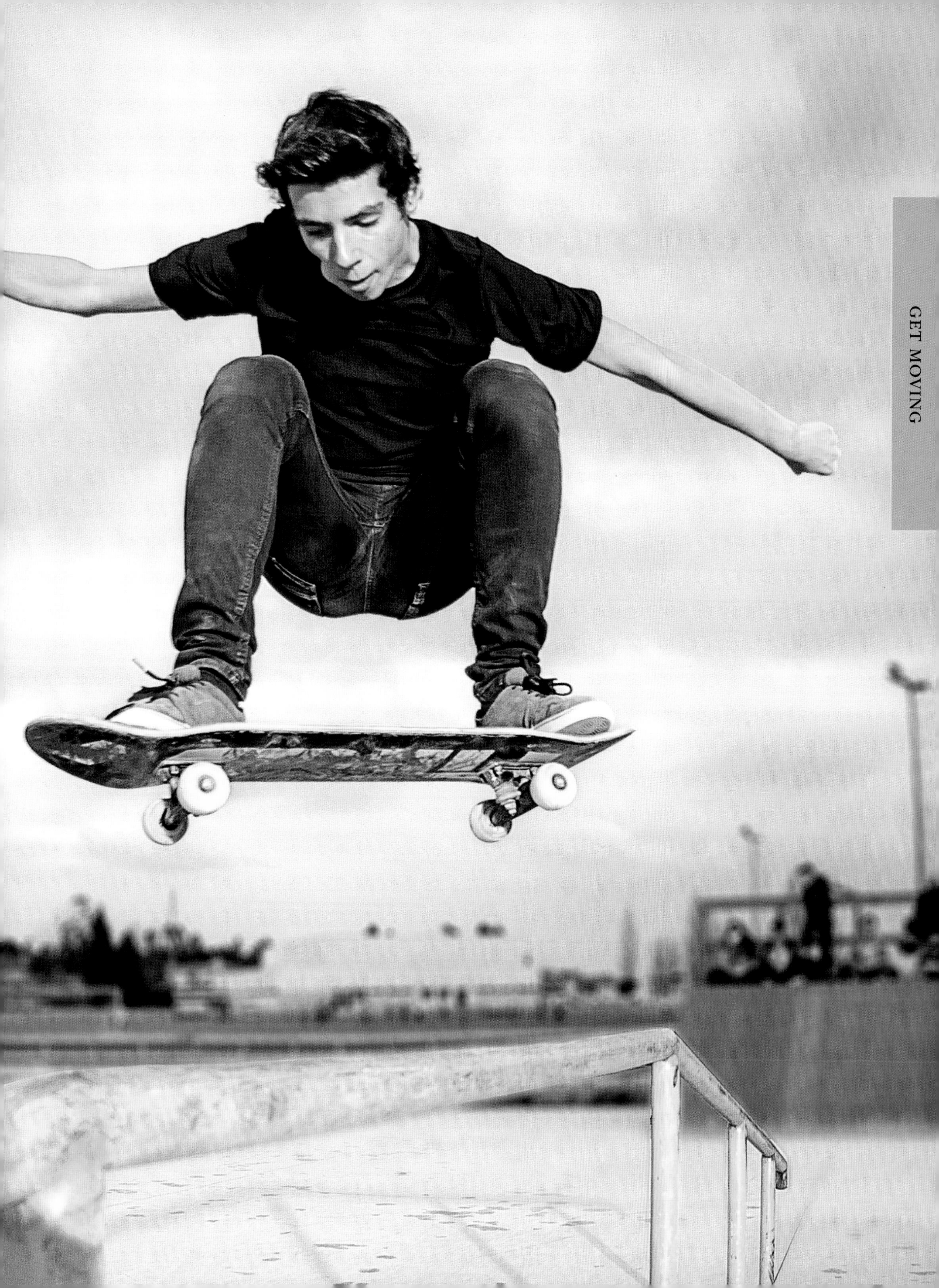

Motorbikes

Although the American inventor Sylvester Roper built the first motorbike in 1869, powering it by steam, the motorbike's story really took off in 1885 with Daimler and Maybach's motorbike. This vehicle had a petrol engine to power the rear wheel via a moving belt. Motorbikes have come far since then, but most still have a petrol engine and a drive belt, or chain.

Handlebars swivelled the front wheel to steer.

Padded saddle for comfort

First motorbike

- **What?** Daimler Reitwagen
- **Who?** Gottlieb Daimler and Wilhelm Maybach
- **Where and when?** Germany, 1885

In 1885, the German engineer Gottlieb Daimler and German designer Wilhelm Maybach pioneered the Reitwagen (riding wagon) – a motorbike that was a test for the first petrol-engined, four-wheeled car built the following year. They took the basic idea of the bicycle introduced by the British inventor J K Starley (see p.84) and attached an engine to power the rear wheel using a leather belt.

Daimler added two tiny wheels to balance the bike.

First production motorbike

- **What?** Hildebrand & Wolfmüller Motorrad
- **Who?** Heinrich and Wilhelm Hildebrand, and Alois Wolfmüller
- **Where and when?** Germany, 1894

In 1894, the German Hildebrand brothers teamed up with the German engineer Wolfmüller to create the first production bike. It was the first to be called a motorbike, and more than 2,000 of them were made between 1894 and 1897.

First bike with telescopic forks

- **What?** BMW R12
- **Who?** BMW
- **Where and when?** Germany, 1935

The BMW R12 was the first bike with telescopic forks, which connect a bike's front wheel and axle to its frame.

The telescopic forks are crucial to motorbike handling and safety, ensuring the front wheel stays on the ground. While earlier bikes had springs, a fluid-filled telescopic fork in the BMW R12 helped to reduce bouncing.

Telescopic fork

▼ WOODEN BICYCLE

Daimler and his colleague Maybach made the Reitwagen from wood, and the drive belt from leather.

Iron-rimmed front wheel

Vespa 125, 1951

Vespa scooter

- ■ **What?** Vespa
- ■ **Who?** Piaggio
- ■ **Where and when?** Italy, 1946

The Italian Piaggio company decided to build a comfortable, stylish, easy-to-ride two-wheeler for zipping through the country's narrow and bumpy streets. The result was the Vespa (wasp) scooter, which continues to be a huge success.

First superbike

- ■ **What?** Honda CB750 Dream
- ■ **Who?** Honda
- ■ **Where and when?** Japan, 1969

The Honda 750 Dream was the first "superbike" – a comfortable and extremely powerful modern bike. Up until then, bikes had to be started with a kick-start ignition. The CB750 was a high-performance bike with a simple push button electric start and disc brakes for stopping quickly.

Water-cooled superbike

- ■ **What?** BMW R1200GS
- ■ **Who?** BMW Motorrad
- ■ **Where and when?** Germany, 2012

Typically, bike engines are cooled by flowing air, but that works well only when the bike is moving fast. So, some bikes have a jacket of cooling water circulating around the engine to make the engine quieter and more reliable. The BMW R1200GS is a powerful superbike that is cooled using both air and water.

First electric superbike

- ■ **What?** Lightning LS218
- ■ **Who?** Lightning
- ■ **Where and when?** USA, 2010

Most people thought electric bikes were slow and dull. Nobody imagined a bike that could whiz along almost silently, driven by only an electric motor. The Lightning LS218 changed people's minds by becoming the fastest bike on the road at the time, with a top speed of 350.8 km/h (218 mph).

Futuristic motorbike

- ■ **What?** BMW Vision Next 100
- ■ **Who?** BMW Motorrad
- ■ **Where and when?** Germany, 2016

Some bike manufacturers are developing bikes with an amazing gyroscopic system that keeps them upright under all circumstances, no matter what the rider does. The BMW Vision Next 100 is one such test bike. When riding, the biker wears a special visor, with a data display that is activated when required. This bike might be a one-off or a sign of motorbikes to come in the future.

Cars for the masses

The very first cars from the late 19th century were hand-built for the rich. The American industrialist Henry Ford (see pp.96–97) dreamed of building a car cheap enough for ordinary people to buy, so, in 1908, he started making the Ford Model T. By bringing mass-production techniques to his motor car – which was made on an assembly line at low cost – Ford revolutionized car manufacturing. Today, there are more than a billion cars on the world's roads.

Most metal fittings on early cars were made of brass.

ONE MODEL

To keep costs down, it is said that Ford told customers they could have the car "in any color you like as long as it's black". This is a myth, since the Model T came in various colours. However, Ford pioneered the idea that all cars need to follow a standard template.

THE MODEL T

In Ford's Model T factory, each worker added only a single part – always the same one – to each car as it slid past on the assembly line. This ensured that every car produced was identical, and built quickly and cheaply. This method of mass production was so successful that, by the time the last Model T came out of the factory in 1927, more than 15 million cars had been built.

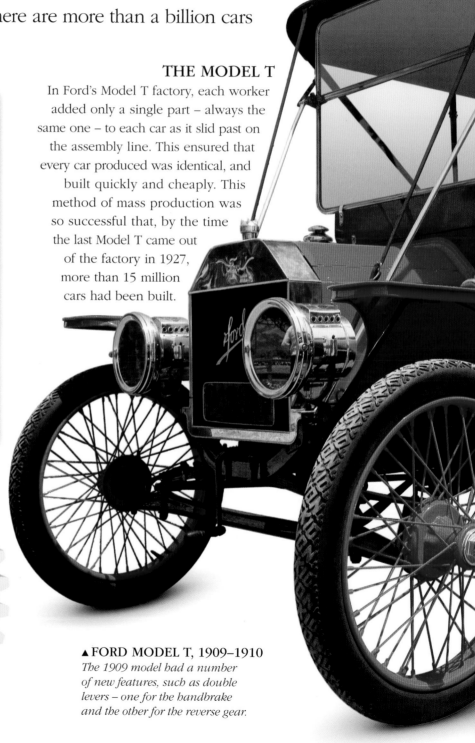

WOW!

Every year, cars burn 1.5 trillion gallons of oil – enough to fill more than two million Olympic swimming pools.

▲ FORD MODEL T, 1909–1910
The 1909 model had a number of new features, such as double levers – one for the handbrake and the other for the reverse gear.

HOW A CAR WORKS

GET MOVING

Most early Ts were open-top, with a fold-back soft top to keep off the rain.

In cars that run on petrol or diesel, the engine is powered by burning the fuel inside cylinders. As the fuel burns, it expands and pushes on pistons, rotating a crankshaft. The crankshaft then turns gears, which adjust the balance between speed and power. The gears turn rods called half-shafts to drive the wheels.

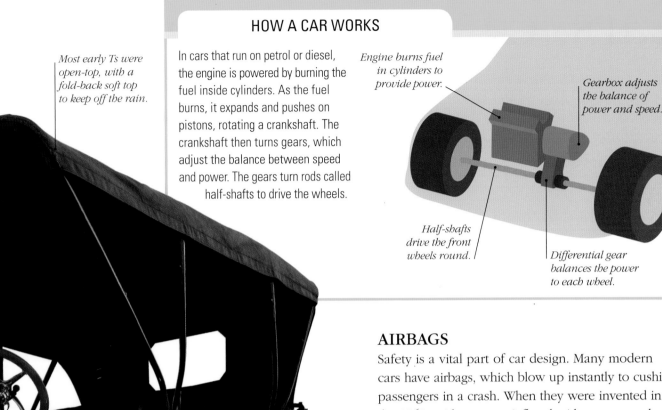

Engine burns fuel in cylinders to provide power.

Gearbox adjusts the balance of power and speed.

Half-shafts drive the front wheels round.

Differential gear balances the power to each wheel.

AIRBAGS

Safety is a vital part of car design. Many modern cars have airbags, which blow up instantly to cushion passengers in a crash. When they were invented in the 1960s, airbags were inflated with compressed air. Now, the impact triggers a chemical reaction, which instantly creates swelling bubbles of gas to fill the bag.

Airbag and dummy used in a crash test

The wheels, like those of a bicycle, were wire-spoked, making them cheap and light.

ADDED FEATURES

Cars are developing all the time – existing features are improved and new features are added. Cars may also be built with extra technology, including parking sensors (left), defoggers, navigation systems, backup cameras, and automatic emergency brakes. In a few years, people may be able to sit back and command the car to drive them to a destination.

Front parking sensors alert the driver to nearby obstacles.

Cars, cars, cars

The earliest cars, or "horseless carriages", were just carts powered by an engine instead of being pulled by a horse. Many of the first cars used steam engines. The big breakthrough came in 1862, when the Belgian engineer Étienne Lenoir created a car powered by his newly designed "internal combustion" engine, which burned gas inside a cylinder to create the power.

Petrol-engined car

■ **What?** Hippomobile
■ **Who?** Étienne Lenoir
■ **Where and when?** France, 1863

Lenoir's first car from 1862 had three wheels and was powered by burning gas, which was ignited repeatedly by an electric spark. The next year, Lenoir modified his engine and switched to petrol as a fuel for a new car, which he named the Hippomobile.

First practical electric vehicle

■ **What?** Electric car
■ **Who?** William Ayrton and John Perry
■ **Where and when?** UK, 1881

The first practical electric car was a battery-powered tricycle made by the British engineers William Ayrton and John Perry. Electric cars are now thought of as cars for the future because they create less pollution.

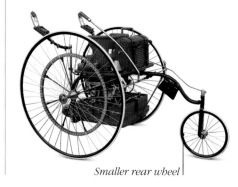

Smaller rear wheel

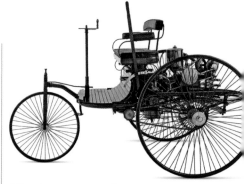

First car on sale

■ **What?** Motorwagen
■ **Who?** Karl Benz
■ **Where and when?** Germany, 1888

In 1888, the German engineer Karl Benz built the first car for sale to the public – the Benz Patent Motorwagen. To show people how well the new car worked, his wife, Bertha, made the first long car trip in it, travelling 180 km (111 miles). This car would become a huge success, and Benz was soon selling 600 cars a year.

People's car

■ **What?** Volkswagen Beetle Model 1300
■ **Who?** Ferdinand Porsche
■ **Where and when?** Germany, 1938

The Volkswagen Beetle was commissioned as a "people's car" – an inexpensive vehicle that was affordable for everyone. It was launched commercially in 1945, and proved to be the most popular car ever. By the time production ended in 2003, 21.5 million Beetle cars had been made.

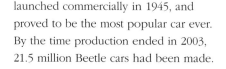

Volkswagen Beetle, 1948

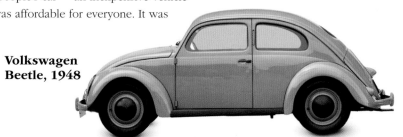

The compact car

- **What?** BMC Mini
- **Who?** Alec Issigonis
- **When?** UK, 1959

The Mini was one of the first successful tiny cars designed for the city. It saved space by mounting the engine sideways and using front-wheel drive, not the back. This idea proved so good that now most small cars are made like this.

BMC Austin Seven Mini

Hybrid

- **What?** Toyota Prius
- **Who?** Toyota
- **Where and when?** Japan, 1997

A hybrid car has both a battery-powered electric motor and a fuel-powered engine. The electric motor powers the car whenever it is fully charged, but the car can also run on the fuel engine. The first successful commercially available hybrid car was the Toyota Prius, which was introduced in 1997.

Electric car

- **What?** Tesla Roadster
- **Who?** Martin Eberhard and Marc Tarpenning
- **Where and when?** USA, 2008

Cars that use petrol and diesel produce air and noise pollution. So, in 2008, the American car company Tesla revived the idea of the electric car with the Roadster, their stylish sports car. Though these cars do not use gas or diesel, they can take a long time to recharge after each trip. Electric cars are better for the environment.

Driverless car

- **What?** Audi A8 L
- **Who?** Audi
- **Where and when?** Germany, 2017

An autonomous, or driverless, car can sense its environment and steer without a human driver, using radar, lasers, and GPS (see p.265) to "see" where it is going. The

Audi A8 L is the first fully driverless car to go into production. It can drive for long distances, brake, and even park on its own.

Retractable roof panel

Batteries are stored in the rear of the car.

▲ CLEANER AND FASTER
The Roadster produces no pollution. It runs on electricity supplied by a pack of powerful lithium-ion batteries.

Henry Ford

The American industrialist Henry Ford made history by launching the affordable Ford Model T (see pp.92–93). By using a simple design and mass-producing this car in a giant factory, he turned the motor vehicle from a luxury item for the rich into an everyday item for the masses. If it weren't for Ford, cars today might have been as rare as luxury yachts.

A CAR FOR EVERYBODY

The speed of the production line meant that Ford could keep up with demand. By 1914, Ford was rolling out more than a quarter of a million cars every year – half of all cars made in the USA.

▶ **THE MODEL T**
Henry Ford stands next to one of his Model Ts, c.1920. Made of lightweight steel, this car was robust and easy to maintain.

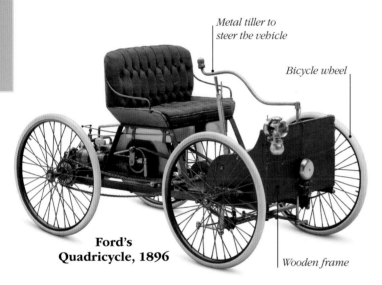

Metal tiller to steer the vehicle

Bicycle wheel

Ford's Quadricycle, 1896

Wooden frame

KEEPING IT SIMPLE

Ford's first car – the simple, cheap Quadricycle of 1896 – was little more than a gasoline engine mounted on four bicycle wheels. This single-seater had twin drive belts (see p.90) that could be operated using a floor-mounted clutch. His idea was to build a car that could be manufactured quickly and in large numbers by labourers, not carefully crafted by skilled coachbuilders.

ASSEMBLY LINE

Ford factory manager Charles Sorensen introduced the assembly line in 1913. Each car was dragged along rails by a chain and each worker added a part, the same one each time. This non-stop process churned out a new car every 10 seconds.

LIFE STORY

1863	1876	1879	1896
Son of William and Mary, Henry Ford is born on 30 July in Wayne County, Michigan, USA.	He dismantles and rebuilds a pocket watch given to him by his father. The young Ford starts repairing watches for others.	He leaves home to become an apprentice machinist in Detroit, where he learns to handle steam engines.	Ford makes the Quadricycle, and test-drives it in Detroit, USA.

1903–1908	1913	1917	1947
He starts the Ford Motor Company and sells his first car, the Model A (left) for US$850. In 1908, he launches the Model T.	Ford's company introduces the moving assembly line for mass production of their cars in Michigan.	He builds the world's largest factory at Dearborn, Michigan, which houses every type of part needed to produce a car on one site.	Ford dies at his home in Dearborn. By this time, nearly all the cars in the world are mass-produced.

PICK A CAR!

The Car Tower (seen from above here) has 400 compartments and is automatically refilled with new cars using a vertical conveyor belt. It is located near the Volkswagen factory in Wolfsburg, Germany. When a customer wants to pick up a car, the tower dispenses it like a giant vending machine, with robot arms pulling the correct car out and bringing it down.

Public transport

As industrial cities, such as London and Paris, grew bigger in the early 19th century, a growing number of people lived further away from their places of work. This spurred the growth of public transport systems. Some commuters caught trains to work, and more and more people had to use horse-drawn buses, and later motorbuses and trams.

First travel coach

- **What?** Mercedes-Benz O 10000
- **Who?** Mercedes-Benz
- **Where and when?** Germany, 1938

Until the 1930s, buses were mostly used for short city rides, but with the creation of autobahns (see p.103) in Germany, German bus-makers began to build large, fast coaches for long journeys. The powerful, long-nosed Mercedes-Benz Ó 10000 was the biggest of these.

Arm in contact with overhead cable

First electric tram

- **What?** Siemens tram
- **Who?** Werner von Siemens
- **Where and when?** Germany, 1881

The world's first electric tram system opened in St Petersburg, Russia, but Berlin was the first city to develop it properly with the Siemens tram of 1881. Berlin had already run horse-drawn trams for 20 years, so the switch to electric was simple. These electric trams ran on tracks and were powered by electricity from overhead cables.

The motorbus

- **What?** B-type bus
- **Who?** Frank Searle
- **Where and when?** UK, 1909

London led the way with motorbuses, especially its famous red-painted, open-topped double deckers. The legendary B-type was the world's first mass-produced bus. About 900 of these buses were also adapted for carrying troops during World War I.

Luxury coach

- **What?** GM Scenicruiser GX-2
- **Who?** Raymond Loewy
- **Where and when?** USA, 1951

Designed for the Greyhound bus company, the Scenicruiser was an American icon. With its ultra-modern design and unparalleled comfort, it was tailor-made for the vast distances between American cities, cruising the highways in style from the mid-1950s right through to the 1970s.

Scenicruiser, 1958

H₂ Fuel Cell Bus

Rail to Beach Shuttle
FREE SERVICE

Mercedes-Benz

ECOBUS 3

Tram-train

- **What?** Tram-train
- **Who?** Karlsruher Verkehrsverbund (KVV)
- **Where and when?** Germany, 1992

With cities needing clean transport, trams have been revived. A new concept is the tram-train, which can run on the city's tramway lines as well as the rail networks that connect to other cities. The idea started in Karlsruhe in Germany and has spread to other cities around the world.

Modern tram-train in Mulhouse, France

Zero-emission bus

- **What?** Citaro FuelCELL
- **Who?** Daimler Benz
- **Where and when?** Germany, 2003

Motorbuses emit lots of polluting fumes. That's why "zero-emission" fuel cell buses may be the future. In a fuel cell, hydrogen combines with oxygen to generate electricity. The only by-product is water, so there is no pollution.

Podcar

- **What?** ULTra
- **Who?** Martin Lowson
- **Where and when?** UK, 2005

Personal Rapid Transport (PRT) systems are a cross between driverless cars and trams. Small electric vehicles, called "podcars", move in quick succession on a track. They can each carry six to ten people at a time.

On the road

The building of roads goes back thousands of years. Ancient Sumeria, Egypt, the Roman Empire, and the Incas all made paved roads. Ancient Islamic cities even made roads using tar. However, it was not until the Industrial Revolution (see pp.52–53) and the motor car (see pp.92–93) that the world saw a major explosion in road building. Today, there are more than 65 million km (40 million miles) of road in the world.

(see pp.52–53)
(see pp.92–93)

Lights are programmed to turn on and off to control traffic flow at every junction.

FAST FACTS

- Most roads are laid with tarmac, which is a mix of bitumen and tiny stones called aggregate.
- Roads are now often made of concrete, which costs more than tarmac to lay but lasts longer.
- Every year, 102 million tonnes of bitumen is used to make roads and airport runways.

TRAFFIC LIGHTS

Traffic lights are vital for controlling the movement of traffic and ensuring safety at busy junctions. In the early days of motoring, drivers relied on hinged signals and traffic police. Then, in 1912, in Salt Lake City, Utah, USA, the American electrician Lester Wire installed the first coloured electric traffic lights. Now, typically, traffic lights use LEDs (see p.181) controlled by computer systems.

(see p.181)

EARLY ROADS

The ancient Romans were great pioneers of road building. To ensure the swift movement of their armies and trade around their empire, the Romans replaced winding tracks with 80,000 km (50,000 miles) of long, straight road paved with stone. They would have a slope in the middle so rainwater ran off properly.

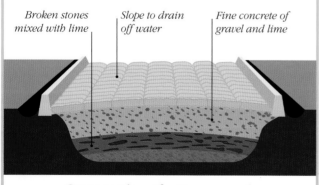

Broken stones mixed with lime *Slope to drain off water* *Fine concrete of gravel and lime*

Cross-section of a Roman road, a forerunner of modern roads

CAT'S EYES

As the story goes, while the British inventor Percy Shaw was driving home one night in 1933, he saw the eyes of a cat glowing in his headlights. It gave him the idea of reflectors – now called cat's eyes or studs – to show the centre of a road at night. Modern studs often have solar-powered LEDs, which glow all night.

Cat's eyes on a road in the UK

WOW!

In 2010, in one of the world's biggest traffic jams, thousands of cars were stuck on a Chinese highway for more than 10 days.

Transparent blocks placed on top of solar panels

ENERGY-GENERATING ROADS

Road engineers are now experimenting with the idea that roads could produce energy. In the future, roads may not just be a flat tarmac surface, but they could be built with solar panels, or "piezo-electric" panels, which use the pressure of vehicles passing over them to generate an electric current.

THE OPEN ROAD

Motorways, freeways, and expressways are wide roads for motor vehicles to travel fast. These have separate lanes to allow safe overtaking, with no signals and road junctions, allowing a continual flow of traffic. Opened in 1908, the Long Island Motor Parkway was the first motorway in the USA. Italy opened its first motorway in 1921, but it was in Germany in the 1930s that the idea really took off.

▼ AUTOBAHN, 1935
Multilane highways in Germany are called autobahns. These were first planned in the 1920s, but were not completed until 1935.

Sail power

Early sailing ships mostly had square sails, which worked only with the wind pushing from behind. Then, 2,000 years ago, the Romans invented triangular sails, which came to be called Latin or lateen sails. These can be set at an angle, allowing a ship to sail almost directly into the wind.

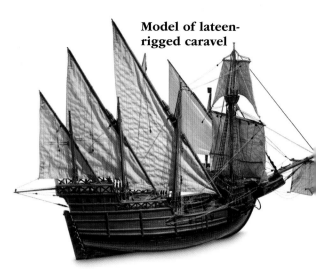

Model of lateen-rigged caravel

THE CARAVEL

Sturdy, square-sailed ships were fine for coastal waters, but not for oceans. In the 1400s, European sailors began to use fast, light vessels called "caravels", which had lateen sails. In the caravels, sailors could travel across the ocean, knowing they could sail long distances quickly, and get home whatever the wind direction.

THREE-MASTERS

From the 1500s, big sailing ships with two, three, and even four masts sailed the oceans. The huge sail area caught enough wind for the vessels to carry heavy cargo. The first battleships were warships, known as "men o' war", which could even carry many heavy cannons.

Cannons mounted on the ship

Model of 1660 Dutch man o' war

▶ THE FLYING YACHT

The Oracle team's yacht for the America's Cup race is designed almost to fly over the water at speeds of 96.5 km/h (60 mph). Hydrofoils, or "daggerboards", help lift the yacht to glide above the water, reducing friction.

Streamlined twin hulls made of tough, light carbon fibre

LIFE JACKET

The forerunner of modern life jackets was invented by the British Arctic explorer Captain John Ward in 1854. Made from blocks of cork, it was uncomfortable to wear. Modern life jackets use soft foam-filled bags, or inflate with gas from a carbon-dioxide cylinder when needed.

Modern J-class racing yacht

BERMUDA RIG

The layout of the sail and mast is called the rig. The Bermuda rig was invented in the 17th century to help small boats wind through the tricky waters around Bermuda in the Atlantic Ocean. This rig has just two triangular sails hung from a single mast. There is a small "headsail" at the front and a large "mainsail" on a swinging arm, or boom, behind. Modern racing yachts use the Bermuda rig as it makes the boat fast and easy to manoeuvre.

AUTOMATIC SAILS

In the 1960s, the German engineer Wilhelm Pröls designed a rig called the Dyna-Rig. In this arrangement, tall masts carry sails that are moved by motors, so a giant sailing ship can be sailed by just one person. The Maltese Falcon (above), the first Dyna-rig yacht, is one of the world's largest yachts.

Sails have adjustable flaps, like aeroplane wings, to reduce wind drag.

TAG HEUER

PUMA

ORACLE TEAM USA

YANMAR

On the water

The steam engine (see pp.52–53) made ships driven by paddle wheels or propellers a practical alternative to sail power. Today, ships for carrying passengers or cargo, as well as warships, have engines that turn propellers underwater to push the vessels forwards or backwards. While the first steam-powered ships appeared in the 1830s, most ships now have diesel engines.

PROPELLER IN ACTION

Propellers were first developed by the ancient Greek inventor Archimedes 2,300 years ago, but they only came into their own with the invention of steamships. A ship's propeller, or "screw", works by moving water as it spins. The angled blades push the water backwards, which pushes the boat forwards.

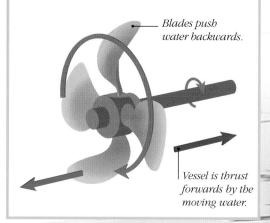

Blades push water backwards.

Vessel is thrust forwards by the moving water.

Screw propeller

Model of hull of SS *Francis Smith*, 1836

A NEW SCREW

Early steamships had paddle wheels, which were easily damaged by waves. In the 1830s, the Swedish inventor John Ericsson and British inventor Francis Pettit Smith developed a propeller shaped like a corkscrew. These "screw" propellers were more powerful than paddle wheels and worked better in stormy seas.

Launch of the SS *Great Britain*

PROPELLING FORWARDS

In 1843, the British engineer Isambard Kingdom Brunel launched his pioneering steamship, SS *Great Britain*, the most innovative passenger liner of its time. It was the first vessel to combine steam power, a screw propeller, and an iron hull. The SS *Great Britain* was the biggest ship in the world at the time, built to cruise quickly across the ocean. By the mid-19th century, propellers would replace paddle wheels on most ships.

NUCLEAR VESSEL

Ships venturing into the frozen waters of the Arctic Ocean need to be strong enough to break through thick ice sheets and to run for a long time. Russian "icebreakers" are powered by nuclear reactors, which allow them to be at sea for years without refuelling.

JET PROPULSION

Some boats are driven along by a powerful whoosh of water. These "pump-jet" boats, or jet skis, have a device called an impeller. Hidden inside a tube in the hull, the impeller draws in water through an intake, then shoots it out at the back to drive the boat along. Jet-propelled boats are very fast.

HYBRID POWER

In most ships, engines turn the propellers directly, but more and more naval vessels and a few passenger liners, such as the *Queen Mary 2* (right), turn their propellers in a different way. In these "hybrid" vessels, the engine powers electrical generators. These run electric motors, which turn the propellers. Hybrid ships are more energy-efficient than standard vessels.

◄ GLIDING THROUGH ICE
One of the world's largest nuclear icebreakers, the Russian ship 50 Years of Victory carried the Olympic flame to the North Pole to launch the 2014 Winter Olympics.

The smooth body and rounded prow of an icebreaker help it to move easily through frozen sea, using its weight to smash the ice.

Boats and ships

The first powered vessels were little more than rowing boats fitted with steam engines and paddle wheels. Over time, the combination of steel hulls and powerful engines allowed all kinds of gigantic ships to be created – from vast supertankers to liners carrying thousands of passengers.

First commercial passenger steamer

- **What?** *Clermont*
- **Who?** Robert Fulton
- **Where and when?** USA, 1807

Although the first working steamboat was the French *Pyroscaphe* of 1783, the first steamer to carry passengers regularly was the *Clermont*. It was built by the American engineer Robert Fulton in 1807, and carried people up and down the River Hudson from New York City to Albany, USA.

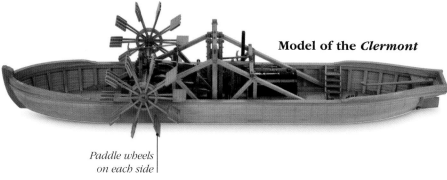

Model of the *Clermont*

Paddle wheels on each side

Round-the-world steamship

- **What?** SS *Great Eastern*
- **Who?** Isambard Kingdom Brunel
- **Where and when?** UK, 1857

After his success with SS *Great Britain*, Isambard Kingdom Brunel wanted to build a massive steamship that could carry enough fuel to sail around the world. His answer was the SS *Great Eastern*. At 211 m (692 ft) long, it was six times bigger than any ship previously built. Although it made many crossings of the Atlantic Ocean, it never sailed around the world and was not a commercial success.

▼ SS *GREAT EASTERN*
The ship's size allowed it to carry 4,000 passengers at a time.

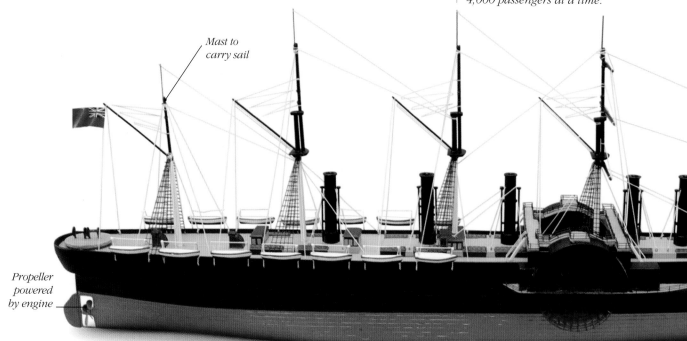

Mast to carry sail

Propeller powered by engine

First turbine-powered boat

- **What?** *Turbinia*
- **Who?** Charles Parsons
- **Where and when?** UK, 1894

In 1884, the British engineer Charles Parsons invented the steam turbine, using high pressure steam to turn a turbine or fan. A decade later, he launched the first turbine-powered ship, the *Turbinia*. It was the fastest ship in the world at the time, reaching speeds of up to 64 km/h (40 mph). Most big ships today use diesel or diesel-electric engines.

WOW!

At 364 m (1,194 ft) long, the French-built *Harmony of the Seas* is the largest ever passenger ship.

Two-layered iron hull strengthened the ship.

Container ship

- **What?** *Ideal X*
- **Who?** Malcom McLean
- **Where and when?** USA, 1956

In 1956, the American transport tycoon Malcom McLean came up with the idea of putting loose cargo in standard metal boxes or containers. These could be stacked high in specialized ships that would be easy to load and unload. The idea worked so well that most standard cargo is now carried in container ships.

MSC *Agata*, a container ship

Identically sized containers are stacked up on the deck of the ship.

Largest solar-powered boat

- **What?** *Tûranor* PlanetSolar
- **Who?** Knierim Yachtbau
- **Where and when?** Germany, 2010

The *Tûranor* PlanetSolar is the world's largest solar-powered boat, and the first to sail right around the world. It is driven by motors entirely powered by solar cells. The word "Tûranor" was invented by the British writer J R R Tolkien in his famous book *The Lord of the Rings* and means "the power of the Sun".

Robotic ship

- **What?** YARA *Birkeland*
- **Who?** Yara International
- **Where and when?** Norway, 2019

The YARA *Birkeland* will be the world's first autonomous ship – a robotic ship that can sail without a crew. It is also a zero-emission container ship that will carry fertilizers between small ports in Norway. While it will have a small crew for the first year, it is expected to be able to run without any crew at all by 2020.

Navigating at sea

Sailors venturing out to sea need navigational aids to help them find their way. Over the centuries, instruments such as the quadrant and sextant were developed. These tools helped sailors to work out their location from the height of the Sun and the stars. Sailors also relied on the magnetic compass. Today, ships rely entirely on electronic satellite systems.

These oscillating weights are not affected by the rolling motion of a ship on water.

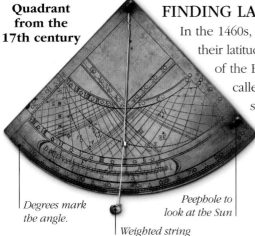

Quadrant from the 17th century

Degrees mark the angle.

Peephole to look at the Sun

Weighted string

FINDING LATITUDE

In the 1460s, navigators began working out their latitude – their position north or south of the Equator – using an instrument called the quadrant. They would see the Pole Star at night, or the Sun at midday, through two peepholes along an edge of the quadrant. Once the star and peepholes aligned, a weighted string showed the latitude on the dial.

▶ **THE SEA CLOCK**
John Harrison's marine chronometer solved the problem of timekeeping at sea.

An explorer uses a sextant in Antarctica, 1930

SEXTANT

In the 1730s, the Englishman John Hadley and American Thomas Godfrey invented the sextant, independent of each other. Looking into the sextant's telescope, a navigator could find out the angle of the Sun and stars relative to the horizon by lining up two mirrors. Printed tables then gave the latitude for the angle. For years, this became the ultimate navigation tool.

KEEPING PERFECT TIME

To find out their longitude – how far east or west they had sailed – navigators needed to check at midday what the exact time was back home. The time difference showed the distance. However, ordinary pendulum clocks lose time on a rocking ship. In 1735, English clockmaker John Harrison made a marine chronometer, which kept perfect time on the move.

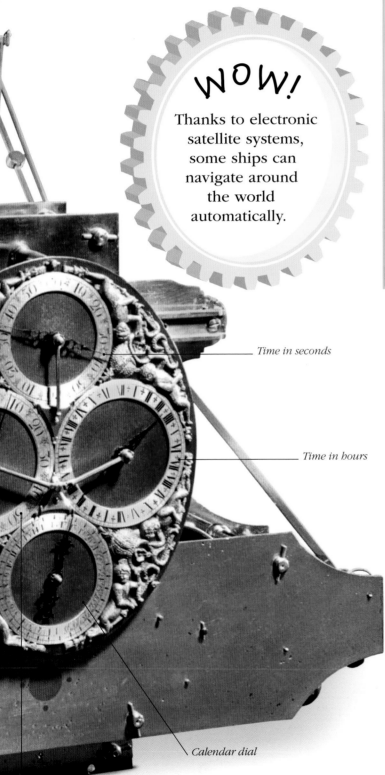

Time in seconds

Time in hours

Calendar dial

Time in minutes

WOW!

Thanks to electronic satellite systems, some ships can navigate around the world automatically.

GET MOVING

SONAR

This system uses sound waves to detect objects under the sea. It sends out "pings" and antennas pick up the ways they bounce back or echo. The American naval architect Lewis Nixon invented the first sonar-like listening device in 1906 to detect icebergs. In 1915, during World War I, the French physicist Paul Langévin built the first functional sonar to detect submarines.

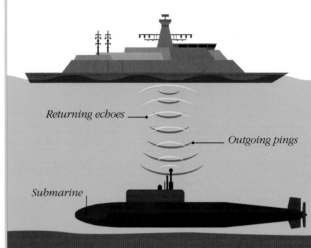

Returning echoes

Outgoing pings

Submarine

RADAR

In 1904, radar systems were pioneered by the German inventor Christian Hülsmeyer. He realized he could reveal hidden objects, such as ships shrouded by dense fog, by bouncing radio waves off them. These resulted in echoes, which made a bell ring or, in later versions, made a glowing spot on a screen. During World War II, radar was used to detect enemy ships. Since then, radars have become key navigation aids.

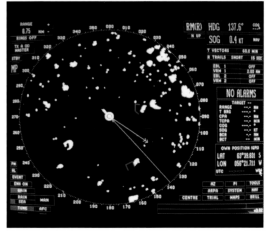

Radar screen of a research ship shows a field of icebergs

Diving propeller for up-and-down movement

Wooden body

Going underwater

The early pioneers of the submarine were inspired by stories of what lay in the ocean depths. According to legend, the ancient Greek king Alexander the Great dived into the sea inside a large glass jar. In the 1500s, air-filled chambers called "diving bells" became popular with underwater explorers. As people experimented with designing craft that could submerge in water, the modern-day submarine began to take shape.

TURNING "TURTLE"

The American inventor David Bushnell's *Turtle* is said to be the first functional, modern submarine. It was a one-man wooden barrel with a propeller, steering gear, and viewing windows. Built in 1773, the *Turtle* was used in the American War of Independence to secretly put explosive charges on British ships, but its mission never succeeded.

THE FIRST AIRLOCK

In 1894, the American engineer Simon Lake pioneered the airlock with his underwater craft, the *Argonaut Junior*. The airlock system is a two-door chamber. When a diver leaves the craft, the chamber is filled with water so the outer door can be opened. When the diver returns, the outer door is closed, the water drained, and inner door opened.

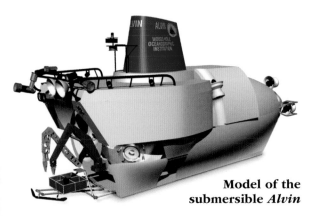

Model of the submersible *Alvin*

The vessel is bullet-shaped so water can flow around it easily.

TAKING A DIVE

Built in 1964, the American research vessel *Alvin* is a submersible. Unlike a submarine, a submersible needs a support crew on the surface for power and air supply. The *Alvin* can run for up to nine hours, carrying two scientists and a pilot to depths of up to 4,500 m (14,764 ft). After half a century and more than 4,000 dives, this craft is still operational.

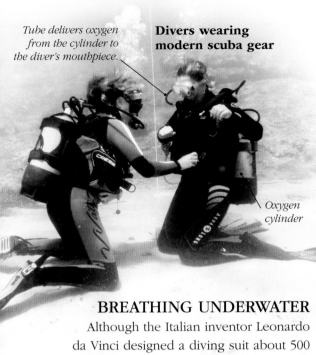

Tube delivers oxygen from the cylinder to the diver's mouthpiece.

Divers wearing modern scuba gear

Oxygen cylinder

BREATHING UNDERWATER

Although the Italian inventor Leonardo da Vinci designed a diving suit about 500 years ago, it was not until 1943 that the first practical diving system became a reality. The Frenchmen Jacques Cousteau and Émile Gagnan invented the self-contained underwater breathing apparatus (SCUBA), which allowed divers to swim underwater, while breathing oxygen from cylinders strapped to their backs.

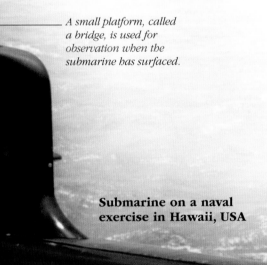

A small platform, called a bridge, is used for observation when the submarine has surfaced.

Submarine on a naval exercise in Hawaii, USA

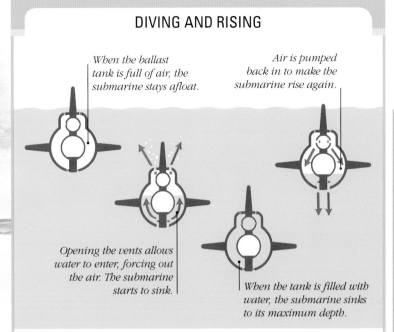

DIVING AND RISING

When the ballast tank is full of air, the submarine stays afloat.

Air is pumped back in to make the submarine rise again.

Opening the vents allows water to enter, forcing out the air. The submarine starts to sink.

When the tank is filled with water, the submarine sinks to its maximum depth.

All submarines have a double skin. In between the inner skin and the outer skin are large spaces, called ballast tanks, that can hold water. To dive, the submarine pumps water in to flood these tanks, making the vessel heavy enough to sink. To resurface, the submarine pumps the water out to make it lighter.

SUBMARINES TODAY

Built for stealth, most modern submarines are used as machines of war. Navies today have both diesel-electric (below) as well as nuclear-powered submarines. The nuclear-powered vessels can stay at sea for months without needing to resurface, and can travel around the world without needing to refuel. The nuclear reactors driving these submarines produce an unlimited amount of power without the need for oxygen. The only reasons a submarine may need to return to the surface are to replenish food and to remove waste.

Marino Branch
Brainse Marino
Tel: 8336297

FLOATING CARRIERS

A fighter plane takes off from the USS *Gerald R Ford*, a US Navy carrier. Aircraft carriers are the biggest naval vessels, with a top flight deck up to 305 m (1,000 ft) long for planes to land and take off. The commander of the carrier's tower is responsible for managing the planes' access to the boat.

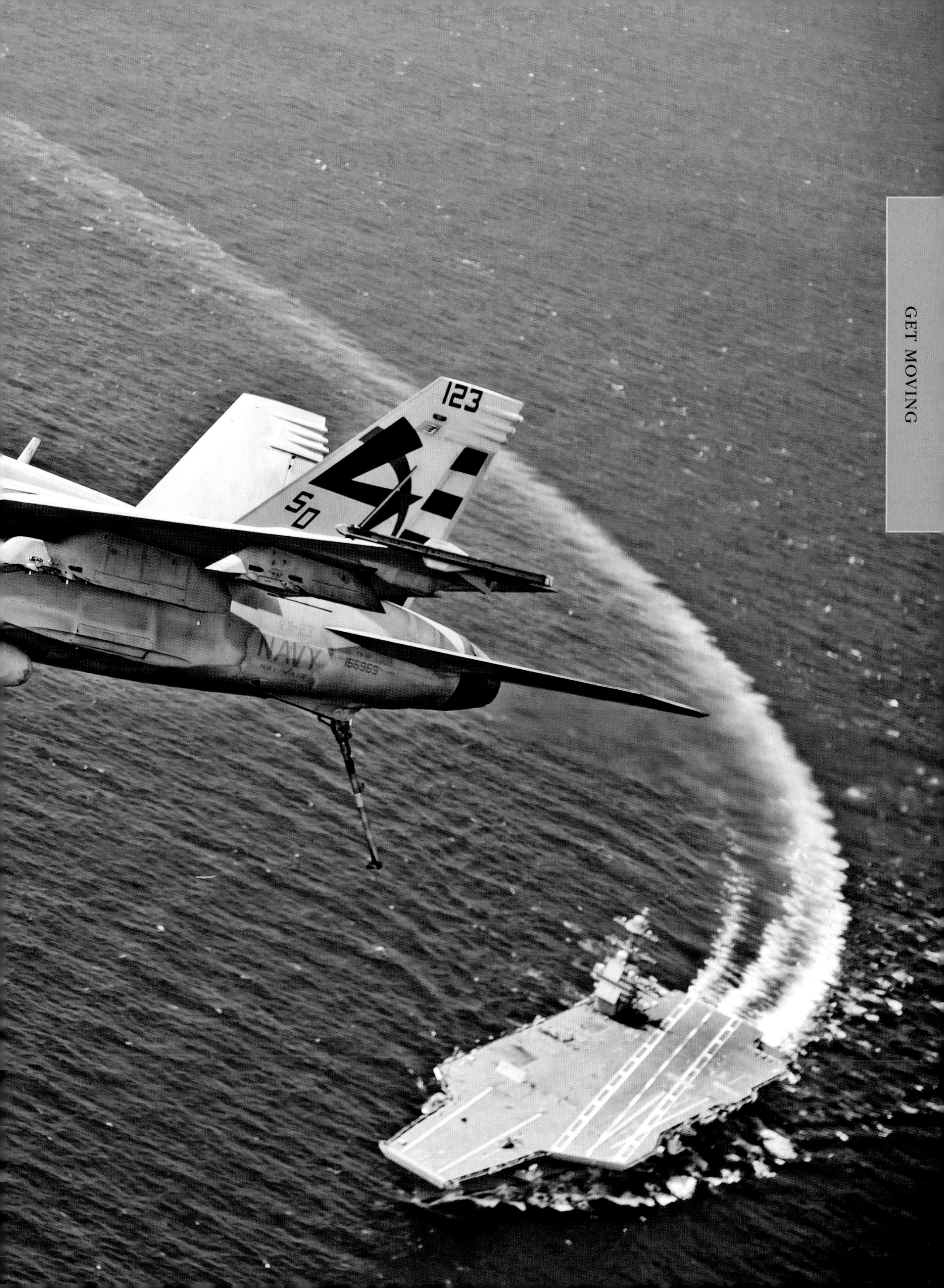
123
SD
NAVY
166969

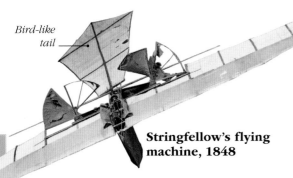

Bird-like tail

Stringfellow's flying machine, 1848

Taking to the skies

Over the centuries, people have attempted to fly by strapping on wings and lunging into the air to try to flap like a bird, but their efforts often ended in tragedy. The breakthrough for winged aircraft came when the British engineer Sir George Cayley recognized the forces that act on a plane in flight, including "lift". It was not until 1903, however, that the Wright brothers (see pp.118–119) mastered controlled, powered flight.

POWERED FLIGHT

In 1847, the English inventors John Stringfellow and William Henson built a model aeroplane powered by tiny steam engines, but it failed to fully take flight. Stringfellow then built a half-size version and, in 1848, it made the first ever powered flight.

DISCOVERING LIFT

Although people flew balloons in the early 1800s, the British engineer Sir George Cayley believed wings were the future of flight. He experimented with kites and developed theories about wing shapes. He also built full-size gliders. In 1849, a 10-year-old boy was lifted into the air in one of Cayley's gliders – this was the first ever manned aeroplane flight.

FLYING BOATS

The Wright brothers' breakthrough flight in 1903 led to the rapid development of planes. The age of air travel began in the 1930s with giant "flying boats", such as the Short Empire, Martin M-130, and Boeing 314. In many places around the world, there were no airports yet built, but most cities have rivers. So, these planes were designed to take off and land on water. The famous American "Clipper" flying boats were huge, and carried passengers like they were on luxury liners.

Tail and wings were made of linen stretched over a frame made of cane.

Cayley's glider

FLY BY WIRE

In older planes, the wing flaps that control a plane's motion were moved mechanically by rods and levers. The supersonic (faster-than-sound) jet Concorde was one of the first "fly-by-wire" plane. In these, the pilot operates the flight controls and his movements are converted into electrical signals. These are sent to electric motors, which move the wing flaps. In autopilot mode, the plane is controlled automatically by a computer.

The nose can be adjusted up or down for better visibility.

Concorde

GLASS COCKPIT

In the late 1960s, analogue gauges gave way to electric displays. The display in modern aeroplanes is sometimes called a "glass cockpit" because it is full of screens that show data readouts, computer updates, and the plane's flight path.

◀ BOEING 314
Air travel was a luxury for the rich and the Boeing 314 was one of the most luxurious aircraft from 1938–1946. It could carry 74 passengers in seats or 40 in sleeping berths. It also had a lounge, dressing rooms, and a dining salon onboard.

FORCES OF FLIGHT

When a plane moves, its wings slice through the air at an angle, forcing the air downwards and producing a force called "lift". This balances the plane's weight, so it stays airborne. To keep the plane moving, the engines produce a force called "thrust", which balances the "drag" of the air.

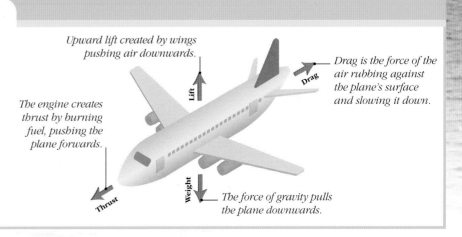

Upward lift created by wings pushing air downwards.

Drag is the force of the air rubbing against the plane's surface and slowing it down.

The engine creates thrust by burning fuel, pushing the plane forwards.

The force of gravity pulls the plane downwards.

117

The Wright brothers

The age of aviation began when the American brothers Wilbur and Orville Wright made the first successful powered aeroplane flight. This was accomplished in their *Flyer* at Kitty Hawk in North Carolina, USA, on 17 December 1903. Many pioneers had tried to fly planes with engines before, but they always crashed. The Wright brothers' breakthrough was controlling the flight – the *Flyer* travelled just 37 m (120 ft), but it took off and landed in full control.

WOW!

The brothers tossed a coin to decide who would fly first. Although Wilbur won, the engine stalled on the first attempt.

LIFE STORY

1867–1871

Wilbur Wright is born on a farm near Newcastle, Indiana, USA. His brother Orville is born four years later in Dayton, Ohio, USA.

1896

The brothers begin as bicycle makers, but turn to flying after hearing of the German aviator Otto Lilienthal's pioneering hang-glider flights.

1899

The brothers move to Kitty Hawk in North Carolina, USA, and they begin building trial planes to improve their flying skills.

1903

Orville makes the first powered, controlled flight in the *Flyer*. This kick-starts a new age in aviation.

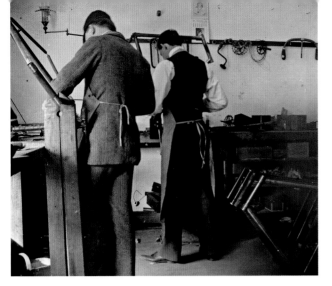

IN THE BICYCLE WORKSHOP

The Wright brothers began their working lives by repairing and making bicycles. They used these skills – and bicycle parts – to build their first plane, the *Flyer*. The aircraft had a wooden frame, and bicycle chains connected the plane's propellers to its engine.

THE GLIDER

Before they built their first powered plane, the Wright brothers experimented with wire-controlled gliders. They launched these gliders by running down sand dunes. The pilot steered the glider by moving a cradle attached to his hips, which then pulled wires to bend the wings to change the direction.

Wright brothers test a glider, c.1901

FLIGHT CONTROL

Orville Wright controlled *Flyer* by pulling wires to "warp", or twist, the wings to lift one side or the other. This is called wing warping. Today, aeroplanes use hinged wing sections instead, but the idea of altering the wing shape to control a plane in the air was the big breakthrough.

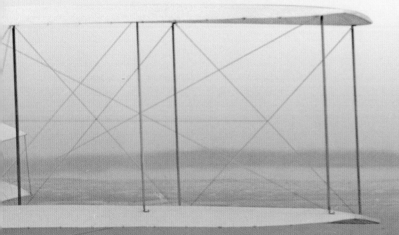

▲ **THE FIRST FLIGHT**
Orville Wright lies across the wing controls of the Flyer *during its historic first flight, which lasted 12 seconds.*

1905

Orville makes a flight of 38.9 km (24 miles) in just 38 minutes at Huffman Prairie, Ohio, USA, in a modified version of the *Flyer*.

1912

Wilbur dies at the age of 45, at the Wright family home, on 30 May 1912. Orville became the president of the Wright company before selling it in 1915.

1948

Orville continues to work as a flight consultant for many decades. He dies on 30 January 1948, at the age of 70.

Jets to solar planes

Early aircraft were all driven by propellers and mostly flew slowly. Passenger planes also flew low through the clouds, where they were buffeted by air turbulence. The invention of the jet engine in the 1930s changed all that. Jet engines could power planes much faster, high above the clouds in calmer air, and made possible modern air travel, which takes people across continents in just a few hours. Today, scientists continue to develop alternative ways of powering flight.

Wings made mostly of wood

Heinkel He-178 aircraft

First jet plane

- **What?** Heinkel He-178
- **Who?** Hans von Ohain
- **Where and when?** Germany, 1939

The first jet engine was developed in the 1930s by the German scientist Hans von Ohain and the British engineer Frank Whittle, each working independently. Ohain then teamed up in 1935 with the German aircraft-maker Ernst Heinkel, who realized that the jet engine could power superfast planes. On 27 August 1939, Heinkel's test pilot made the first successful jet flight.

Jet airliners

- **What?** de Havilland Comet DH 106
- **Who?** Ronald Bishop
- **Where and when?** UK, 1952

In 1952, the de Havilland Comet DH 106, or Comet 1, was the first jet aircraft to go into regular passenger service. It immediately halved the time for long journeys, such as that between the UK and South Africa. Today, there are more than 20,000 jet airliners flying people all around the world.

▼ BOEING 777-300ER
This typical mid-sized airliner can carry almost 400 people at once.

The Boeing 777 is the world's biggest twin jet – an aircraft powered by a pair of jet engines.

Fastest jet plane

- **What?** Lockheed SR-71 Blackbird
- **Who?** Clarence "Kelly "Johnson
- **Where and when?** USA, 1964

Military jets can fly three times as fast as sound. The Lockheed SR-71 could cross the Atlantic Ocean in less than two hours and, on 28 July 1976, it reached 3,529.6 km/h (2,193.2 mph) – the top speed achieved by a jet plane. The SR-71 was a "stealth" plane, carefully shaped and painted with a special "radar-absorbent" black paint to hide it from enemy radar.

Engine attached below the plane collects oxygen.

Illustration of NASA's X-43A in flight

Heat-resistant titanium body was lightweight and helped the plane fly at very high speed.

WOW!

Of the world's 20,000 or so commercial jet airliners, more than 11,000 are in the air at any one moment.

Fastest powered plane

- **What?** X-43A
- **Who?** NASA
- **Where and when?** USA, 2004

Rockets travel at high speeds, but they have to carry a heavy load of liquid oxygen to mix with their fuel. NASA developed superfast scramjets to solve this problem – these scoop oxygen from the air as they fly. The X-43A scramjet was an experimental, faster-than-sound, unmanned plane, which was first launched in 2001. Only three X-43As were built. The third was tested in 2004, when it screeched through the air at almost 11,200 km/h (7,000 mph).

Solar-powered plane

- **What?** *Solar Impulse 1*
- **Who?** André Borschberg and Bertrand Piccard
- **Where and when?** Switzerland, 2009

Jet planes cause pollution, so innovators look for alternative ways to power planes, including solar power. Swiss pilots André Borschberg and Bertrand Piccard made a breakthrough with *Solar Impulse 1*, which combined rechargeable batteries with solar cells on its wings. The next model, *Solar Impulse 2* (above), completed the first ever solar-powered flight around the world in 2016, and also showed that clean technologies can help achieve goals nobody thought possible.

Fastest glider

- **What?** DARPA Falcon HTV-2
- **Who?** DARPA and US Air Force
- **Where and when?** USA, 2011

Imagine travelling around the world in less than two hours. That's how fast the DARPA Falcon Hypersonic Test Vehicle 2 (HTV-2) rocket-launched glider can fly. It is carried high up in the sky by a rocket before gliding back to Earth. It is an experimental craft, but during a test flight in 2011, it reached a top speed of 21,000 km/h (13,000 mph) before crashing.

Illustration of HTV-2

Other flying machines

Planes rely on wings to fly, but they must fly forwards non-stop for the wings to produce "lift". Other ways of flying include the use of whirling rotor blades that generate lift in helicopters simply by spinning round. That's why helicopters and drones can take off and land almost vertically, and hover in mid-air.

TAKING TO THE SKIES

In 1783, the Montgolfier brothers made the first successful human flight, in a silk balloon (left) filled with hot air. Hot air is lighter than cool air, and it made the balloon rise upwards. Other early balloons were filled with hydrogen gas, which is lighter than air. For a century, people flew using balloons.

GIANTS IN THE AIR

A hundred years ago, large airships carried passengers in luxury across the Atlantic Ocean. Like balloons, airships are lifted by a lighter-than-air gas, such as helium, but they also have engines to help them fly in any direction. Today, the largest aircraft in the world is the Airlander 10 airship (below), with a length of 92.05 m (302 ft). This experimental craft doesn't need a runway and can carry heavy cargo to remote places.

Tail rotor

Twin-blade main rotor

Replica of the Bell 47 helicopter

SPINNING BLADES

Used mainly by the armed forces in the beginning, helicopters were developed in the 1920s by the German engineer Anton Flettner and the Russian aeroplane designer Igor Sikorsky, among others. Helicopters really took off in 1946 with the Bell 47, made for civilian use. It had a cleverly balanced two-blade rotor, which made it compact and stable.

FORCES IN FLIGHT

As a helicopter's rotor spins, it creates lift. With a collective pitch control, the pilot can increase the angle or "pitch" of all the blades at once to get more lift.

Each blade can tilt to steer the helicopter in a particular direction.

Blades cut through the air like aeroplane wings to create lift.

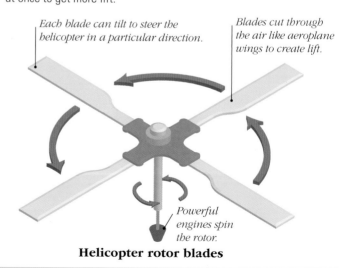

Powerful engines spin the rotor.

Helicopter rotor blades

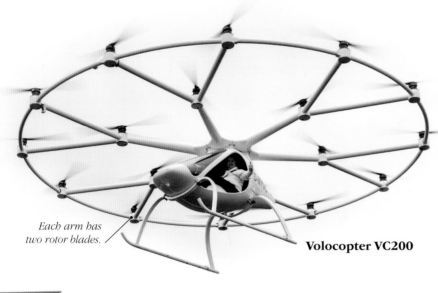

Each arm has
two rotor blades.

Volocopter VC200

PASSENGER DRONES

Drones are small robotic craft that either fly by themselves or are remote-controlled. Multiple rotors allow a drone's position in the air to be controlled precisely. Most drones are tiny remote-controlled flying cameras that give a bird's-eye view of places too difficult or dangerous for people to go to. An experimental German craft, the electric-powered Volocopter is like a small flying car that can carry two people.

ELECTRIC AIR TAXI

Although just at the trial stage, the Lilium air taxi concept could be the way people get around in the future. It's a flying car powered by non-polluting and silent electric jet engines (not powered by fossil fuels). The craft has 12 flaps that help engines provide lift. At take-off, the flaps are tilted vertically, and once the craft is in the air, they tilt horizontally to provide acceleration.

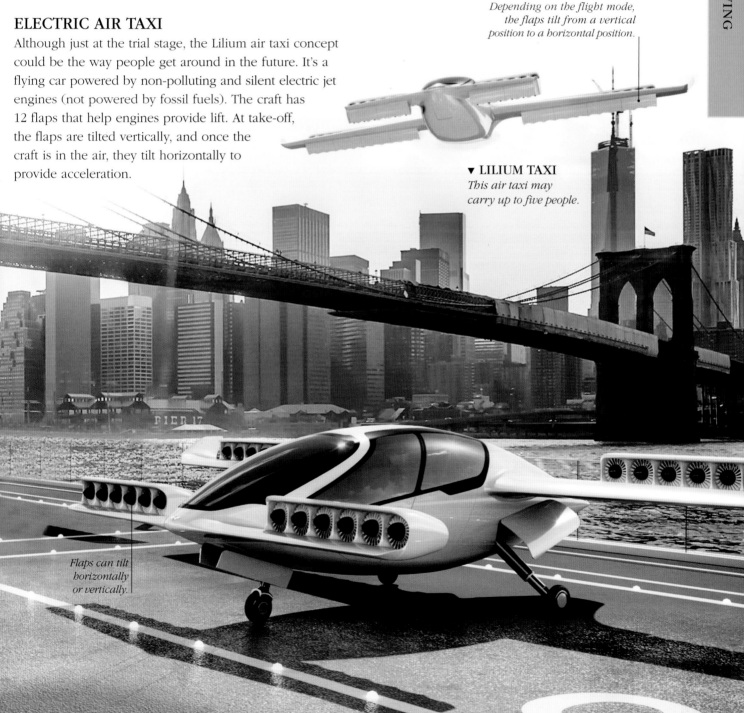

Depending on the flight mode, the flaps tilt from a vertical position to a horizontal position.

▼ LILIUM TAXI
This air taxi may carry up to five people.

Flaps can tilt horizontally or vertically.

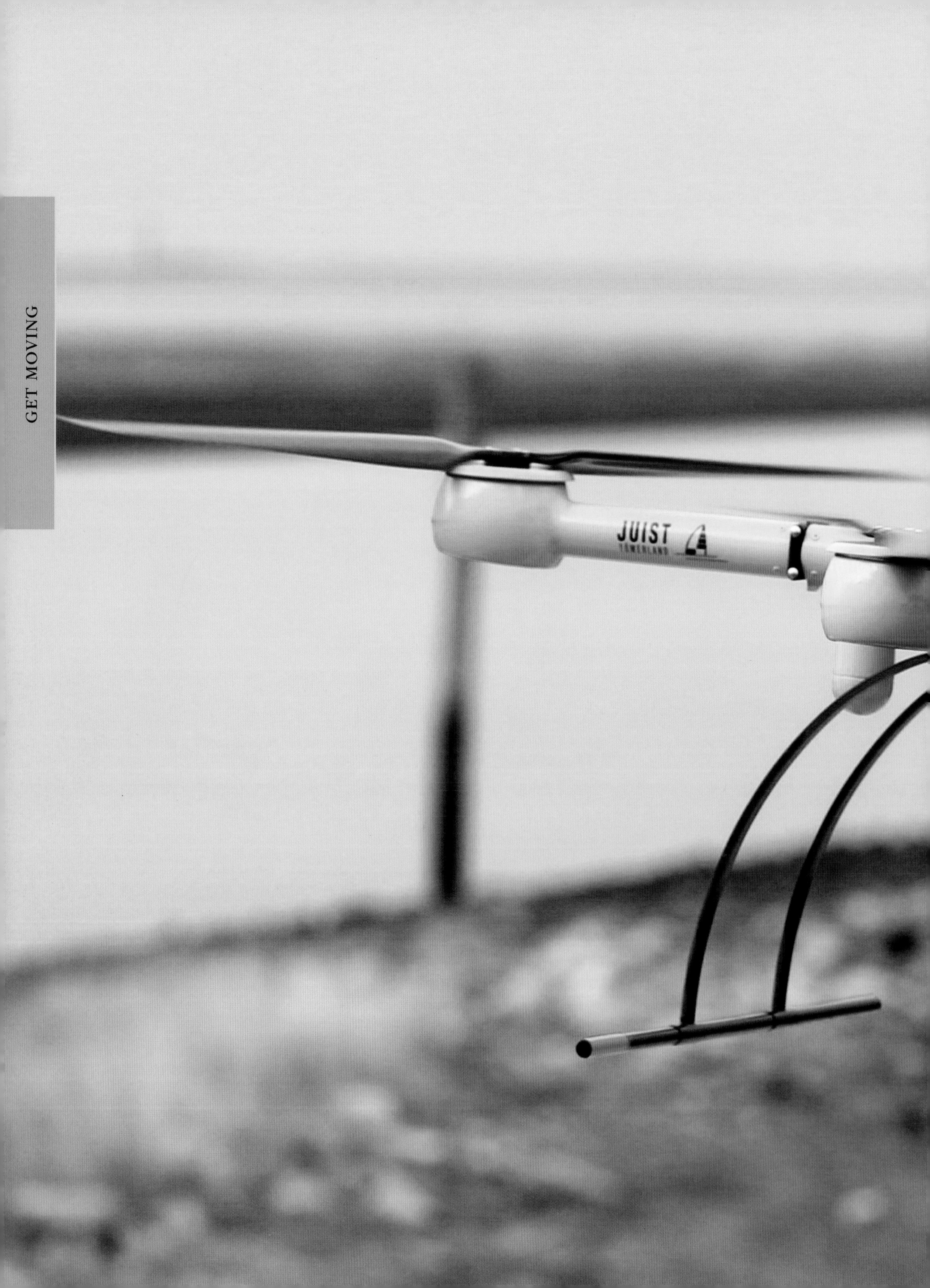
JUIST

DRONE DELIVERIES

Remote-controlled, pilotless aircraft, called drones, are designed for a wide range of purposes, including spying and warfare. Today, delivery companies are developing drones to carry items such as goods ordered online, medical supplies, and possibly even takeaway meals. The drone shown here making a test flight is called the Parcelcopter. Produced in Germany, it is part of an ongoing research project started in 2013 on how to use drones to deliver consumer goods.

Railways

While early carriages relied on human power or animals (horses or donkeys) to move them along tracks, it was the invention of the steam locomotive that spurred the development of railways. Early steam engines (see pp.52–53) were fixed in place and mainly ran pumps and machines in factories, but they were too bulky to use in locomotives. The breakthrough for railways came in about 1800, with the development of small, powerful, high-pressure steam engines.

THE FIRST PUBLIC RAILWAY

In 1825, Stockton and Darlington, UK, became the first railway line to open to the public. It was built to carry coal, but on the day it opened, people jumped into the open wagons and rode all the way. The 36 wagons were pulled by a locomotive called *Locomotion No 1*, and carried coal, flour, workmen, and passengers. Seen above is a 1925 re-enactment of the event.

>> FAST FACTS >>

■ The first high-pressure steam engine was built by the American inventor Oliver Evans in the 1790s.

■ Three years before he built the first steam locomotive, Richard Trevithick made a steam-powered cart called the *Puffing Devil*.

■ The first steam locomotive to officially hit a speed of 160 km/h (100 mph) was the *Flying Scotsman* in the UK in 1934, but another called the *City of Truro* may have done it 30 years earlier.

STEAMING AHEAD

In 1804, the British engineer Richard Trevithick invented the world's first steam locomotive, *Pen-y-Darren*. Trevithick fitted it with his own high-pressure steam engine, and to prove that it worked, he bet it could haul 10 tonnes of coal along rail tracks laid for horses to pull trains of wagons. The locomotive travelled 14 km (9 miles) and Trevithick won his bet.

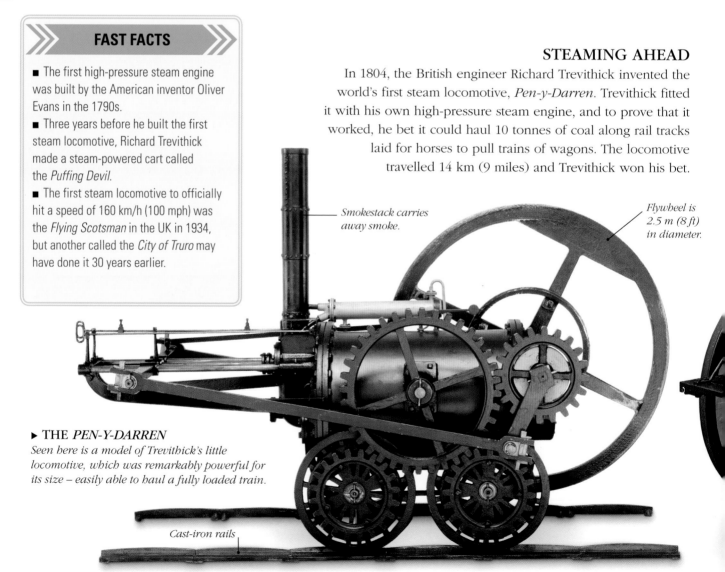

Smokestack carries away smoke.

Flywheel is 2.5 m (8 ft) in diameter.

▶ **THE *PEN-Y-DARREN***
Seen here is a model of Trevithick's little locomotive, which was remarkably powerful for its size – easily able to haul a fully loaded train.

Cast-iron rails

STEPHENSON'S *ROCKET*

In 1829, five locomotives competed before a huge crowd at Rainhill, Lancashire, UK, to decide which would haul carriages on the world's first passenger railway, between Liverpool and Manchester in the UK. The winner was the British engineer Robert Stephenson's *Rocket*, which at one point reached a speed of 40 km/h (25 mph). It soon became the world's most famous locomotive.

Chimney releases hot air and smoke via the boiler.

WOW!
Within 45 years of the *Rocket*, over 257,000 km (160,000 miles) of railway track had been built around the world.

WARNING SIGNALS

Semaphore signals are hinged arms that can be set at different angles to send messages to a train driver. First used in 1842 by the British engineer Charles Hutton Gregory, semaphore signals warned train drivers about hazards ahead. They have been replaced by coloured light signals over the years.

Red, square-ended horizontal arm means "stop".

Yellow indicates that this is a distant signal and the horizontal arm indicates "caution".

Water barrel supplies water to the boiler.

Firebox heats the boiler.

Boiler heats the water to make steam, which drives the pistons.

Mechanical semaphore signal

On the tracks

Since the world's first railway opened between Stockton and Darlington in the UK in 1825, train technology has come a long way. For well over a century, steam locomotives dominated the railways, but in the last 50 years, diesel and electric locomotives have almost entirely replaced them.

Diesel-electric locomotive

- **What?** EMD FT
- **Who?** General Motors, EMD
- **Where and when?** USA, 1939

By the time this powerful locomotive began its run, diesel locomotives were replacing the steam engines. Unlike electric locomotives, which are usually powered by overhead electric lines, diesel-electric engines could be operated on existing tracks with no modification. The "F" stood for Fourteen Hundred horsepower, and the "T" for Twin, because FTs were always sold in pairs.

First underground railway

- **What?** Metropolitan Railway
- **Who?** John Fowler
- **Where and when?** UK, 1863

The problem of building railways in crowded cities was solved by putting them underground. The world's first was the Metropolitan Railway, which opened in January 1863 in London. It had gas-lit wooden carriages hauled by steam locomotives, but smoke was a choking hazard in the confined tunnels.

Deep-tube electric railway

- **What?** City and South London Railway
- **Who?** James Henry Greathead
- **Where and when?** UK, 1890

Electric underground railways are now the way people get around in many of the world's biggest cities. The first one was built in London in 1890, between the city and Stockwell (a suburb of London). The tunnels were so small and the carriages so tiny that the carriages were nicknamed "padded cells".

Fastest steam locomotive

- **What?** *Mallard*
- **Who?** Sir Nigel Gresley
- **Where and when?** UK, 1938

Steam locomotives reached their peak in the 1930s, and the *Mallard* was cutting-edge technology of the day. On 3 July 1938, *Mallard* set the world speed record for a steam locomotive when it reached 203 km/h (126 mph) on the line from London to Edinburgh, in the UK.

WOW!

In 2016, an experimental Japanese maglev train hit a top speed of 603 km/h (374 mph).

First bullet train

- **What?** *Shinkansen*
- **Who?** Japan Railways
- **Where and when?** Japan, 1964

In 1964, railways were given a dramatic new lease of life when streamlined electric "bullet" trains, or *Shinkansen*, were introduced in Japan. They ran very fast on specially constructed tracks with gentle curves. Today, high-speed trains run in many countries around the world.

Maglevs

- **What?** Shanghai Maglev Train (SMT)
- **Who?** Siemens and ThyssenKrupp
- **Where and when?** China, 2004

The fastest trains in the world have no wheels and no engine. High-powered magnets move the trains and make them float above the track. These trains are called "maglevs", which is short for magnetic levitation. The SMT airport train runs at up to 430 km/h (267 mph).

A magnet on the track repels the magnet on the underside of the train to make the train float above the track.

Fastest bullet train

- **What?** *Fuxing*
- **Who?** China Railway Corps
- **Where and when?** China, 2017

China now has the world's fastest bullet trains. Their newest trains, named *Fuxing* (which means "regeneration"), can reach a maximum speed of 400 km/h (248 mph) and operate at an average speed of 350 km/h (217 mph). The trains can complete the 1,318-km (819-mile) journey from Beijing to Shanghai in China in just four and a half hours.

FLYING TRAIN

The carriages of the world's oldest suspended monorail have been gliding 12 m (40 ft) above the traffic, crowded streets, and river of Wuppertal, Germany, since 1901. The 13.3 km- (8.3 mile-) long track, slung beneath a towering iron structure, provides daily transport for local people and a thrilling tourist ride. The model for this railway was an experimental electric hanging monorail built in 1897 by the German engineer Carl Eugen Langen.

The Stephensons

Although the first steam locomotive was built in 1804, it was the British father-and-son engineers George and Robert Stephenson who made steam railways a reality. They built the first public railway in 1825 (see p.126) and created the famous *Rocket* (see p.127) – a locomotive that pulled trains on the first passenger railway, between Liverpool and Manchester in the UK, when it opened in 1830.

▶ **FATHER AND SON AT WORK**
The Stephensons were practical engineers, who had the foresight and inventiveness to realize the potential of railways.

SAFETY LAMP

Candles can easily set off explosions in mines because of flammable gases in the air. So in 1818, George Stephenson and the British scientist Humphry Davy both came up with designs for safety lamps for miners. In these designs, the flame would be kept covered, out of reach of the gases in the mines. Stephenson's lamp was soon widely used in mines across the northeast of England until the advent of electric light.

Safety lamp based on George Stephenson's design

ENGINEERS AND DESIGNERS

As well as designing tracks and engines, the Stephensons were also bridge engineers. Robert Stephenson's design for the railway bridge across the Menai Straits in North Wales, UK, was revolutionary. The trains ran inside two box-shaped iron tubes, supported by huge brick pillars. With the load of the trains spread through all four sides of the boxes, it was very strong. Stephenson's design was hugely influential and is still used in some bridges today.

LOCOMOTION

The Stephensons built the world's first public steam railway between the English towns of Stockton and Darlington in the UK. George Stephenson was at the controls when their locomotive, *Locomotion No 1*, pulled the first train in 1825. The Stephensons had the brilliant idea of laying the boiler flat to deliver power to the wheels more effectively.

Artist's impression of George Stephenson's 1825 locomotive, *Locomotion No 1*

Boiler laid flat

LIFE STORY

1781	1803	1818	1823
George Stephenson is born in Northumberland, UK. His parents are too poor to send him to school, so he starts working at a local mine.	George's son, Robert, is born. Robert's mother and baby sister die the following year.	George Stephenson invents a safety lamp for miners, which provides light while avoiding the danger of flammable gases in mines catching fire.	The Stephensons make a company to develop steam railways and set up the world's first locomotive works in Newcastle, UK.

George and Robert Stephenson

1825	1830	1848
The Stephensons build the Stockton and Darlington Railway. Although it was built for transporting coal, it also carries passengers.	The world's first passenger railway opens with locomotives built by the Stephensons, including the *Rocket*. 	George dies, aged 67. By this time, nearly 65,000 km (40,000 miles) of railway have been built. Robert dies in 1859, aged 55.

COMMUNICATION

For most of human history, the only way you could talk to someone who was not in hearing distance was by written word. Now, we can reach anyone, anywhere, at any time.

The telegraph

In 1820, Hans Christian Ørsted discovered that electricity could create magnetism. From this, William Sturgeon and Joseph Henry developed the electromagnet – in which an electric current creates a strong magnetic field. In turn, this led Samuel Morse to resume his experiments in electricity and, eventually, a new way of communicating was born.

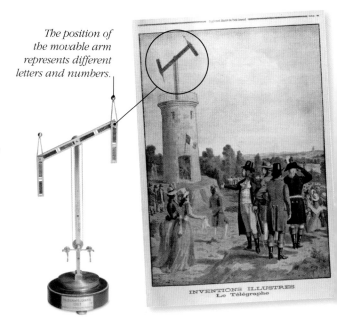

The position of the movable arm represents different letters and numbers.

INVENTIONS ILLUSTRES
Le Télégraphe

SYNCHRONIZED SEMAPHORE

The French inventor Claude Chappe developed a semaphore system. In 1794, this chain of towers topped by movable arms carried news between Lille and Paris, France, a distance of 205 km (128 miles), in less than an hour.

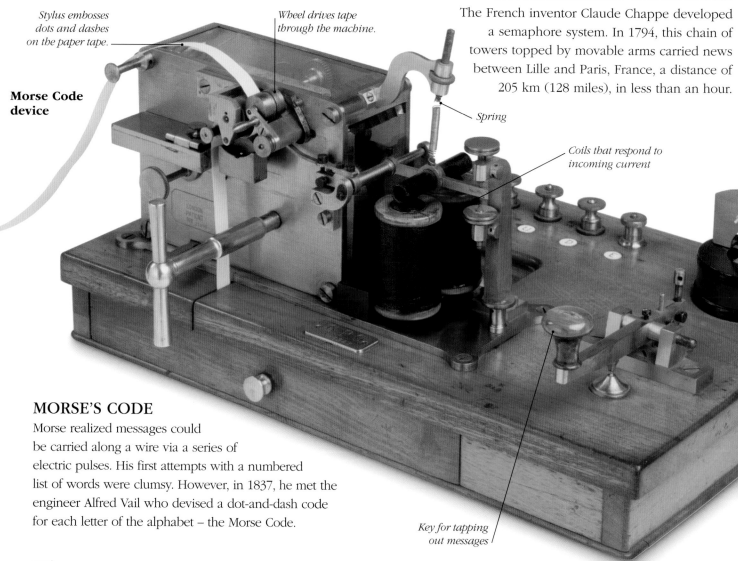

Stylus embosses dots and dashes on the paper tape.

Wheel drives tape through the machine.

Morse Code device

Spring

Coils that respond to incoming current

MORSE'S CODE

Morse realized messages could be carried along a wire via a series of electric pulses. His first attempts with a numbered list of words were clumsy. However, in 1837, he met the engineer Alfred Vail who devised a dot-and-dash code for each letter of the alphabet – the Morse Code.

Key for tapping out messages

THE NEEDLE TELEGRAPH

In 1837, the Englishmen William Cooke and Charles Wheatstone patented the first practical telegraph. Activated by electric currents, its five needles could point to 20 letters of the alphabet to spell out received messages. By 1839, it was in use on the railways.

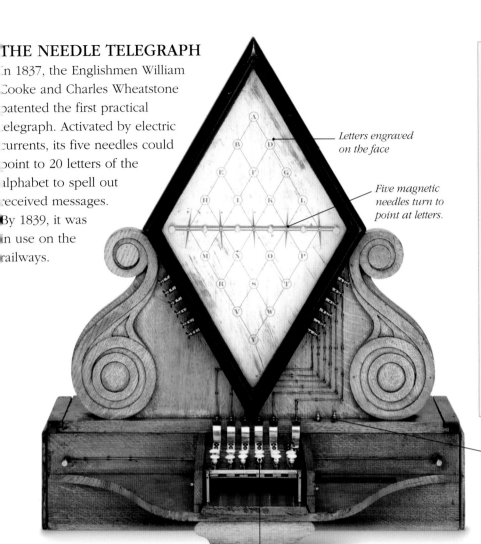

Letters engraved on the face

Five magnetic needles turn to point at letters.

Terminals used to connect the wires

Cooke and Wheatstone's electric telegraph

Keys pressed in pairs to send letters.

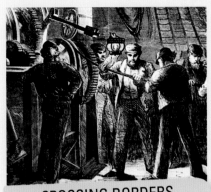

CROSSING BORDERS

The first transatlantic telegraph cable was laid under the sea between Ireland and Newfoundland, Canada, in 1858, by the SS *Great Eastern* ship, above. This reduced communication time between Europe and North America from 10 days (a ship's crossing time) to just 17 minutes.

WOW!

The first words transmitted by Morse's telegraph in 1844 were, "What hath God wrought", sent between Baltimore and Washington, DC, USA.

SENDING MESSAGES BY ELECTRICITY

Morse and Vail created a machine that worked by pushing the operator key down to complete the electric circuit of the battery. This sent the electric pulse along a wire to a receiver at the other end. Here, a small electromagnet powered by the electric pulse attracted a stylus that marked the paper tape with either short or long marks, representing dots and dashes.

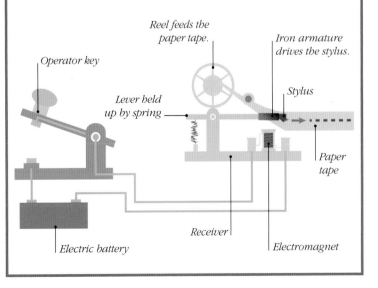

Reel feeds the paper tape.

Operator key

Iron armature drives the stylus.

Lever held up by spring

Stylus

Paper tape

Electric battery

Receiver

Electromagnet

SUNDIALS

Some 3,000 years ago, the astronomers of ancient Egypt used the regular movement of the Sun through the sky to tell the time. Early Egyptian clocks, called sundials, indicated time by the position of a shadow falling across markers.

The "gnomon" casts a shadow onto the dial.

9th-century sundial, Northern Ireland

MECHANICAL CLOCKS

The first mechanical clocks were invented in Europe around the start of the 14th century. Nobody had clocks at home, so clocks were put on towers at the centre of towns and cities.

Clock towers had bells to chime out the hours.

Town clock tower, Tavira, Portugal

Measuring time

Keeping track of time became important as soon as people began to live in towns and cities. Clocks were set by the Sun, which meant time differed between locations, even within the same country. This worked up until the arrival of the railways, when train schedules demanded that time be standardized.

British station masters set station clocks according to signals from Greenwich, UK.

STANDARDIZING TIME

Trains run to timetables, which means every part of the railway network has to operate on the same time. This was first applied by the Great Western Railway in England in 1840. By 1855, nearly all public authorities – including churches and town halls – set their clocks to "railway time".

London

Brussels

New York

Hong Kong

Moscow

TIME ZONES

The Italian mathematician Quirico Filopanti proposed a worldwide system of time zones in 1858, as did the Scottish-born Canadian Sir Sandford Fleming in 1879. Filopanti suggested that time zones be centered on Rome's meridian, while Fleming proposed that the Greenwich Meridian become the international standard for zero degrees, from which 24 hourly time zones are calculated.

▲ **TIME DIFFERENCE ACROSS THE WORLD**
Each 15 degrees of longitude from Greenwich adds or subtracts one full hour.

Steel sculpture on the prime meridian, pointing at the North Star

GREENWICH MEANTIME

At the International Meridian Conference, held in October 1884 in Washington, DC, in the USA, delegates decided on Greenwich, UK, as the meridian to be employed as a common zero of longitude.

The prime meridian is symbolized by a steel strip.

WOW!

NIST-F1, an atomic clock in the USA, is said to be so accurate that it would neither gain nor lose a second in over 30 million years.

◄ **THE FIRST ATOMIC CLOCK**
The world's first properly functioning atomic clock, which was built in 1955.

ATOMIC CLOCK

The first usable atomic clock, built by Louis Essen and Jack Parry at the National Physical Laboratory in England in 1955, provides the most accurate measure of time. It measures time according to vibrations within atoms.

Telling the time

Early devices for telling the time depended on the regular burning of a candle, or the flow of water through a small hole. The first mechanical clocks used the regular rocking of a metal rod, called a foliot, to control the movement of a hand around a dial. Later clocks used pendulums, which swing back and forth. The movement is transferred to gears that drive the hands.

It is called a Japanese lantern clock because it looks like a lantern.

Day and night clock

- ■ **What?** Japanese lantern clock
- ■ **Who?** Unknown
- ■ **Where and when?** Japan, 19th century

Before about 1870, Japan divided both the day and the night into six equal hours. A daylight hour was a different length from a night hour and both varied according to the season. This clock has two timekeeping mechanisms, one for day and one for night.

19th-century Japanese lantern clock

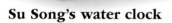

Small-scale model of Su Song's clock

Su Song's water clock

- ■ **What?** Water clock
- ■ **Who?** Su Song
- ■ **Where and when?** China, around 1090

Water clocks were among the earliest devices for telling the time that did not depend on observation of the Sun. Su Song's water clock, made in China in 1088, was one of the most complicated designs and was housed in a tower 10 m (35 ft) high. It was driven by a waterwheel and included 117 figures that came out of the tower on the hour and banged gongs.

The first watch

- ■ **What?** Pocket watch
- ■ **Who?** Peter Henlein
- ■ **Where and when?** Germany, early 1500s

In the early 1500s, Peter Henlein, a locksmith from Nuremberg, Germany, miniaturized the large components of a clock into more portable devices, known as "pocket watches". These small, drum-like clocks were usually worn around the neck or attached to clothing – at this time they could not actually fit into a pocket. It was not until about a century later that smaller versions – the first true pocket watches – were designed.

Early pocket watch

A single hand marks the hours.

Terry balance wheel skeleton clock from the 19th century

A more accurate clock

- **What?** Pendulum clock
- **Who?** Christiaan Huygens
- **Where and when?** The Netherlands, 1657

A physicist, astronomer, and mathematician, Christiaan Huygens also invented the pendulum clock. Until then, the best clocks were accurate to about 15 minutes a day, whereas the pendulum clock was accurate to about 15 seconds.

Model based on the design of Huygens's first pendulum clock

HUYGENS FIRST PENDULUM
DUTCH MATHEMATICAN
ASTRONOM R - 1657

Electric watch

- **What?** Hamilton Electric 500
- **Who?** Hamilton Watch Company
- **Where and when?** USA, 1957

The Hamilton Electric 500 was the first battery-operated electric wristwatch and the first never to need winding. It was marketed as the watch of the future and issued in several suitably modern designs, including the shield-shaped Ventura (left).

Using weights

- **What?** Balance wheel
- **Who?** Unknown
- **Where and when?** Europe, 17th century

The balance wheel is a weighted device that swings back and forth, winding and unwinding a spring in a constant cycle. Each swing of the balance wheel creates a tick or a beat and drives the gears that make the hands move one position.

Hamilton "Ventura" electric watch

Digital watch

- **What?** Hamilton Pulsar P1
- **Who?** Hamilton Watch Company
- **Where and when?** USA, 1972

Luxury watch brand Hamilton was the first to release a digital display watch, in 1972. It was ridiculously expensive, but then the case was 18 carat gold. Cheaper, mass-market versions soon followed.

WOW!

Early wristwatches were designed as jewellery for women. The first was probably made for an aristocrat some time in the mid-19th century.

Smartwatch

- **What?** TrueSmart
- **Who?** Omate
- **Where and when?** USA, 2013

The first smartwatch to have all the functions of a smartphone was the TrueSmart, which appeared in early 2013. Since then, many larger companies have launched smartwatches, including Samsung, Sony, and Apple.

Seiko 06LC digital watch from 1973

SEIKO QUARTZ

10:58 00

141

The telephone

Long before the telephone was invented, people knew that sound could travel along a wire – children could do it with two tin cans and some string. In the second half of the 20th century, many individuals searched for a better way to transmit speech. The Scotsman Alexander Bell made a breakthrough in 1876, by converting sound into an electric current that could be sent along wires.

ALEXANDER GRAHAM BELL

In 1876, scientist Alexander Graham Bell, working on the invention of the telephone in the USA, became the first person to receive a patent for it. A keen business sense and flair for promotion kept him ahead of his rivals.

Bell's telephone was given a beautiful wooden case for the royal demonstration.

FIT FOR A QUEEN

In 1878, in the UK, Queen Victoria was given a demonstration of the telephone by Bell on the Isle of Wight. Bell called Southampton and London in the UK. The queen liked the telephone so much that she wanted to buy it.

The caller speaks into the receiver.

The receiver is then held to the ear to hear the reply.

Bell's telephone from 1878

◄ GETTING CONNECTED

Callers would lift the phone and ask an exchange for the number they wanted, then the operator plugged the line into a switchboard to make the connection.

Finger-sized holes allow the caller to turn the dial and select a telephone number.

THE TELEPHONE EXCHANGE

Early telephones came in pairs and connected only with each other. It needed the invention of a central exchange, to which all local telephones were connected, to allow any person to call any other.

GOING MOBILE

The first portable phones without cords appeared in the 1970s. Networks had relatively few radio frequencies, but millions of users, and calls could be handled automatically without an operator.

Dr Martin Cooper, the inventor of the first practical mobile phone

▲ AUTOMATIC TELEPHONE EXCHANGE PHONE

This 1905 phone was designed for use with an automatic exchange, which first appeared in 1889.

TEXTING

The first text message ever sent was in 1992 and read "Happy Christmas". Texting was slow to catch on as the first phone with a full keyboard did not appear until 1996.

WOW!

The first words ever spoken on a telephone were, "Mr Watson, come here, I want you", said by Alexander Graham Bell.

143

Taking a call

The earliest telephones had two sets joined by a single cord, connecting just two places. Now, phones are wireless and we can talk to anyone anywhere in the world. We can now even see the person we are talking to, thanks to smartphones and phone apps such as Apple's FaceTime.

Candlestick phone

- **What?** Candlestick phone
- **Who?** American Bell Telephone Company
- **Where and when?** USA, 1892

The candlestick phone was the first stand-up telephone and one of the earliest models of telephone to be mass-produced. It featured a mouthpiece (transmitter) at the top of the stand, and an ear phone (receiver) that was held to the ear by the user during a call – similar to those seen on the Western Electric candlestick (right). This type of phone lasted well into the 1920s.

Receiver

Transmitter

Later candlesticks, like this one, had a rotary dial.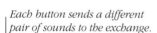

Western Electric nickel candlestick phone, 1920s

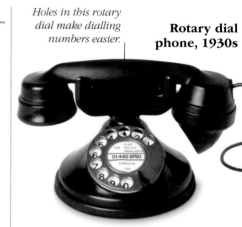

Holes in this rotary dial make dialling numbers easier.

Rotary dial phone, 1930s

Rotary dial phone

- **What?** Model 50AL Candlestick
- **Who?** Bell Systems
- **Where and when?** USA, 1919

Automatic exchanges had allowed people to call each other directly since 1892, but the rotary dial, introduced in about 1905, made the process simpler. Later, handsets became popular, which combined the rotary dial with a handset containing both the transmitter and receiver in the same unit.

Each button sends a different pair of sounds to the exchange.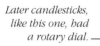

A push-button telephone

Push-button dialling

- **What?** Western Electric model 1500
- **Who?** Bell Systems
- **Where and when?** USA, 1963

The push-button phone had electronic keys for dialling a number and was far easier and quicker to use than a rotary-dial phone. Although it was introduced in the 1960s, it was not until the 1980s that most users had push-button phones at home.

WOW!

It is estimated that more than 60 per cent of people in the world will own a mobile phone by 2019.

Talking on the move

- **What?** Cordless phone
- **Who?** Sony
- **Where and when?** Japan, 1980s

A prototype cordless phone was patented in the 1960s by former US Army radio operator George Sweigert. However, most of us had to wait until the 1980s, when Japanese company Sony introduced the first commercially available cordless phones to the market.

Cordless phone, 1993

Early mobile phone

- **What?** Nokia 3210
- **Who?** Nokia
- **Where and when?** Finland, 1999

The Nokia 3210, launched in 1999, became one of the most popular and successful phones in history. Its inclusion of three games, changeable covers, and customizable ringtones, along with an affordable price, made it popular with teenagers. It became many people's first-ever mobile phone.

Nokia 3210

Satellite phone

Antenna

- **What?** Globalstar GSP-1700
- **Who?** Iridium and Globalstar companies
- **Where and when?** UK, 1998/1999

A satellite phone connects to orbiting satellites, rather than ground-based towers. This means it can make a call from essentially anywhere in the world. Satellite phone services are not cheap, but they are invaluable in remote areas where landline or mobile phone networks don't exist.

An early satellite phone

FAST FACTS

- Alexander Graham Bell recommended answering the telephone with the word "Ahoy".
- The number of mobile phones in the world overtook the number of people in 2014.
- The Nokia tone for receiving SMS text messages is Morse code for "SMS".
- The first mobiles had to be charged for 10 hours to give 30 minutes of battery life.
- The 555 prefix is reserved for fictional US telephone numbers.

Early smartphone

- **What?** Nseries
- **Who?** Nokia
- **Where and when?** Finland, 2005

When Nokia launched the N70, it introduced the world to a phone that could double up as a portable computer, camera, GPS, and music player. However, just two years later, Apple launched the iPhone – a touchscreen smartphone that dominated the market.

Hands-free wireless technology

- **What?** Bluetooth unit
- **Who?** Ericsson
- **Where and when?** Sweden, 1994

Devised in Sweden, Bluetooth is a way of exchanging data wirelessly. Using a special radio frequency to transmit data, it creates a short-range network. It connects with a phone to leave your hands free, or with your desktop computer so you don't need cables to transfer files.

Bluetooth headset

Smartphone

Part phone, part palm-sized computer, life without a smartphone today is unimaginable. We do not just communicate through them, we use them to listen to music, watch videos, play games, shop, take photos, look up information, and document our own lives on social media apps such as Instagram. Yet, a little over 10 years ago, they did not exist.

Ericsson R380, 2000

The iPhone looks radically different from any other device before it, with its large screen and slim profile.

The large screen and unique operating system makes it the first phone suitable for Internet browsing.

TOUCH AND TAP

When Apple launched its first iPhone in 2007, it changed the industry. It was simpler to use than anything that had come before and, through its groundbreaking touchscreen, it offered many more functions, such as music and video.

The "home" button is the only button on the iPhone.

EARLY SMARTPHONES

The Ericsson R380 was the first device to be called a "smartphone" when it was launched in 2000. The hugely popular BlackBerry followed soon after, which was one of the first devices to have a full keyboard and provide access to emails and limited Internet browsing on the move.

▲ APPS
Uniquely, the iPhone allowed users to easily add new software to their phone in the form of apps (applications).

Apple was most famous for its iPod music player, but now the iPhone does everything that the iPod did, and more.

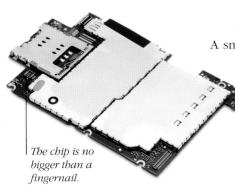

The chip is no bigger than a fingernail.

SMARTPHONE COMPUTER

A smartphone is powered by a chip. Not to be confused with the SIM card, which communicates with external networks, a chip is a small computer processor that makes all the phone's many features work.

SAY CHEESE

Historically, self-portraits were only painted by artists, or taken by cameras set on a timer. Thanks to innovations such as the smartphone's front-facing camera and selfie-sticks we have all gone selfie crazy.

EMOJIS

The earliest emojis were designed in 1998 by Shigetaka Kurita, an employee of a Japanese mobile phone carrier. They convey complex information about human emotions in a single character.

WOW!

A poll by smartphone-maker Samsung found that selfies make up 30 per cent of the photos taken by people aged 18–24.

SMART TECH

In the race to entice consumers, smartphones have become thinner, faster, and, well, smarter. New, clever technology includes use of the camera as a scanner, for instance, to translate foreign text on a menu.

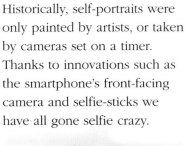

◄ FACIAL RECOGNITION

Several phones have facial recognition as a security device to unlock a phone's screen. Some identify patterns in the iris of the eye, others use infrared to scan the whole face.

▼ FINGERTIP SCAN

A smartphone with a fingerprint scanner appeared in 2007 but the technology became widespread with the iPhone 5S in 2013.

147

THE SUPERCOMPUTER

In 2018, the Sunway TaihuLight was the world's fastest supercomputer. Housed in the city of Wuxi, in eastern China, it can carry out 93 quadrillion calculations per second. That's twice as fast as the next-most-powerful supercomputer in existence, Tianhe-2, which also happens to be in China.

Radio

German physicist Heinrich Hertz discovered radio waves in 1888. He understood they were a form of energy, like light, that travelled in waves, but he did not see any potential practical uses. However, other scientists seized on his discovery and, within a decade, it was possible to send signals around the world without the need for wires.

WOW!

Early crystal radios required earphones, so only one person could listen at a time.

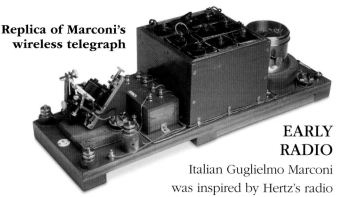

Replica of Marconi's wireless telegraph

EARLY RADIO

Italian Guglielmo Marconi was inspired by Hertz's radio waves discovery. Starting in 1894, his experiments saw him transmit a radio signal a distance of 3.2 km (2 miles). In 1896, he received the world's first patent for "wireless telegraphy", which became known as radio communication. Although Marconi was awarded the patent, Nikola Tesla invented the technology almost simultaneously.

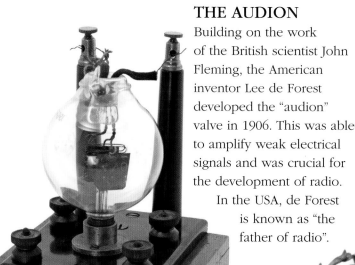

Audion valve with mounting, 1906

THE AUDION

Building on the work of the British scientist John Fleming, the American inventor Lee de Forest developed the "audion" valve in 1906. This was able to amplify weak electrical signals and was crucial for the development of radio. In the USA, de Forest is known as "the father of radio".

ALEXANDERSON ALTERNATOR

The Alexanderson Alternator was a rotating machine invented by electrical engineers Ernst Alexanderson and Reginald Fessenden in 1904. It produced a high-frequency alternating current and was one of the first devices capable of generating continuous radio waves.

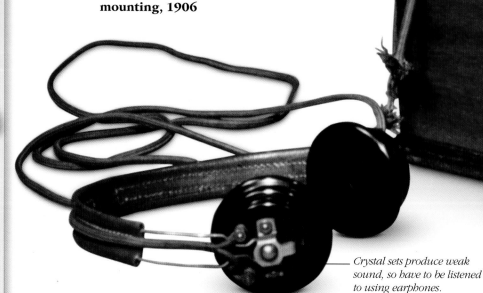

Crystal sets produce weak sound, so have to be listened to using earphones.

DEVELOPMENT OF RADIO

Early transmitters could send out radio waves only in short bursts and used Morse code. For proper sound, continuous waves are needed. In 1906, Canadian-American engineer Reginald Fessenden invented an electric generator that could produce such waves. His first broadcast was on Christmas Eve, 1906. Regular broadcasting began in 1909, but it was not widely used until after World War I.

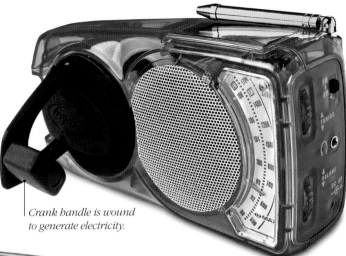

Crank handle is wound to generate electricity.

WIND-UP RADIO

In the early 1990s, the English inventor Trevor Baylis designed a radio for use in remote places, where there was no electricity. It was powered by a clockwork motor that stored energy in a spring. Later radios, like this one, use energy from winding the handle to charge the battery.

DIGITAL RADIO

Digital broadcasting was first pioneered in the early 1980s, developed at the Institut für Rundfunktechnik in Munich, Germany. It was not popularly adopted until the 2000s, but now broadcasters can offer more services and a higher-quality signal than ever before.

A "crystal set", the simplest type of radio receiver common in the early days of radio

▲ CRYSTAL SET
Household radios first became popular in the 1920s, when this radio was made.

Listen to the radio

The invention of radio was so revolutionary that developments since have made only minor improvements. Digitial radio has massively increased the range of what we can listen to, but the experience of listening to the radio today remains little altered from a century ago.

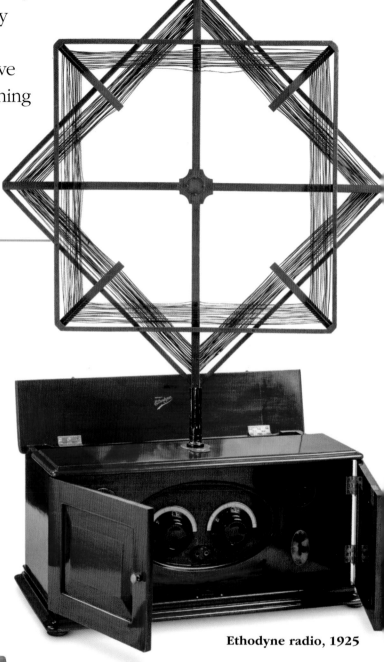

Ethodyne radio

- **What?** Superheterodyne circuit
- **Who?** Edward Howard Armstrong
- **Where and when?** USA, 1919

New York-born Edward Howard Armstrong was fascinated by radios from childhood. As an adult, he invented FM radio, now the most popular system, and also a way in which radio receivers could in effect shift every station to the same frequency. This greatly simplified their design and made them more sensitive and easier to tune.

> ### FAST FACTS
>
> - In 1908, while in Paris, France, on his honeymoon, Lee de Forest broadcasted music from the top of the Eiffel Tower, becoming the first radio DJ in history.
> - In 1920, the world's first commercial radio station, KDKA, went on the air in Pittsburgh, USA.

Ethodyne radio, 1925

Backpack military radio

- **What?** SCR-300
- **Who?** Motorola
- **Where and when?** USA, 1940

In 1940, Motorola was asked by the US War Department to develop a portable, battery-powered radio for use by the military during World War II. It was the first radio to be nicknamed a "walkie-talkie".

Handheld walkie-talkie

- **What?** AM SCR-536
- **Who?** Motorola
- **Where and when?** USA, 1940

What we now know as a walkie-talkie was originally called a "handie-talkie" – in other words, a handheld, two-way radio. The first example to appear was the AM SCR-536, made by Motorola. It was made for the military and was quite bulky. It was soon succeeded by smaller, lighter models, popular with service organizations and on worksites.

Antenna

WOW!

More than half the world's population is not connected to the Internet, so for many, radio is still the most accessible form of communication.

UFT 432 walkie-talkie, 1970s

Transistor radio

- **What?** Regency TR-1
- **Who?** Texas Instruments and Idea Inc.
- **Where and when?** USA, 1954

The Regency TR-1 transformed the radio from a piece of bulky furniture to something that could be put in a pocket. What made this possible was the transistor, a tiny, solid device developed in 1947 that replaced bulky glass valves for amplifying signals. Texas Instruments supplied the transistors and Idea Inc. designed and produced the gadget that changed the way the world listened to music.

Portable radio

- **What?** TR82
- **Who?** Bush
- **Where and when?** UK, 1959

The first transistor radios were expensive, but soon other manufacturers entered the market with cheaper models. One of the most iconic of the first wave of portable radios was the TR82 transistor radio by British company Bush, which launched in 1959. Its fashionable design by David Ogle, with a large central dial inscribed with the names of various radio stations, made it immensely popular, especially with teenagers. It is now considered a design classic.

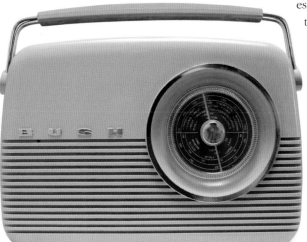

Buttons make switching stations and modes easier.

Digital radio

- **What?** Alpha 10
- **Who?** Arcam
- **Where and when?** UK, 1999

Although digital broadcasting was pioneered in the 1980s, the world's first digital radio tuner intended for home use did not go on sale until 1999. It was big and expensive. Smaller, more affordable units began to appear over the next few years, such as the pioneering Evoke 1 from British company Pure in 2002.

CONNECTING CONTINENTS

Submarine communications cables at the bottom of the ocean transmit 99 per cent of data – including Internet data – around the world. The cables are installed by special boats and land equipment and can be sunk as deep as Everest is tall – that's 8,848 m (29,028 ft) deep! When laying cables, care must be taken to avoid obstructions such as reefs and sunken wrecks.

The camera

Pinhole cameras were used in ancient times to project images, but they couldn't take a picture – that had to wait until the 1820s. The first photographs took several hours of exposure in the camera. Now, with digital technology, we can take pictures and view them instantly.

WOW!

The earliest known photograph was taken by Joseph Nicéphore Niépce in 1826. It shows the view from an upstairs window at his country estate in France.

An aperture allows light into the camera.

THE FIRST SNAPS

The first photographs, taken by Joseph Nicéphore Niépce in the 1820s, were very crude. It was his colleague, Louis Daguerre, who developed the first viable photographic process. The 1839 Giroux Daguerreotype was the world's first commercially produced camera.

SILVER SHOTS

Daguerreotype images, like this one (right) from 1843, were made by exposing a silver-coated copper plate for a few minutes. The faint image was developed to full visibility using mercury fumes. William Fox Talbot created the "calotype", another early photographic process, in 1841. Unlike the daguerreotype, an unlimited number of prints could be made from one calotype.

A tripod holds the camera steady during the exposure.

Giroux Daguerreotype, 1839

CAMERA OBSCURA

The camera obscura, a bigger version of the simple pinhole camera, was refined in 1570. Inside a dark room, a tiny hole is made in one wall. Natural light is focused through it, and an image of the outside scene is projected onto the opposite wall. There is a working example (left) in Edinburgh, Scotland.

SEEING IN COLOUR

The earliest colour pictures required photographers to take three photographs using red, blue, and green filters, and then superimpose them using projectors. In 1907, the French Lumière brothers patented a way of combining the colours on a single plate in a process they called "autochrome".

The photographic plate is at the rear of the case.

Autochromes needed long exposures so most were of still scenes.

◄ **PEGGY IN THE GARDEN, 1909**
This autochrome picture was taken by pioneering English photographer John Cimon Warburg, who took up photography in the 1880s.

IN A FLASH

For lighting in dark places, early photographers used flash powder – a mix of magnesium powder and potassium chlorate, ignited in a pan. It was very dangerous. In 1929, a German company introduced the flashbulb, with magnesium contained in the bulbs.

Magnesium foil is electrically ignited by the wire filament.

Wire filament

German flashbulb, 1929

GELATIN DRY PLATES

Developed in 1871, the gelatin dry plate was more sensitive than previous film plates and reduced exposure time. For the first time, a tripod or other support was not necessary. Small cameras could be handheld while taking "snapshots".

ON A ROLL

In 1885, the American George Eastman introduced transparent, flexible photographic film. This allowed multiple images to be taken using a roll of film rather than a single plate. Eastman introduced a camera for his film, the Kodak, which was first offered for sale in 1888. The Kodak camera was handheld and easy to use, making photography accessible to more people, not only professional photographers.

The Kodak came with a 100-exposure film inside it.

Kodak camera, 1888

The camera had to be returned to the factory when film was finished so the photos could be developed.

Original Kodak film pack from 1890

Snap away!

Until relatively recently, photography was reserved for special occasions, such as holidays and weddings, due to the cost and time involved in buying film and having it developed. Now we can take pictures all day long and we no longer even need a special camera – our mobile phones do the job.

WOW!

It is estimated that every two minutes we snap as many photos as the whole of humanity took in the entire 19th century.

Kodak No.3a, made from 1903 to 1915

Pocket camera

- **What?** Folding Pocket Kodak No.1
- **Who?** Eastman Kodak Co Ltd
- **Where and when?** USA, 1897–1898

Pioneers in the camera business, Kodak produced ever smaller and cheaper models for the amateur photographer, including one of the first folding cameras. This was followed by an even smaller "vest pocket" camera in 1912.

Press camera

- **What?** Speed Graphic
- **Who?** Graflex
- **Where and when?** USA, 1912

A press camera shot pictures that were bigger than average, but the camera was still relatively compact and very easy to handle. It was used by press photographers and anybody that needed a reliable camera that could shoot pictures quickly.

Flash bulb

Graflex Speed Graphic camera

Twin-lens reflex camera

- **What?** Rolleiflex K1
- **Who?** Franke & Heidecke
- **Where and when?** Germany, 1929

TLR (twin-lens reflex) cameras have two lenses, one to take the picture and one for viewing, as pictured above on the later 2.8 F model. A 45-degree mirror allows the user to view the shot from above, with the camera held at waist height. With this technique, the camera could also be held more steadily.

Leica Standard, 1932

35 mm camera

- **What?** Leica Standard
- **Who?** Oskar Barnack
- **Where and when?** Germany, 1932

In the first quarter of the 20th century, 35 mm (the width of the film) became the primary format for cameras. Cameras using 35 mm film were available as early as 1913, but the compact cameras made by Leica, such as the iconic Leica Standard (left), really popularized the format.

Brownie Flash IV

Brownie Flash series

- **What?** Brownie Flash II
- **Who?** Eastman Kodak Co Ltd
- **Where and when?** UK, 1957

In 1898, Kodak-founder George Eastman asked his camera designer to design the cheapest camera possible, and the Brownie was created – a camera so simple to use, anyone could operate it. The Brownie range continued with the popular Brownie Flash series in the 1950s, which was even more useful as it allowed the user to attach a flash.

SX-70 onestep, 1978

Polaroids

- **What?** Polaroid SX-70
- **Who?** Edwin Land of the Polaroid Corporation
- **Where and when?** USA, 1972

Jennifer Land, after having her photo taken, asked her father, "Why can't I see them now?" Her father was Edwin Land of the Polaroid company, who went on to invent the first commerical instant camera. The innovation continued with the iconic SX-70, which delivered a print shortly after taking the picture and was popular in the 1970s.

Hasselblad cameras

- **What?** Hasselblad 500 EL
- **Who?** Victor Hasselblad
- **Where and when?** Sweden, 1969

A former trading company, Hasselblad started making cameras during World War II. Their cameras are regarded as being of the highest quality, and they became well known when NASA chose the Hasselblad 500 EL to be the camera used on the legendary Moon landing in 1969.

Digital camera

- **What?** Minolta RD-175
- **Who?** Minolta
- **Where and when?** Japan, 1995

Cameras that do not use film but capture and save photographs electronically first appeared commercially in the mid 1990s. The first properly portable digital camera was probably the Minolta RD-175, released in 1995, followed by the Nikon D1 in 1999.

Action cameras

- **What?** GoPro HERO
- **Who?** Nick Woodman
- **Where and when?** USA, 2004

Beloved of adventure-sports enthusiasts, the GoPro range of cameras was dreamed up by a surfer who could not find the right kind of equipment he needed to shoot while riding waves. The original camera, developed in 2001, used 35 mm film, but later models incorporated digital and video technology, as well as special wide lenses.

GoPro HERO 4

Drone photography

- **What?** SOLO Drone
- **Who?** 3D Robotics
- **Where and when?** USA, 2015

Originally designed for military use, small drones equipped with GPS navigation and digital cameras have become commonplace, allowing increasing numbers of photographers to capture stunning aerial images.

Olympus digital SLR camera, 2015

Cinema

In 1891, the American Edison company demonstrated its Kinetoscope – a camera designed for "moving pictures" to be watched by one person at a time through a viewer window. Four years later, films were shown to audiences of hundreds, but it wasn't until 1927 that the first film, *The Jazz Singer*, was made with recorded sound.

GLORIOUS TECHNICOLOR®

Early attempts at colour involved hand-tinting the film. Beginning in 1932, the Technicolor company introduced a camera, below, that used three separate films to record red, blue, and green, which were then combined to develop a full-colour print. This became the standard process until the mid-1950s.

CAUGHT ON CAMERA

Early films lasted only a minute or so and showed just a single scene. This cinematograph camera, left, from 1896 could be swivelled to follow the action. It was probably used to film Queen Victoria's Diamond Jubilee procession in the UK in 1897.

Protective canisters contain the film reels.

Reels hold the three lengths of film that record the three different colours.

Technicolor three-strip camera, 1932

Muybridge's galloping horse, 1877

MOVING PICTURES

Cinematography is the illusion of movement by the rapid projection of photographs. Englishman Eadweard Muybridge was a pioneer photographer who shot still images of animals and projected them as moving sequences, a key moment in the development of cinema.

A PAYING AUDIENCE

The first public cinema screening shown to a paying audience was presented by the French brothers Auguste and Louis Lumière in Paris, France, in December 1895. They showed 10 short clips they had filmed.

Toshiba DVD player, 1996

LASER TECHNOLOGY

In the mid-1970s, cinema moved into the home with the debut of video cassette players. The experience improved considerably with the first Hollywood studio-release of DVDs in 1997, thanks to higher-quality picture and sound, more user-friendly menus, and sometimes interactive games.

DVD

SEEING IN 3-D

Experiments in 3-D film date back as far as the late 1890s, but the earliest 3-D film shown to a paying audience was *The Power of Love*, shown in Los Angeles, USA, in 1922. This was also the first film to use anaglyph 3-D glasses that had lenses of opposite colour. 3-D quality improved with the introduction of polarized lenses in 1986. The popularity of 3-D peaked with the most successful 3-D film, *Avatar*, released in 2009.

Modern 3-D glasses

MODERN "FILM" CAMERA

The modern camera no longer uses reels of celluloid film; instead, it records using digital technology. The "films" are supplied to cinemas as digital files. The first digital screening was *Star Wars Episode I: The Phantom Menace*, in 1999.

Genesis digital movie camera, first used to shoot *Superman Returns*, 2006

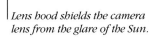

Lens hood shields the camera lens from the glare of the Sun.

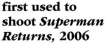

Television

Several different people were working on the invention of the television at around the same time. John Logie Baird developed a mechanical system for the BBC, an important British broadcaster, in 1923. In the USA, Philo Farnsworth demonstrated an electronic television in 1934. However, it was Russians, Isaac Shoenberg and Vladimir Zworykin, who created the electronic television we know today.

WOW!

The first TV images ever broadcast in public were of a scary-looking ventriloquist's dummy called Stookie Bill in 1926.

EARLY BROADCASTING

Although there were earlier broadcasts, including the 1936 Olympic Games in Berlin, the BBC service that started on 2 November 1936 is regarded as the world's first regular public TV broadcast.

CATHODE RAY TUBE

The first important step was the invention of the cathode ray tube (CRT). The first was built by the German Ferdinand Braun in 1897. It fired electrons down a glass tube at a phosphor screen, which lit up. Controlling which bits of phosphor lit up created a picture.

Glass tube with phosphor screen at the end

Cathode that sends out electrons when heated

SPINNING DISC TELEVISION

Scottish engineer John Logie Baird used a rotating disc to sweep a spotlight over the subject to be televised, with a matching disc in the receiver. He gave public demonstrations in 1926. However, the pictures produced by this mechanical system were not as good as those made using electronics.

Baird Televisor made in 1929

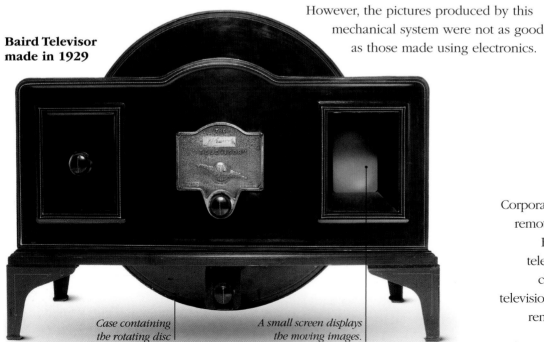

Case containing the rotating disc

A small screen displays the moving images.

REMOTE CONTROL

The American Zenith Radio Corporation created the first television remote control in 1950, called "Lazy Bones" (above). It could turn a television on and off, and change channels. It was attached to the television by a cable. The first wireless remote control appeared in 1955.

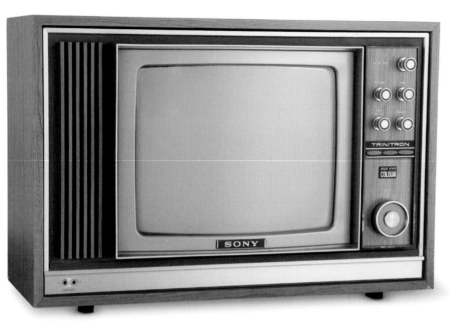

COLOUR TELEVISION

The American television broadcaster CBS showed the first colour TV programme on 25 June 1951. Unfortunately, few viewers saw the benefit, as most people had black-and-white televisions then. Britain produced its first colour TV in 1967, but it was not until the 1970s that more colour TV sets were bought than black-and-white ones.

Sony Trinitron, a popular colour TV of the 1970s

DIGITAL TELEVISION

The biggest evolution since colour has been the possibility to receive television signals in a digital format rather than analogue. Beginning in the 2000s, this allowed TV companies to broadcast better quality sound, a higher definition picture, and a wider range of channels than they ever could before.

BT Vision TV digital set-top box

Professional digital HD camera

HD TELEVISION

HD (high definition) is a television display technology that provides picture quality similar to a cinema experience – pictures have more detail and are much sharper and more colourful. The first HD TV broadcast was of the Statue of Liberty and New York Harbor, shown in Japan in 1989, but HD broadcasts only became common in the 2000s.

Server racks in a data centre in Germany

STREAMING

In recent years, TV has changed enormously. Thanks to the Internet and the ability to watch shows live, we can now view whatever we want, wherever we want. We don't even need a television – we can use our phones or laptops – and we are not dependent on broadcasters, just a fast link to a computer server.

Big screens

Most items of technology get smaller as they are developed. Think of how large the earliest phones, computers, or cameras were. Television screens have done the opposite and become bigger. The earliest TV screens were about the size of those on laptop computers. The latest models today are like mini cinema screens.

WOW!

The world's largest TV screen, made by an Austrian company, is over 6.6 m (22 ft), measured diagonally.

Early household television

- **What?** Telefunken FE-1
- **Who?** Telefunken
- **Where and when?** Germany, 1934

The earliest TV sets used John Logie Baird's mechanical system, which was scrapped in the 1930s when the first electronic televisions were made in Germany. France, Britain, and the USA soon followed with their own models. Early TVs were large pieces of wooden furniture with small, 30 cm (12 inch) screens.

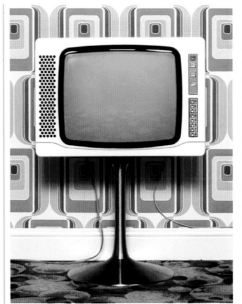

Colour television, 1970s

Colour television

- **What?** Westinghouse H840CK15
- **Who?** Westinghouse
- **Where and when?** USA, 1954

Although the first colour broadcasts were made in the USA in 1951, Westinghouse's colour television set was not available to the public until three years later. Other companies produced colour TVs, too, but they sold slowly because they were so expensive and there were few programmes in colour. It was not until the 1970s, when all programming was in colour, that colour television really took off.

Modern-age television

- **What?** Philco Predicta
- **Who?** Philco
- **Where and when?** Philadelphia, USA, 1958

Televisions did not stay in their heavy wooden cases for long. Improved technology allowed them to become more movable and to include new ideas. This Philco Predicta, for example, had the world's first swivel screen. In the 1950s, TVs were still a luxury and designers wanted to make them look as futuristic as possible.

The Philco Predicta could be swivelled in any direction.

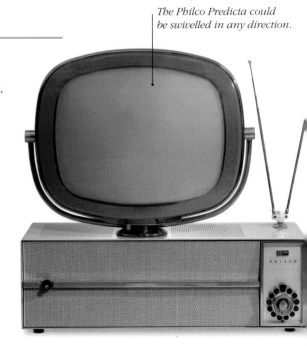

Portable television

- **What?** Philco Safari
- **Who?** Philco
- **Where and when?** Philadelphia, USA, 1959

The first truly portable TV set was the Philco Safari, which was about the size of a backpack and was powered by a small battery. By 1970, Panasonic had a handbag-sized TV, the TR-001, and in 1978, the British inventor Clive Sinclair released his near pocket-sized MTV1, seen here.

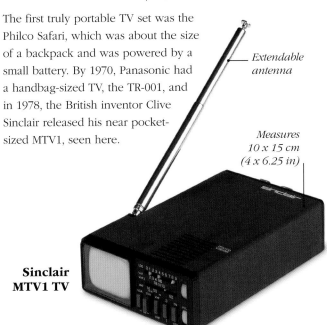

Extendable antenna

Measures 10 x 15 cm (4 x 6.25 in)

Sinclair MTV1 TV

OLED television

Flat-screen plasma television

- **What?** Flat-screen TV
- **Who?** Panasonic
- **Where and when?** Japan and USA, 1997

This flat-screen TV was thin and light enough to be hung on a wall. The technology was invented in 1964 by two University of Illinois professors. The screen is made from thousands of tiny, gas-filled tubes that can glow red, green, or blue when excited by electricity. These are controlled by circuits that make each tube vary continually in brightness to form the moving picture. It was not until 1997 that the first flat-screen TVs went on sale to the public.

The huge, slim screen provides a high-quality picture.

Organic light-emitting diode (OLED) television

- **What?** Sony XEL-1
- **Who?** Sony
- **Where and when?** Japan, 2008

An OLED is a device containing a plastic-like material that glows when electricity passes through it. The screen uses thousands of these to form the picture. OLED TVs are much more energy efficient. They have incredibly thin screens and a much better picture than any seen before. Sony released the first version in 2008, but they are so expensive that many people are unable to afford them.

3-D television

- **What?** Viera VT20 plasma 3D HDTV
- **Who?** Panasonic

- **Where and when?** Japan, 2010

In 2009, with the release of films like James Cameron's science-fiction film *Avatar*, 3-D seemed to be the future of cinema. Electronics companies rushed to produce 3-D televisions, and the first sets appeared the following year. It proved to be a passing trend, and by 2017, no one wanted 3-D.

Written communication

People were communicating via marks inscribed on clay tablets 5,000 years ago in Mesopotamia (modern-day Iraq), and more than 2,000 years ago, on paper in China. The next great leap was not until about 1450, with the invention of the printing press in Germany. This paved the way for printed books, newspapers (introduced in the 17th century), and magazines (in the 18th century).

Bic biro

Ballpoint pen

PENNY POST
Postal services date back to ancient times. However, the first postage stamp, known as the Penny Black (right), was issued on 1 May 1840 in the UK, as a part of postal reforms introduced to make sending letters affordable for all.

A STEADY INK FLOW
Early pens had to be dipped in or filled with ink, which leaked or dried up. In the 1880s, American John J Loud developed an early version of the ballpoint pen that had ink inside it ready for writing. This was later improved by the Hungarian Lázló Bíró.

In 1870, postcards were issued with a stamp as part of the design.

German postcard, 1870

WISH YOU WERE HERE
The earliest known postcard was posted in London, UK, by the writer Theodore Hook – to himself – in 1840, using a Penny Black stamp. In the USA, the first postcard-like piece of mail was sent in 1848 and was paid for by advertising printed on it.

FINGERTIP READING

As a student, the blind Frenchman Louis Braille, encountered a way of writing messages with raised dots that was used by soldiers to communicate at night. He improved the system and published it in 1829. It is known as Braille and is still in use today.

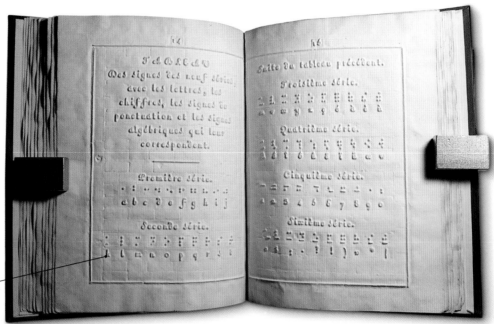

Braille's system works with a six-dot code, used to identify the letters of the alphabet.

First Braille book, 1829

By using carbon paper, multiple copies of one document could be made.

Ink-soaked ribbon transfers marks to the paper when hit by levers carrying the type.

The Crandall typewriter, 1875

PUNCHING KEYS

Appropriately, the US inventor of the typewriter was an ex-newspaper editor. Christopher Sholes wanted something that would "write" faster than a pen. With the help of two fellow inventors, Carlos Glidden and Samuel Soule, he created such a machine in 1873.

Fast typists jammed keys on early keyboards such as this one, so Sholes came up with the QWERTY keyboard in 1875.

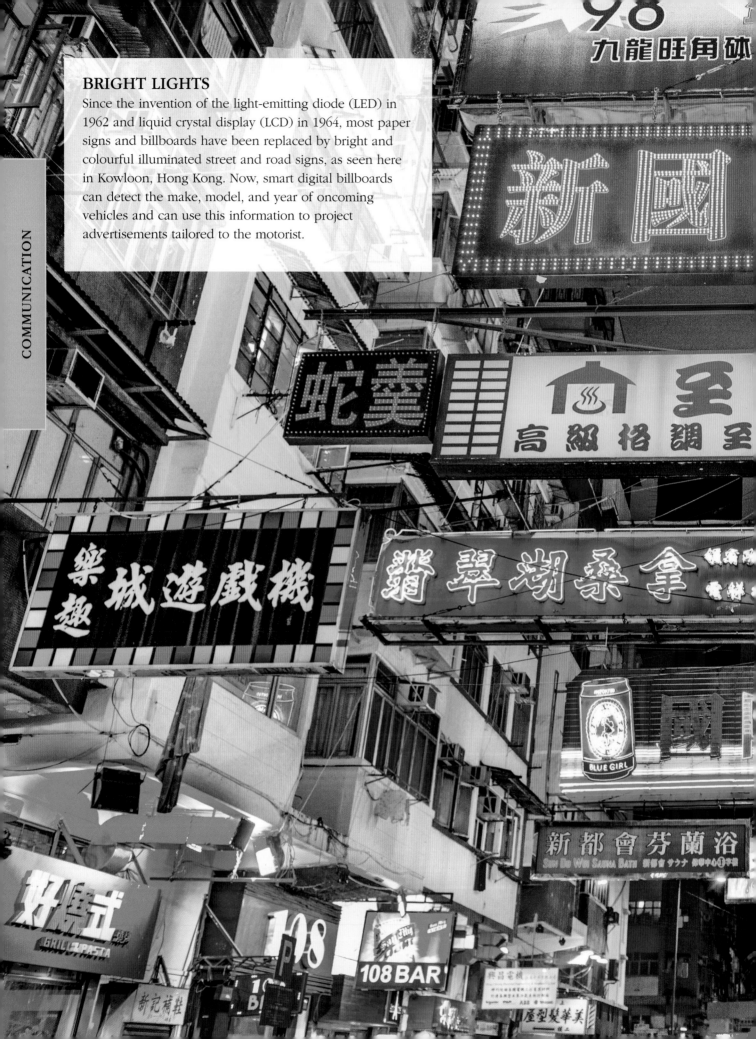

BRIGHT LIGHTS

Since the invention of the light-emitting diode (LED) in 1962 and liquid crystal display (LCD) in 1964, most paper signs and billboards have been replaced by bright and colourful illuminated street and road signs, as seen here in Kowloon, Hong Kong. Now, smart digital billboards can detect the make, model, and year of oncoming vehicles and can use this information to project advertisements tailored to the motorist.

The computer

English inventor and mathematician Charles Babbage famously designed three computing machines. Their purpose was to store and process numbers, and output the results of calculations. Babbage's designs were groundbreaking, leading many to regard him the "father of the computer".

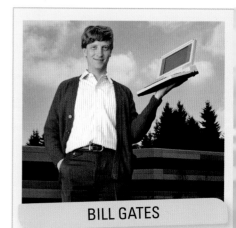

BILL GATES

Every computer uses software – a set of instructions that tells a computer how to perform a task. In 1975, US computer scientist Bill Gates co-founded Microsoft, which became the world's largest software company and made him one of the world's richest men.

COMPUTING ENGINE

Although Charles Babbage designed the first automatic computing engines, he failed to build them. His "Difference Engine No. 2" was completed in London, UK, in only 1991, 142 years after it was designed.

Part of Babbage's "Difference Engine No. 1"

EARLY COMPUTING

The era of modern computing began during World War II. In 1941, the German engineer Konrad Zuse completed the Z3, the world's first general-purpose, programmable digital computer, which was non-electronic and large enough to fill a room. It helped Zuse in his calculations for aeronautical design.

▶ COMPUTING GIANT

The Colossus was a computer developed by the British in 1943–1945 during World War II to help break Germany's wartime secret codes.

Grace Hopper is seen here programming Howard Aiken's "Mark 1" computer, which made calculations used to design the atomic bomb during World War II.

GRACE HOPPER

In the 1940s, Grace Hopper joined the US Navy and became one of the first computer programmers. She helped develop one of the first programming languages, called COBOL, which is still in use. She also coined the term "computer bug" when she took a trapped moth out of a computer.

GETTING SMALLER AND FASTER

A microprocessor is a computer's "engine". Early computers were the size of a large wardrobe, or bigger. In 1947, the creation of transistors shrunk the workings down to a small integrated circuit board that could carry out operations at incredible speeds, and computers became smaller.

Each sub-circuit of this early processor contains thousands of transistors.

COMPUTER MOUSE

In 1964, American engineer Douglas Engelbart came up with a wheeled device that could move a computer cursor. He called it a "mouse" because it looked like a mouse with a tail.

First mouse, made of wood

COMMUNICATION

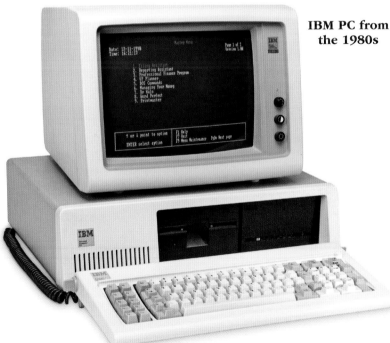

IBM PC from the 1980s

PERSONAL COMPUTER

The first personal computers (PCs), created in the 1970s, were self-assembly kits for experts only. The personal computer revolution truly began in 1981 when IBM launched its first PCs, changing forever the way people work, play, and communicate.

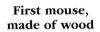

Home computers

Since the arrival of the earliest personal computers, which were boxy and heavy, the trend has been towards ever smaller devices with greater processing power. The power of our smartphones is far greater than that of early computers that were the size of a wardrobe.

Build-it-yourself computer

- **What?** Altair 8800
- **Who?** MITS
- **Where and when?** USA, 1974

Many of the earliest personal computers were sold as build-it-yourself kits to hobbyists. After the Altair 8800 appeared on the cover of Popular Electronics magazine, it sold in large numbers and kick-started a personal computing revolution.

Computing at home

- **What?** Atari 400/800
- **Who?** Atari
- **Where and when?** USA, 1979

The first home computers, intended for non-technical users, arrived in 1979. Leading the pack were models by manufacturers Texas Instruments and, particularly, Atari. Their most common uses were playing video games, but some people used them for word processing and basic programming.

Steve Wozniak's Apple II

- **What?** Apple II
- **Who?** Apple Computer, Inc
- **Where and when?** USA, 1977

The Apple II was designed by Steve Wozniak, co-founder of Apple Computer Inc (now just Apple), in 1977. It was one of the first consumer products to be sold by Apple. With colour graphics, sound, and a plastic casing, it set the template for all personal computers to follow.

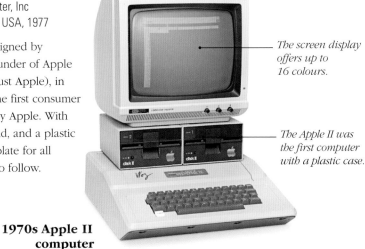

The screen display offers up to 16 colours.

The Apple II was the first computer with a plastic case.

1970s Apple II computer

The first laptop

- **What?** Epson HX-20
- **Who?** Yukio Yokozawa of Seiko
- **Where and when?** Japan, 1981

The Epson HX-20 was the first laptop computer. It was developed by the Seiko company in Japan and marketed internationally by Epson. It was about the size of an A4 sheet of paper and weighed 1.6 kg (3.5 lb). The monitor screen was no bigger than that of a calculator.

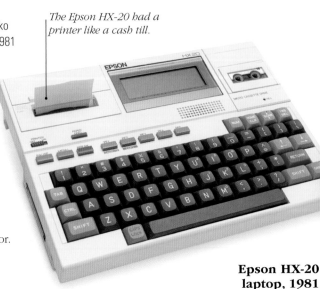

The Epson HX-20 had a printer like a cash till.

Epson HX-20 laptop, 1981

GRiD compass laptop, 1982

Folding-screen laptop

- **What?** GRiD Compass
- **Who?** GRiD Systems Corporation
- **Where and when?** USA, 1982

The first laptop to have the features of a modern laptop – in particular, a screen that folds flat – came out in 1982. It was very expensive and the main buyer was the US government. The laptops were used by the US Navy and NASA carried them onboard some Space Shuttle missions.

Apple Macintosh

- **What?** Apple Macintosh
- **Who?** Apple
- **Where and when?** USA, 1984

The Macintosh (named after the McIntosh variety of apple) was designed as an easy-to-use, low-cost computer for the average person. It was launched in 1984, but was not actually that cheap. It did not take off until the early 1990s, when Apple launched more price-competitive machines.

A handle built into the top of the case makes it easier to lift and carry.

Apple Macintosh 128k

Psion 3a PDA notebook, 1993

Touchpad

- **What?** Psion MC 200
- **Who?** Psion
- **Where and when?** UK, 1989

A touchpad is a specialized surface that can track the position and motion of a finger and translate that to the screen. Touchpads are used instead of a mouse and first appeared on a range of laptops made by the British company, Psion.

Touchscreen revolution

- **What?** Microsoft Tablet PC
- **Who?** Microsoft
- **Where and when?** USA, 2002

Many companies worked on the idea of a tablet computer during the 1990s, but the first commercial model was designed by Microsoft and appeared in 2002. It was heavy and not very user-friendly. When Apple released the iPad in 2010, tablets became much more popular, thanks to improved touchscreen technology and lots of cool apps.

Apple iPad

Convertible laptop computer

The 2-in-1 computer

- **What?** Compaq Concerto
- **Who?** Compaq
- **Where and when?** USA, 1993

The 2-in-1 portable computer is both a laptop and a tablet. An early version, the Compaq Concerto, was developed in 1993. However, the idea did not catch on until almost 20 years later, when Asus launched the Eee Pad Transformer in 2011.

World Wide Web

So much of what we do in our daily lives relies on the World Wide Web – an easy-to-use system that has made the Internet available to all. For many of us, social media is our preferred way of communicating. We use the Internet to shop, pay bills, watch TV, and play games. In some countries, people even vote in elections online.

MAKING CONNECTIONS

British computer scientist Tim Berners-Lee was working at CERN, the European particle physics laboratory, near Geneva, Switzerland, when he developed the "World Wide Web" in 1989. He imagined an open platform of connected computers that would allow people around the world to share information and collaborate.

Berners-Lee's own computer was the Web's first server – to ensure the Web was not switched off, a label read, "This machine is a server. DO NOT POWER DOWN!!"

▼ **TIM BERNERS-LEE**
The inventor of the Internet stands by the NeXT computer on which he developed the World Wide Web.

CAFÉ CULTURE

In the early 1990s, nobody had access to the Internet at home. In 1991, a number of cafés in San Francisco, USA, had computers that were connected to other cafés. The first café with full Internet access arrived in early 1994 at the Institute of Contemporary Arts in London, UK.

Users at Vietnam's first cyber café, 1996

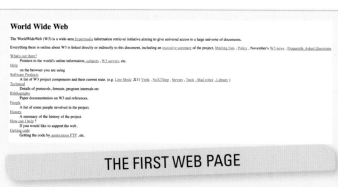

THE FIRST WEB PAGE

The first ever web page, above, went live on 6 August 1991. It was made by Tim Berners-Lee. He shared information about the World Wide Web project and outlined how to create web pages.

WORDS AND PICTURES

Early websites only had words, no pictures. In 1993, the National Center for Supercomputing Applications at the University of Illinois, USA, released Mosaic – an interface, or browser, that supported graphics. Websites now looked much more appealing and were easier to read. Mosaic helped to popularize the World Wide Web.

WOW!

There are more devices connected to the Internet than there are human beings living on Earth.

Web browsers enable users to view pages on the Internet.

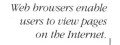

GLOBAL NETWORKS

Online communities have existed since before the World Wide Web. However, they became more popular with the arrival of sites such as Classmates (1995), Six Degrees (1997), LinkedIn and MySpace (both 2003), Facebook (2004), and Twitter (2006).

▲ BUILDING WEBSITES

The arrival of website-creation platforms such as WordPress, launched in 2003, has made it easy for users to create their own websites.

Ada Lovelace

Ada Lovelace was born Ada August Gordon in 1815. Her father was the romantic English poet George Gordon, better known as Lord Byron. Ada became a mathematician in later life. She wrote what is regarded as the first computer program and her ideas inspired work on early computing in the mid-20th century.

A SCIENTIFIC EDUCATION

Ada's parents divorced when she was young. Fearing Ada would inherit her father's unpredictable temperament, her mother raised her on science and mathematics. The young Ada was fascinated by the new inventions of the Industrial Revolution.

ANALYTICAL ENGINE

Around the age of 17, Ada met mathematician and inventor Charles Babbage. She became intrigued by his ideas for an "analytical engine", which could perform complicated calculations. It had all the essential elements of a modern computer.

**Modern model
of the Analytical Engine**

▶ ADA LOVELACE
*Ada married the Earl of Lovelace –
her proper title is Lady Ada King,
Countess of Lovelace.*

LIFE STORY

1815	1816	1828	1833
In December, Ada Gordon is born in London, UK, the only legitimate child of the romantic poet George Gordon, or Lord Byron.	In January, her mother, Annabella, leaves her father, whom she considers insane, and takes one-month-old Ada with her.	Ada is a clever and gifted child and, at the age of 13, designs her own flying machine.	She is introduced to mathematician and inventor Charles Babbage.

**Punched cards
for Babbage's
machine**

COMPUTER PROGRAMMING

Ada wrote notes on the potential of Babbage's machine including, in the letter below, that calculations "may be worked out by the engine without having been worked out by human head and hands first" – in other words, a computer program.

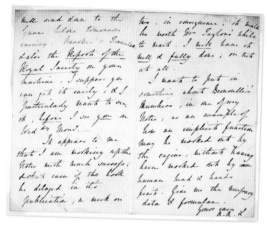

Letter from Ada to Babbage, 1842

ADA'S LEGACY

Sadly, Babbage's Analytical Machine was never built and Ada's ideas remained theoretical. However, her foresight was impressive. In fact, it would take another hundred years and the invention of the computer for the real significance of her work to become apparent.

▶ **IDEAS IN PRACTICE**
The concept of programming Ada proposed has influenced applications in many fields, not least aerospace.

1843	1844	1851	1852
Ada publishes her notes on Babbage's Analytical Engine, including algorithms for calculating complex number sequences.	She designs a mathematical model to understand human feelings, calling it a "calculus of the nervous system".	Ada is a gambling addict and creates a mathematical model for betting on horses. It fails.	At the young age of 36, Ada dies from cancer. She is buried next to her famous poet father.

AT HOME

From cooking and cleaning appliances to gadgets and games for play and relaxation, our homes are full of inventions that help make life comfortable.

The light bulb

Scientists spent much of the 19th century trying to turn electricity into light. Their goal was to create a long-lasting electric light for home use. Two inventors – Joseph Swan and Thomas Edison – working independently on either side of the Atlantic Ocean, came up with the solution: the incandescent light bulb. This invention transformed the world.

LIFE IN THE DARK

Before the invention of the electric light, the world was a much darker place. People lit up their homes using candles made of animal fat and beeswax, as well as oil lamps and gas lamps. All were much less effective than electricity – a 100-watt light bulb is more than 100 times brighter than a candle flame.

LIGHTING THE WAY

Invented by the British scientist Humphry Davy in 1809, the arc lamp worked by passing a bright arc of electricity through the air between two charcoal rods – like a controlled lightning strike. Although it was the first practical light, it was too powerful for home use. Arc lamps were used mainly for street lighting.

Arc lamps illuminate a street in New York, USA, in 1881

▶ SWAN'S BULB
This is a replica of Swan's electric filament bulb, which was first demonstrated in 1878–1879. While Swan's bulbs worked, they did not last very long and were not commercially viable.

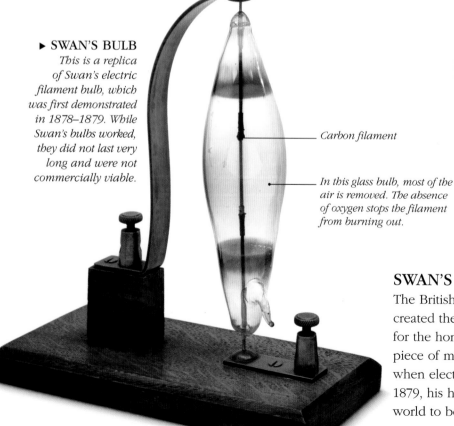

Carbon filament

In this glass bulb, most of the air is removed. The absence of oxygen stops the filament from burning out.

WOW!

In the USA, sales of light bulbs rocketed – from roughly 300,000 in 1885 to 795 million in 1945.

SWAN'S LIGHT

The British scientist Joseph Swan created the first light bulb suitable for the home, using a filament (a thin piece of material that glows brightly when electricity passes through it). In 1879, his home became the first in the world to be lit by electric light bulbs.

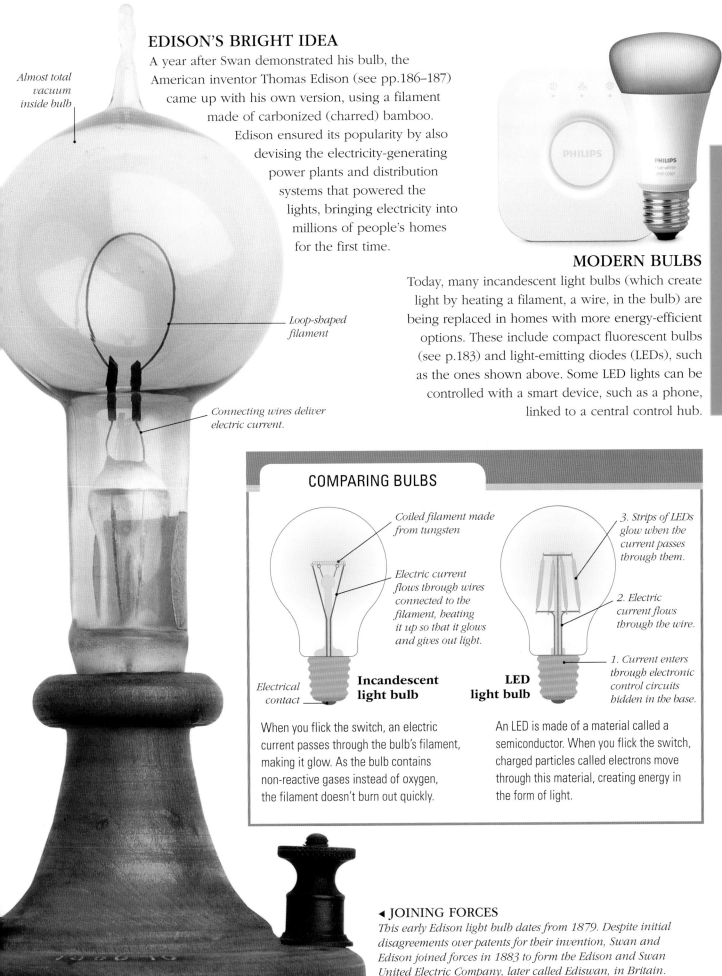

EDISON'S BRIGHT IDEA

A year after Swan demonstrated his bulb, the American inventor Thomas Edison (see pp.186–187) came up with his own version, using a filament made of carbonized (charred) bamboo. Edison ensured its popularity by also devising the electricity-generating power plants and distribution systems that powered the lights, bringing electricity into millions of people's homes for the first time.

Almost total vacuum inside bulb

Loop-shaped filament

Connecting wires deliver electric current.

AT HOME

MODERN BULBS

Today, many incandescent light bulbs (which create light by heating a filament, a wire, in the bulb) are being replaced in homes with more energy-efficient options. These include compact fluorescent bulbs (see p.183) and light-emitting diodes (LEDs), such as the ones shown above. Some LED lights can be controlled with a smart device, such as a phone, linked to a central control hub.

COMPARING BULBS

Coiled filament made from tungsten

Electric current flows through wires connected to the filament, heating it up so that it glows and gives out light.

Electrical contact

Incandescent light bulb

3. Strips of LEDs glow when the current passes through them.

2. Electric current flows through the wire.

1. Current enters through electronic control circuits hidden in the base.

LED light bulb

When you flick the switch, an electric current passes through the bulb's filament, making it glow. As the bulb contains non-reactive gases instead of oxygen, the filament doesn't burn out quickly.

An LED is made of a material called a semiconductor. When you flick the switch, charged particles called electrons move through this material, creating energy in the form of light.

◀ **JOINING FORCES**
This early Edison light bulb dates from 1879. Despite initial disagreements over patents for their invention, Swan and Edison joined forces in 1883 to form the Edison and Swan United Electric Company, later called Ediswan, in Britain.

Lighting up the world

The invention of the electric light bulb lit up the world at night as never before. It paved the way for many other types of light and also brought electricity into people's homes for the first time. Electricity would soon power a wide range of domestic devices.

>> **FAST FACTS** >>

- First switched on in 1901 and still burning to this day, the Centennial Light in Livermore, California, USA, is the world's longest lasting light bulb.
- In 1881, London's Savoy Theatre became the first public building in the world to be lit entirely by electricity.
- On a clear night, the light on the Luxor Hotel in Las Vegas, USA (right), is visible from more than 440 km (274 miles) away.
- The "World's Largest Light Bulb", on top of the Thomas Edison Memorial Tower in New Jersey, USA, is actually now lit by LEDs.

Moving lights

- **What?** Electric headlamps
- **Who?** Electric Vehicle Company
- **Where and when?** USA, 1898

Car headlamps were originally fuelled by oil or gas, which made them a fire risk. The first electric car headlamps didn't work very well, as their filaments tended to burn out quickly. They also required their own supply of electricity, which made them expensive to run. Technology improved in the early 20th century and, in 1912, the American car company Cadillac came up with a method of powering headlamps using the car's ignition system. Pictured above are the electric headlamps of a Ford Model T from 1915.

Gas lights

- **What?** Neon lights
- **Who?** Georges Claude
- **Where and when?** France, 1910

The French physicist Georges Claude discovered that passing an electric current through a glass tube filled with neon gas produced an intense orange light. The light wasn't bright enough to light up homes, but Claude thought it might work well as an advertising sign. In 1912, the first neon sign was switched on outside a barber shop in Paris. Neon advertisements were soon appearing around the world.

▶ GLOWING LIGHTS
The colours of this neon sign in California, USA, are produced by different gases: neon for red, hydrogen for blue, helium for pink-orange, mercury for blue, and krypton for white-yellow. As neon was the first gas to be used in this way, all gas-filled tubes that emit light are called neon lights.

Energy-efficient lights

- **What?** Fluorescent lights
- **Who?** Edmund Germer, Friedrich Meyer, and Hans Spanner
- **Where and when?** Germany, 1926

In a fluorescent light, electricity is passed through vapour of the element mercury, creating invisible ultraviolet light. When this hits a fluorescent coating lining the inside of the bulb, it is converted to visible light. Early fluorescent lights were large, but in the 1970s, small compact fluorescent lights (CFLs) were developed by the American engineer Edward E Hammer.

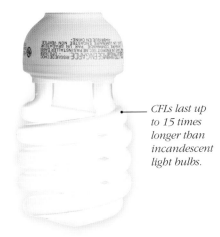

CFLs last up to 15 times longer than incandescent light bulbs.

Searchlights

- **What?** Xenon arc lamp
- **Who?** Osram Licht AG
- **Where and when?** Germany, 1940s

A type of arc light, a xenon lamp is filled with high-pressure xenon gas. When electricity passes through it, the xenon glows brightly. Xenon lamps are used in movie projectors, searchlights, lighthouses, and to create the most powerful light beam in the world – on top of the Luxor Hotel in Las Vegas, USA (above).

Laser light

- **What?** Laser
- **Who?** Theodore H Maiman, Arthur Schawlow, Charles Townes, and Gordon Gould
- **Where and when?** USA, 1960

A laser is a powerful but very narrow beam of light. It is produced by providing energy to the atoms of a solid or gas so they give off light. The atoms work in step with each other to produce very pure light. Lasers are mainly used for industrial purposes, such as carrying information along fibre-optic cables and sending information into space.

Lasers can be used to spectacular effect at concerts

LEDs

- **What?** Light-emitting diodes (LEDs)
- **Who?** Nick Holonyak Jr
- **Where and when?** USA, 1962

Because they use less energy, last longer, and are less fragile, LEDs have begun to replace incandescent bulbs in recent times. LEDs work by jiggling the electrons in a material known as a semiconductor, such as silicon, so that an electric current flows, creating light. LED bulbs can be very small – they are used for the tiny lights seen on on/off buttons on remote controls.

Coloured decorative lights are often LEDs.

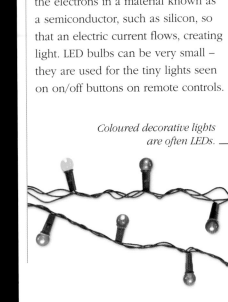

183

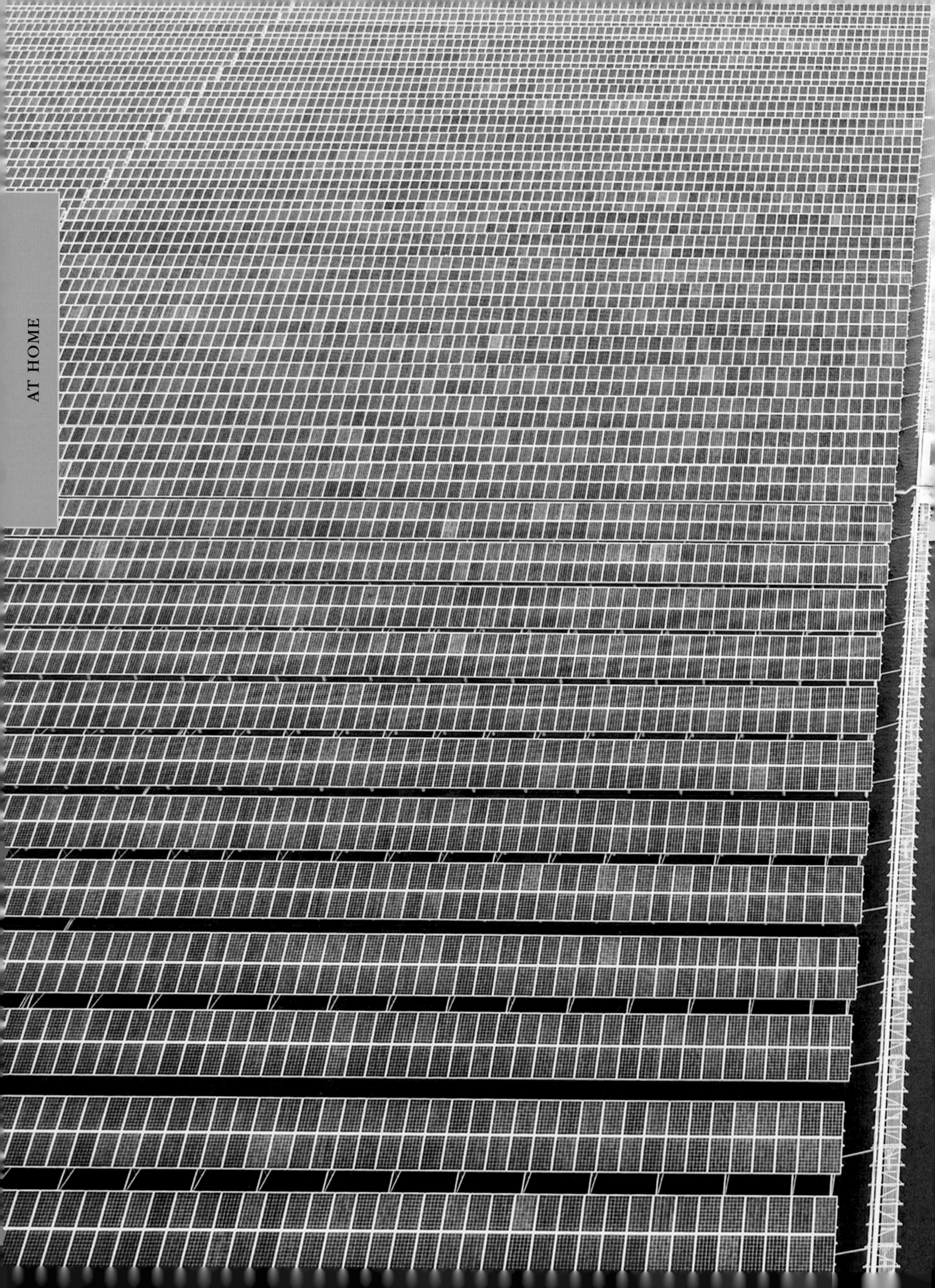

FISH AND SOLAR POWER

As the use of electric lights and other electrical appliances has spread around the world, so has the hunger for energy. Opened in 2017, this giant solar power plant in Zhejiang Province, China, has been built above a fish farm to save space and to provide two sources of revenue – from the fish and from the energy generated by the solar panels. Covering about 2.99 sq km (1.15 sq miles), the plant generates enough energy each year to power 100,000 homes.

Thomas Edison

The man behind the light bulb, the phonograph, and the movie camera, Thomas Edison's inventions have changed the way people live their lives. Edison built up a huge team of researchers and inventors to help him devise and test his remarkable ideas. He was also always quick to challenge his rivals.

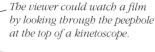

The viewer could watch a film by looking through the peephole at the top of a kinetoscope.

Edison's kinetoscope

MENLO PARK

In 1876, Edison set up a research facility in New Jersey, USA, called Menlo Park. In his lifetime, Edison patented 1,093 inventions in the USA and another 1,200 worldwide, more than anyone else in the 20th century.

THE INVENTING BUSINESS

For Edison, inventing was a business, or, as he put it, "Anything that won't sell, I don't want to invent." One early invention that did sell was the kinetoscope. In 1888, Edison filed a patent on this device, which allowed one person at a time to watch movies.

LIFE STORY

1847	1859	1869
Born in Ohio on 11 February, Edison is raised in Michigan, USA, where he is mainly taught at home by his mother.	Aged 12, he saves a three-year-old child from being hit by a train. The child's grateful father teaches Edison how to use a telegraph as a reward. Edison becomes a telegraph operator, inventing things in his spare time.	Edison's first major inventing success is a device that sends out share prices by telegraph. He sells the rights to it for US$40,000, allowing him to become a full-time inventor at just 22 years old.

Edison's stock ticking device

CURRENT WARS

In the 1880s, Edison entered into a bitter feud with the electrical engineer George Westinghouse over the best way to provide electrical power. Edison favoured direct current (DC) while Westinghouse promoted alternating current (AC). Eventually, Edison had to admit that alternating current was the superior method as it could be sent over longer distances.

Dynamo (an electrical generator that produces direct current) in the first power plant in the USA, built by Edison in 1882

LIMITED SUCCESS

Battery-powered motor

Many of Edison's inventions, including his electric vote counter, concrete houses (with concrete furniture), and electric pen were not successful – although that's not how Edison saw it. While developing the light bulb, he once stated, "I have not failed. I've just found 10,000 ways that won't work."

Edison and his colleagues test a new lamp in Menlo Park, New Jersey

Edison's electric pen

1879	1895	1904	1931
Following his phonograph in 1877 (see p.204), Edison comes up with a more popular device: the light bulb.	He attaches a phonograph to a kinetoscope to create a kinetophone, one of the first sound-film systems.	Edison builds a storage battery for cars, which becomes a huge money-maker.	He dies aged 84 on 18 October. Across the USA, companies dim their lights to pay their respects.

Edison next to an electric car powered by his battery

HIGH VOLTAGE
Here, the Serbian-American scientist Nikola Tesla (see pp.60–61) casually sits by one of his inventions, the Tesla coil, as it sends powerful bursts of electricity through the air. It worked at a very high frequency to produce extremely high voltages and transmitted electricity wirelessly.

The battery

People have known about electricity for a long time. Ancient Greek scholars performed experiments with static electricity and, in the 18th century, the American inventor Benjamin Franklin proved lightning to be a form of electricity. But no one knew how to produce an electric current until the start of the 19th century, when the Italian scientist Alessandro Volta created the first battery.

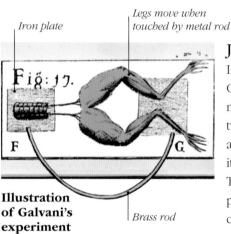

Iron plate

Legs move when touched by metal rod

Fig: 17.

F   G

Illustration of Galvani's experiment

Brass rod

JUMPING FROGS

In 1780, the Italian scientist Luigi Galvani found that he could make the muscles of a dead frog twitch, as if the animal were still alive, by touching the nerves in its legs with different metals. Thinking the force was being produced inside the frog, he called it "animal electricity".

THE VOLTAIC PILE

Another Italian scientist, Alessandro Volta, thought Galvani's explanations were wrong. He believed the metals, not the animal, produced the electric current. To prove it, he created the world's first battery in 1800. This "Voltaic Pile" was made of piled groups of three discs – made of copper, cardboard soaked in seawater, and zinc.

Electric charge flows from one metal to another across the wet cardboard, creating a small electric current.

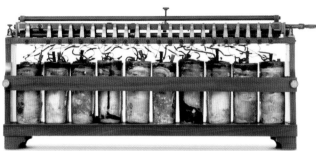

Gaston Planté battery, 19th century

LONGER LIFE

Early Voltaic-style batteries did not last very long. They ran on chemicals and once their supply had run out, they stopped working. The French physicist Gaston Planté overcame this problem with his invention of a rechargeable lead-acid battery in 1859. Many modern batteries, such as the lithium-ion batteries in smartphones, are rechargeable.

SAFER TO HANDLE

Early batteries used liquids, often contained in glass, and had to be moved very carefully. With the invention of his dry battery in 1886, the German scientist Carl Gassner made batteries easier to handle and so usable with more devices. His battery used a dry paste electrolyte (the substance through which an electric current passes) enclosed in a zinc case.

One of Hornsdale Wind Farm's 99 wind turbines

STORING UP ENERGY

Batteries not only provide electricity, they can also be used to store it. Many companies now produce batteries that store electricity gathered from solar panels or wind farms. This electricity can be used to provide energy at times when there is no sunshine or no wind blowing, either locally or to the national electricity supply.

HOW A BATTERY WORKS

When an alkaline dry battery is placed in a device, it causes a chemical reaction to take place between the battery's two electrodes (the anode and the cathode), producing electricity. The electricity is then conducted out of the battery to the device via the collector.

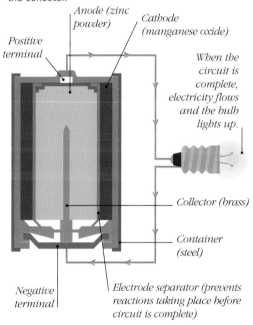

Anode (zinc powder)

Cathode (manganese oxide)

Positive terminal

When the circuit is complete, electricity flows and the bulb lights up.

Collector (brass)

Container (steel)

Negative terminal

Electrode separator (prevents reactions taking place before circuit is complete)

◀ **LARGEST BATTERY**
The world's biggest storage battery was built for the Hornsdale Wind Farm, Australia, in December 2017, by the American company Tesla. This giant array of lithium-ion batteries can store enough electricity to power 30,000 homes.

Washing

The world's first mechanical dishwasher was created by the wealthy American Josephine Cochrane, in the 19th century, supposedly to prevent her servants from breaking her plates. Upon discovering there wasn't already such a machine, she apparently said, "If nobody else is going to invent a dish-washing machine, I'll do it myself." Unveiled in 1893, it was soon followed by many other domestic washing devices.

Dishwasher connected to hot-water tap, 1921

THE FIRST DISHWASHER

Cochrane's dishwasher held the dishes in a wire rack that was turned by hand using a lever. As the dishes turned, they were squirted first with hot, soapy water and then with cold, clean water. The result was sparkling, clean dishes. However, her machine was big and bulky. Small domestic dishwashers wouldn't become popular until the 1950s.

Water from the wet clothes drained back into the tub.

Inside the tub was a motorized arm to spin the clothes around.

MODERN DISHWASHERS

Unlike in Cochrane's invention, the dishes in modern dishwashers are stacked in racks that don't move. Mechanical arms at the top and bottom spin around, squirting water over the dishes – first a cold prewash, then hot, soapy water, followed by clean, rinsing water. Finally, a heating element heats the air to dry the dishes.

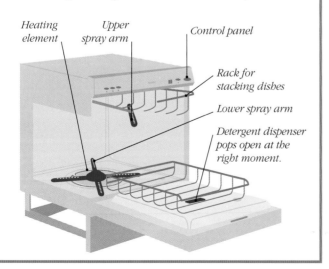

Heating element

Upper spray arm

Control panel

Rack for stacking dishes

Lower spray arm

Detergent dispenser pops open at the right moment.

FRESH LAUNDRY

In the 19th century, some businesses had begun operating laundries with large, steam-powered washing machines. But it wasn't until 1908 that the American inventor Alva Fisher came up with the first commerically successful electric washing machine, the Thor. It had a cylinder, which rotated, containing the water for the wash. Although the design was fairly basic and the clothes had to have the water squeezed out by hand, it sold well, and spurred many imitators. Later models of Thor (right) had rollers for squeezing excess water from clothes.

Wet clothes were placed between rollers to squeeze out excess water.

Handle to turn the rollers

Thor washing machine, c.1929

SPIN DRYER

In the 19th century, before the appearance of dryers, most people dried clothes by hanging them outside or next to a fire. In the 1920s, electric dryers began to appear. They used a motor to spin clothes rapidly in a metal drum, which had holes in it to let the water escape. The dryers produced heat to dry the clothes, something that modern dryers also do.

Early German spin dryer, 1929

MODERN WASHING MACHINES

Today's washing machines are a vast improvement on the Thor. Their drums are positioned horizontally and spin at high speed to remove moisture from clothes. They have compartments for detergent (cleaning liquid) and fabric conditioner (which softens clothes), and a variety of programmes to cope with different materials, ranging from wool to polyester.

DETERGENTS

Modern detergents are made of substances called surfactants – chemicals that work by pulling oil and grease into a water solution, allowing them to be washed off clothes. Discovered by German chemists during World War I, surfactants were refined in the 1940s by the American researcher David Byerly.

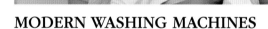

Packets of liquid detergent

Opening a can

- **What?** Can opener
- **Who?** Robert Yeates
- **Where and when?** UK, 1855

Strange as it seems, it took more than 40 years from the invention of tin cans in 1810 for someone to come up with a usable can opener. Early cans were opened with a hammer and chisel, which could be dangerous. In 1855, a British cutlery company invented a simple handheld device with a single blade that was worked around the rim of the can to open it. The opener shown here is from the 1930s.

Magazine advertisement for the Toastmaster, 1951

Toasting bread

- **What?** Pop-up toaster
- **Who?** Charles Strite
- **Where and when?** USA, 1919

The first electric toasters appeared in 1893, but weren't foolproof – they kept on toasting until someone turned them off, resulting in a lot of burnt toast. The American inventor Charles Strite created a toaster that had a timer and springs to pop up the bread when it was ready. It was first used in the catering industry before a model for the home – the Toastmaster – was introduced in 1926. It's been a kitchen essential ever since.

Kitchen devices

In the not-too-distant past, most kitchen and cooking tasks, such as mixing, chopping, and toasting, had to be done by hand and were slow work. From the mid-19th century onwards, inventors turned their attention towards creating devices that not only saved both time and effort with the preparation of food, but also helped with its storage.

Pulling the lever forces hot water through the coffee and into the cup.

Ground coffee is placed in a detachable filter.

Italian espresso machine, 2007

Faster coffee making

- **What?** Lever-operated espresso maker
- **Who?** Achille Gaggia
- **Where and when?** Italy, 1938

Ideas for speedy coffee brewing had been around since 1884, when Angelo Moriondo of Turin, Italy, was granted a patent for a steam-powered coffee maker. The large machine was not a success, and in 1903, two other Italians, Luigi Bezzerra and Desiderio Pavoni, improved its design. Then, in 1938, the Italian engineer Achille Gaggia created the first steam coffee maker to be operated by lever. Smaller, but with much higher water pressure than earlier devices, it produced standard-sized cups of coffee similar to modern espresso.

Non-stick frying pans

- **What?** Teflon™
- **Who?** Roy Plunkett
- **Where and when?** USA, 1938

Like many other inventions, the coating that gives frying pans a non-stick surface was discovered by accident. While researching gases for use in refrigerators at the chemical company DuPont, the American chemist Roy Plunkett stumbled upon polytetrafluoroethylene – a super-slippery substance. Later called Teflon™, the material was applied to frying pans, and has been a boon to pancake flippers ever since.

Keeping food fresh

- **What?** Tupperware®
- **Who?** Earl Tupper
- **Where and when?** USA, 1946

The period just after World War II saw the creation of a number of products for keeping food fresh. These included plastic fridge boxes, Tupperware®, which had airtight lids and a patented "burping seal". Named after their American inventor Earl Tupper, the boxes became popular in the 1950s through "Tupperware parties", pioneered by saleswoman Brownie Wise, held in people's homes.

Superfast cooking

- **What?** Microwave oven
- **Who?** Percy Spencer
- **Where and when?** USA, 1945

The American engineer Percy Spencer was experimenting with a magnetron (a device that emits microwaves) when he found that a chocolate bar in his pocket had mysteriously melted. Spencer realized that the microwaves were causing water molecules in the chocolate bar to vibrate, creating heat and cooking it. The company he worked for, Raytheon, turned his discovery into a new type of cooker – the microwave oven.

RadaRange, an early microwave oven, c.1958

Cutting and chopping

- **What?** Food processor
- **Who?** Pierre Verdon
- **Where and when?** France, 1971

Kitchen food mixers for kneading bread dough and whisking liquids had been around since 1919. But it was not until many decades later that the French engineer Pierre Verdon developed the first food processor, a machine capable of chopping, blending, and mixing solid foods. Verdon called his labour-saving processor the Magimix.

Modern food processor

195

Keeping cool

The invention of refrigeration in the mid-19th century changed forever the way we eat and store food. The cold temperature in a refrigerator slows down the growth of bacteria that make food go bad, keeping items fresh for longer. An understanding of refrigeration led to the development of air conditioning, making it more comfortable to live in hot climates.

In this early fridge, the compressor unit that helps regulate the temperature is on the top. In most modern models, it is at the bottom.

A thick, insulated door keeps the inside cold.

The ice box is used for frozen food and ice cubes.

▶ **GE "MONITOR-TOP" REFRIGERATOR, 1934**
Invented by Christian Steenstrup of the American company General Electric, this was the world's first airtight refrigerator.

HOW A REFRIGERATOR WORKS

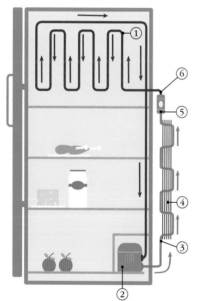

1. Coils absorb heat inside fridge.

2. Compressor squeezes the gas, heating it up as it leaves the fridge.

3. Gas travels through coils on the back of the fridge, cooling and turning back into a liquid.

4. Heat is radiated away from the fridge via the vent fins.

5. Expansion device expands the liquid coolant, turning it rapidly into a gas and making it cold.

6. The coolant goes back inside the fridge and the process repeats.

Refrigerators work by transferring heat from inside to outside the fridge. A substance called a coolant flows through the fridge in a set of coils. When the coolant is inside, it is cold and absorbs heat. As it leaves the refrigerator, it heats up and the heat is radiated away before the coolant re-enters the fridge.

CREATING A CHILL

Artificial refrigeration was invented by the Scottish physician William Cullen in the mid-18th century. It was not until 1899 that a patent was issued in the USA to Arthur T Marshall for the first mechanical refrigerator. The first fridge for home use, called the DOMELRE, was developed by the American engineer Fred W Wolf Jr in 1913.

Frozen tuna is unloaded from a refrigerated ship in Japan, 2005

FLASH FREEZING

The American naturalist Clarence Birdseye developed the rapid refrigeration method known as flash freezing in the 1920s, based on a technique used by the Inuit people of Canada. It involves cooling food quickly at very low temperatures, which keeps it fresher than if it is frozen more slowly.

Workers using flash freezing to preserve seafood

FROZEN CARGO

Refrigeration not only allowed food to be kept longer at home, it has also changed what we eat. The invention of refrigerated ships in the 1870s transformed the global food supply. Easily spoiled items, such as meat and fish, can now be frozen for transport across the world.

SMART REFRIGERATORS

Since the late 1990s, many companies have tried to perfect the smart refrigerator – a device that knows when it's running low on a product and orders new supplies automatically via the Internet. Samsung's Family Hub Refrigerator (below) has a camera inside that lets owners check the contents of their fridge using a smartphone, even if they are not at home.

COOLER INDOORS

Invented in 1902 by the American engineer Willis Carrier, air conditioning works much like refrigeration. A coolant loops between the inside of a building, where it absorbs heat, and the outside, where the heat is released into the air with the help of fan units, as shown in the picture above.

A quick bite

Sometimes a snack or a sweet becomes a hit all over the world. It is almost impossible to predict what will be a success, but inventors can grow rich by making the right judgement about the tastes of the public. However, unless they patent their ideas or (as with Coca-Cola) keep the recipe a closely guarded secret, they may find that rivals beat them to the fame and fortune.

Modern Fry's chocolate bar

Iced desserts

- **What?** Ice cream
- **Who?** Unknown
- **Where and when?** Possibly China, c.200 BCE

The origins of ice cream are unclear. Many ancient cultures – including the Greeks, the Romans, and the Chinese – enjoyed desserts cooled with snow. Recipes for what is now recognized as ice cream were first served to European royalty in the 17th century, and gradually spread to the general public.

▼ ICE-CREAM VANS
Two young boys enjoy ice-cream cones in Hull, UK, in 1961. Travelling ice-cream vans are common in many countries.

Chocolate delights

- **What?** Solid chocolate bar
- **Who?** Francis Fry
- **Where and when?** UK, 1847

The first people to consume chocolate were the Mayans of Mexico in the first millennium CE. They made a bitter drink called *xocolatl* using cocoa beans and spices. In the 16th century, Spanish invaders sweetened the drink with sugar. But it would take until 1847 for the first solid chocolate bar to be produced. It was the creation of a British confectioner, who mixed cocoa powder, cocoa butter, and sugar.

Fizzy drinks

- **What?** Coca-Cola
- **Who?** John Pemberton
- **Where and when?** USA, 1886

One of the world's top drinks began as a herbal medicine created by the American pharmacist John Pemberton. Among its ingredients, which were made into a syrup and mixed with carbonated water, were alcohol and the then-legal drug cocaine, both later removed. More than 1.8 billion Coca-Colas are sold every day.

Breakfast cereal

- **What?** Cornflakes
- **Who?** Dr John Harvey Kellogg
- **Where and when?** USA, 1894

The American doctor John Kellogg ran a health spa where patients were served very plain food, which the doctor thought especially healthy. For breakfast, he gave them a simple cereal he had created using flakes of cooked corn (maize). The flakes proved so popular with the patients that Kellogg's brother, Will Keith, decided to mass-produce them, and they were soon being sold round the world.

Simpler sandwiches

- **What?** Sliced bread
- **Who?** Otto Rohwedder
- **Where and when?** USA, 1928

It took a while for the American engineer Otto Rohwedder to perfect his bread-slicing machine. His biggest problem was the speed at which sliced bread goes stale. He solved this by inventing a machine that not only sliced bread, but also wrapped it, keeping it fresh. Soon, nearly all the bread sold in the USA was pre-sliced.

Modern machines ensure that every slice is the same width.

AT HOME

Blowing bubbles

- **What?** Bubble gum
- **Who?** Walter Diemer
- **Where and when?** USA, 1928

While working for a chewing gum company in Philadelphia, USA, accountant Walter Diemer discovered an extra-stretchy gum that could easily be blown into large bubbles. Called "Dubble Bubble", the new gum was soon being sold across the country. But because Diemer had not patented his invention, rival companies soon copied it.

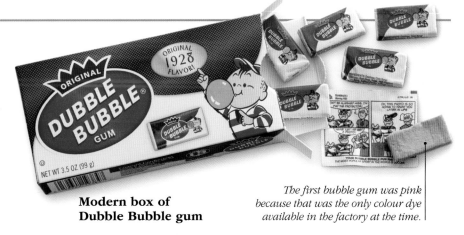

Modern box of Dubble Bubble gum

The first bubble gum was pink because that was the only colour dye available in the factory at the time.

Noodles to go

- **What?** Instant noodles
- **Who?** Momofuku Ando
- **Where and when?** Japan, 1958

The invention of dried noodles, which can be stored for a long time, led to the creation in the 1970s of new snacks called cup or pot noodles. These are plastic pots containing a mixture of dried noodles and flavourings, which become instant snack meals when boiling water is added.

Vacuum cleaner with bellows, 1910

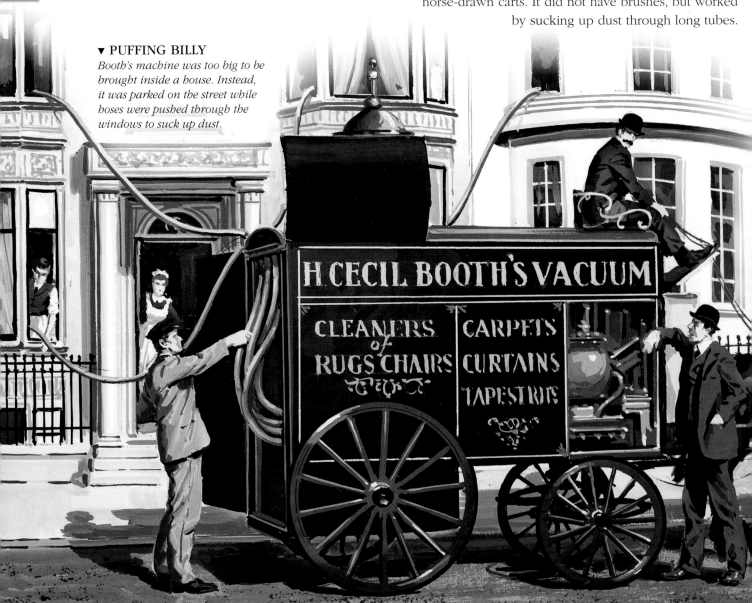

Bellows

Vacuum cleaners

By the middle of the 19th century, scientists understood how vacuum cleaning might work – by creating a partial vacuum within a device so as to suck up dirt and dust. However, it took until the early 20th century for an inventor to design a contraption that worked well enough to become a hit with the public.

EARLY CLEANERS

The American inventor Daniel Hess came up with the first dust-sucking machine for the home in 1860. It consisted of a wheeled carpet sweeper with a rotating brush that was positioned below a device called a bellows (a squeezable air bag), which could be pushed up and down to create a vacuum. This invention was not a success.

POWERED VACUUM CLEANERS

The game changer arrived in 1901 when the British engineer Hubert Cecil Booth created a dust-eating monster, nicknamed "Puffing Billy". Powered by a petrol engine, it weighed 1,800 kg (4,000 lb) and had to be transported by horse-drawn carts. It did not have brushes, but worked by sucking up dust through long tubes.

▼ PUFFING BILLY
Booth's machine was too big to be brought inside a house. Instead, it was parked on the street while hoses were pushed through the windows to suck up dust.

H. CECIL BOOTH'S VACUUM

CLEANERS of RUGS CHAIRS | CARPETS CURTAINS TAPESTRIES

HOOVERING IT UP

In 1907, an American caretaker called James Spangler invented a small, portable cleaner. It had a rotating brush and an electric fan to move dust, a pillowcase to collect it, and a broom handle to move the device around. Spangler sold his device's rights to the American businessperson William Hoover, who would build one of the world's leading vacuum cleaner companies making improved versions of Spangler's invention.

Handle for pushing the cleaner around

Dust collects in this transparent plastic cylinder, which can be emptied when full.

A futuristic-looking Hoover vacuum cleaner, 1954

THE DYSON CLEANER

For much of the 20th century, vacuum cleaners used cloth bags to collect the dust, but the fuller the bags got, the power to suck up dust became weaker. In 1979, the British inventor James Dyson (see pp.202–203) came up with a new type of bagless vacuum cleaner, called a cyclonic vacuum cleaner (right).

Brushes at front sweep up dust

The G-Force, Dyson's first widely sold cyclonic vacuum cleaner, 1990

ROBOT CLEANERS

In the 2000s, a number of robot vacuum cleaners reached the market. These devices are fitted with sensors that automatically guide them around objects, such as pieces of furniture, while they suck up dust. The first one to go on sale was the Electrolux Trilobite (above) in 2001.

CYCLONIC VACUUM CLEANER

In a cyclone vacuum cleaner, rotating fans create a vacuum that sucks dust-filled air into the machine. The air then passes through a series of cone-shaped devices called cyclones where it's spun around very fast, separating the dust from it. This dust falls into a dust collection bin, which is emptied when full, removing the need for a bag.

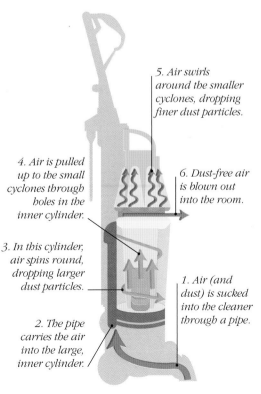

5. Air swirls around the smaller cyclones, dropping finer dust particles.

4. Air is pulled up to the small cyclones through holes in the inner cylinder.

6. Dust-free air is blown out into the room.

3. In this cylinder, air spins round, dropping larger dust particles.

1. Air (and dust) is sucked into the cleaner through a pipe.

2. The pipe carries the air into the large, inner cylinder.

James Dyson

One of the most successful British inventors of recent decades, James Dyson has created numerous devices for use both inside and outside the home, most notably the cyclonic vacuum cleaner. All his inventions have a similar backstory – Dyson spotted a flaw in an existing, widely used device and decided that he could come up with innovations to improve it.

▶ IN THE WORKSHOP
Dyson's workshops have created more than 50 types of cyclonic cleaner, from giant industrial machines to handheld versions.

AT HOME

THE BALLBARROW

Dyson's first major inventing success was a new type of wheelbarrow. He was inspired to create the product by his experiences of getting the narrow wheel of his own barrow stuck in the mud while gardening. Dyson solved the problem by replacing the wheel with a plastic ball, which spread the load, making the barrow easier to use on soft ground.

The ball at the front of the barrow makes it simpler to steer.

THE CYCLONIC VACUUM CLEANER

In 1978, Dyson set about inventing a bagless vacuum cleaner based on cyclonic technology (see p.201). He built 5,127 prototypes before he had a working version. Dyson's first cyclonic cleaner, the G-Force, was launched in Japan in the mid-1980s. A later version, the Dyson DC01, became a global phenomenon, prompting other companies to produce their own cyclonic cleaners.

The Contrarotator's two drums had more than 5,000 holes to remove water quickly.

FAILURES

Along with his successes, Dyson suffered a few failures, including the Contrarotator (also known as the CR01) washing machine in 2000. It had two counter-rotating drums, which were meant to spin clothes drier than other models. However, it was expensive and sold poorly. Its production was stopped after a few years.

TIMELINE

1947	1970	1974	1978
Dyson is born on 2 May. He goes on to study furniture design and interior design at the Royal College of Art in the 1960s.	While studying, he helps to design the Rotork Sea Truck, a high-speed landing craft used by the British military.	Dyson sets up a company to manufacture his first successful invention, the Ballbarrow, which wins the Building Design Innovation Award in 1977.	He starts working on developing the cyclonic vacuum cleaner. By 1983, he has produced a model, but he is unable to find a manufacturer to invest in his product.

1986

With the help of a Japanese company, Dyson launches his first cyclonic vacuum cleaner, the G-Force, in Japan.

1993

The Dyson DC01 is released in the UK. Within two years, it is the country's best-selling vacuum cleaner. By 2002, Dyson has launched it in the USA.

2006

His company enjoys another big success with the Airblade (right), an updated version of the blown-air hand-dryer.

2016

In recent years, Dyson has launched a bladeless fan, a room humidifier, and, in 2016, a hairdryer.

Recorded music

Until the late 19th century, the only way to hear music was to listen to it live. Then the invention of the telephone in 1876 showed that sound could be transmitted electrically. This spurred the American inventor Thomas Edison (see pp.186–187) to explore if it was possible to record sound. His invention, the phonograph, kick-started the recorded music industry.

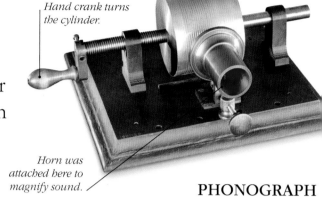

Cylinder

Hand crank turns the cylinder.

Horn was attached here to magnify sound.

PHONOGRAPH

Invented in 1877, Edison's phonograph consisted of a horn, a needle, and a rotating cylinder covered in tin foil. When sound was played into the horn, the needle traced a groove in the foil as the cylinder turned. To play back the recording, the needle was drawn through the groove again. Later phonographs used a wax cylinder to make and play recordings (see p.206).

RECORDING WITHOUT ELECTRICITY

For early recordings, musicians played directly into a large horn, the sound waves moving the recording needle. The horn gathered only a small amount of sound, producing low-quality recordings. Microphones, invented in the 1870s, improved sound, though not as much as the far more sensitive "ultra audible" microphone that appeared in the 1920s.

▼ PLAY IT LOUD
Before microphones, musicians gathered in front of one large horn to record.

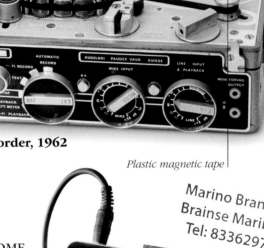

Today, almost everyone carries their own high-tech digital recorder around with them contained in their smartphone.

MAGNETIC TAPE

In 1928, the German-Austrian engineer Fritz Pfleumer found a way to record sound onto tape coated with magnetized iron oxide powder. The magnetic particles stored sounds as patterns. Based on Pfleumer's invention, the first tape recorders were produced in the 1930s.

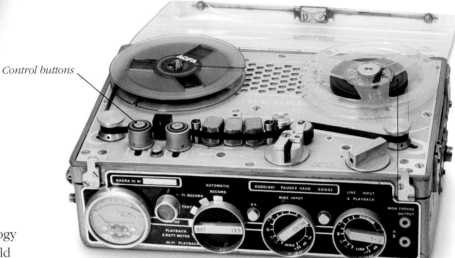

Control buttons

Tape recorder, 1962

Plastic magnetic tape

MULTITRACK RECORDING

Although multitrack recording technology had been around since the end of World War II in the 1940s, it was the American musician Les Paul who pioneered its use for music in the 1950s. He realized that by using many recording heads on a single wide magnetic tape, he could record each musician separately as they played together. His invention gave record producers much greater control over the sound of the finished piece of music.

Multitrack recorder, 1970s

▶ **HOME RECORDING**
Technology is now so advanced that music-lovers can make their own high-quality multitrack recordings on everyday devices, such as smartphones and iPads.

Marino Branch
Brainse Marino
Tel: 8336297

DIGITAL RECORDING

After the late 1970s, tape recording began to be replaced by digital recording. This technology converts sound that has been recorded as electrical signals into a digital code, which can then be converted back into a reproduction of the sound. The idea was first suggested by the British scientist Alec Reeves back in 1937.

Each of Edison's wax cylinders could hold around two minutes of audio.

Listen to the music

The devices we use for listening to music have changed dramatically over the years. For much of the 20th century, most of the developments were aimed at improving sound quality. In recent times, the move has been towards making equipment smaller and lighter. A record collection – along with the device to play the records – has evolved from something taking up shelves of space to something that fits in your pocket.

The first records

- **What?** Sound recording
- **Who?** Thomas Edison
- **Where and when?** USA, 1877

Edison discovered how to record sound in 1877. By 1888, he had developed wax cylinders that were the first widely used method of listening to music. Each cylinder was moulded from hard wax with a groove on the outer surface corresponding to a sound recording. It could be played using a phonograph (see p.204). Early phonographs or "talking machines", as they were originally called, were operated by clockwork.

Early discs were just 13 cm (5.75 in) wide, but would get bigger in time.

Flat discs

- **What?** Berliner gramophone
- **Who?** Emile Berliner
- **Where and when?** USA, 1887

Phonographs were popular but expensive, and took up a lot of space. The German-American inventor Berliner came up with a cheaper, less bulky alternative with his invention of a machine that traced sound grooves onto flat discs. These records were not only more durable, easier to produce (as they could be simply stamped out using a template), and store, in their final form they also held more music – up to five minutes.

FAST FACTS

- The first ever sound recording was of Thomas Edison reciting the nursery rhyme "Mary had a little lamb".
- Early disc records were made of shellac – a type of resin produced by insects.
- Record players didn't become truly loud until the 1920s, after the invention of electric speakers by the American engineers Peter L Jensen and Edwin Pridham in 1915.

Long-playing (LP) records

- **What?** Vinyl 45 and 33 rpm records
- **Who?** RCA Victor (45s) & Columbia Records (33s)
- **Where and when?** USA, 1948

Early discs revolved at 78 rpm (rotations per minute) when played. In 1948, two new longer-playing formats were introduced. Made of a plastic called vinyl, they played at different speeds. The 45 rpm extended play (EP) records could hold around four minutes of sound per side while the 33 rpm long-playing (LP) records could hold 25 minutes per side.

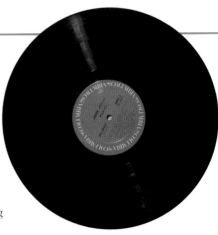

Vinyl record, 1971

Portable sounds

- ■ **What?** Walkman
- ■ **Who?** Masaru Ibuka, Norio Ohga, Nobutoshi Kihara, Akio Monta, and Kozo Ohsone
- ■ **Where and when?** Japan, 1979

In 1962, the Dutch electronics firm Philips introduced compact cassettes, which store music on magnetic tape (see p.205). The invention paved the way for the first truly portable music player, the Sony Walkman, in 1979. It was the brainchild of Sony co-founder Masaru Ibuka who wanted a way of listening to music on plane flights.

The device came with headphones for listening to music privately.

An early Sony Walkman, 1979

Unlike vinyl records, CDs don't scratch easily.

Digital sounds

- ■ **What?** Compact discs
- ■ **Who?** Philips and Sony
- ■ **Where and when?** Netherlands and Japan, 1982

In the 1980s and 1990s, compact discs (CDs) replaced vinyl records as the dominant format. Based on technology invented by the American James Russell in the 1960s, CDs store sound as digital information in pits moulded on plastic discs, which can be read by a laser.

Released in 2001, Apple's iPod made the MP3 player globally popular

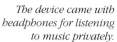

Users rotated a "click wheel" to browse the music stored on the device.

Compressed sounds

- ■ **What?** MP3s
- ■ **Who?** Karlheinz Brandenburg
- ■ **Where and when?** Germany, 1989

Digital recordings take up a lot of computer memory. In 1989, a new technology called MP3 arrived. This significantly reduces an audio file's size by removing the parts people don't normally hear – a 40 MB song can be reduced to just 4 MB. The first MP3 players were released in 1999. Today, people can listen to their entire record collection on an MP3-playing app on their smartphone.

Headphones use radio waves to communicate with a smartphone.

Wire-free sounds

- ■ **What?** Bluetooth headphones
- ■ **Who?** Several manufacturers
- ■ **Where and when?** Various, 2002–2004

A problem with headphones is that they tether the user to the music source. People tried radio to overcome this, but it was not until the 2000s that Bluetooth, invented in the 1990s by the Swedish telecom giant Ericsson, finally solved the problem. This radio-wave technology allows data to be transmitted over short distances, enabling people to enjoy wire-free music on their smartphones. The first wireless headphones were released in 2002.

Games and pastimes

Indoor games and pastimes have been discovered dating back thousands of years, and many are still enjoyed today. Often, these games are played just for fun, but some are also educational, teaching skills such as maths, logical thinking, and how to plan ahead. Many of the games shown here are played worldwide.

Modern jigsaw of a world map

Ancient board games

- **What?** Senet
- **Who?** Ancient Egyptians
- **Where and when?** Egypt, c.3100 BCE

The earliest known board game, Senet was played on a small board marked with 30 squares, set out in three rows of 10 squares each. Players took turns moving small pieces around the squares, the winner being the first to clear all their pieces off the board. The game was supposed to represent the journey of a person's spirit to the afterlife.

Senet board and pieces from c.1285 BCE

Picture puzzles

- **What?** Jigsaws
- **Who?** John Spilsbury
- **Where and when?** UK, 1766

It is believed that the first jigsaw puzzle was made by the British map-maker John Spilsbury in 1766 as an educational tool. He stuck a map of Europe onto a piece of wood, which he then cut into pieces with a jigsaw, so students could learn geography by reassembling the pieces. The term "jigsaw" comes from the type of saw used to create the puzzles.

Modern board games

- **What?** Monopoly
- **Who?** Elizabeth Magie, Charles Darrow
- **Where and when?** USA, 1904 and 1935

One of the most popular board games of all time, Monopoly was originally called the "Landlord Game". It was created by the American games designer Elizabeth Magie, who wanted it to act as a warning against property ownership and greedy landlords. It only became popular when another designer, Charles Darrow, turned it into Monopoly, a board game celebrating property ownership.

Charles Darrow was the first millionaire games designer

WOW!

The largest jigsaw puzzle ever made had 551,232 pieces that formed a picture of a giant lotus flower.

Construction games

- **What?** LEGO® Bricks
- **Who?** Godtfred Kirk Christiansen
- **Where and when?** Denmark, 1958

In 1958, the Danish company, LEGO Group, took out the patent for a new type of interlocking plastic bricks – the now iconic LEGO® Brick. Twenty years later, the company introduced themed building sets, which allowed children to build models, such as a space rocket, a medieval castle, or an entire town. With just a few LEGO bricks, there are almost infinite building possibilities – six classic 2x4 LEGO bricks can be combined in more than 915 million different ways.

The bricks and plates lock together with studs.

Flame-shaped LEGO® pieces are used for the dragon's fiery breath.

◀ **RED DRAGON**
*The bricks in this **LEGO® Creator**: Red Animals set can be used not only to build this fire-breathing dragon but also to make a snake or a scorpion.*

Role-playing games (RPGs)

- **What?** Dungeons & Dragons
- **Who?** Gary Gygax and Dave Arneson
- **Where and when?** USA, 1974

Dungeons & Dragons (D&D) is a fantasy-themed, role-playing game. During the game, players take on the role of a character, such as a warrior or a wizard, for an adventure that can take days, or weeks, to complete. Each action is decided by rolling a multi-sided dice – from four- to 20-sided. The release of D&D inspired a host of similar role-playing games.

Called D20, this dice has 20 sides.

The seven D&D dice

3-D games

- **What?** Rubik's cube
- **Who?** Erno Rubik
- **Where and when?** Hungary, 1974

Invented by a Hungarian professor of architecture, this multi-coloured cube can be twisted in an almost endless number of variations. To be "solved", the cube must be untwisted so that each side shows only one colour. With more than 350 million sold, it is the best-selling puzzle game of all time.

Playing against computers

- **What?** AlphaGo
- **Who?** Google DeepMind
- **Where and when?** UK, 2014

Computers that play complicated board games, such as chess, have been around since the 1960s. Over time, they have become more powerful. In 2014, the British company DeepMind (bought by Google) developed a program to play the ancient Chinese game of Go. Called AlphaGo, the program has defeated many of the world's top Go players.

AlphaGo beats the world's top Go player, Ke Jie, in China, 2017

Video games

The first computers were built to perform serious tasks such as cracking enemy codes. But, in the 1950s, university researchers started using them for creating fun video games. These early experiments led to the development of the first home video-game consoles in the early 1970s. Since then, video games have grown into one of the world's most popular forms of entertainment.

First home-gaming system

- **What?** The Magnavox Odyssey
- **Who?** Ralph H Baer
- **Where and when?** USA, 1972

The first video-games console that could be connected to a television set featured simple games, such as *Table Tennis*. The console was a success and an inspiration for many imitators – kick-starting an entire industry.

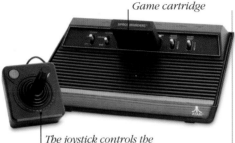

Game cartridge

The joystick controls the player's movement on screen.

Cartridge games

- **What?** Atari 2600
- **Who?** Atari, Nolan Bushnell, and Ted Dabney
- **Where and when?** USA, 1977

Atari dominated the home video-game market in the 1970s. While earlier consoles could play only the pre-installed games, the Atari 2600 gave more options – it was one of the first systems to use games stored on separate cartridges. It helped popularize some of the biggest games of the age, including *Space Invaders* and *Donkey Kong*.

Japanese gaming

- **What?** Nintendo Entertainment System
- **Who?** Nintendo
- **Where and when?** Japan, 1983

The video games industry was initially dominated by the USA, but Japan took over in the 1980s following the introduction of the Nintendo Entertainment System (NES). It became the biggest selling console of the time – owned by around a third of all American households.

The bulky joystick was replaced by slimmer, cross-shaped joy pads and buttons.

NES Classic Edition, 1985

WOW!

The first video game is believed to be *Tennis for Two*, devised by the American physicist William Higinbotham in 1958.

Handheld consoles

- **What?** Nintendo Gameboy
- **Who?** Nintendo, Satoru Okada
- **Where and when?** Japan, 1989

With the release of the Gameboy, Nintendo came to dominate the handheld console market in the 1990s and 2000s. In 2004, it released the Nintendo DS, which sold more than 154 million to become the biggest selling handheld console ever. These consoles helped to popularize character-driven games, such as *Super Mario Brothers*.

Home entertainment consoles

- ■ **What?** Sony Playstation 2
- ■ **Who?** Sony, Ken Kutaragi
- ■ **Where and when?** Japan, 2000

Another Japanese company, Sony, entered the video game industry in the 1990s. Its first console, the PlayStation, was released in 1994 and was reasonably successful. The real game changer was its follow-up, the PlayStation 2. This could also play DVDs and CDs, making it an all-in-one home entertainment console.

Controller vibrates with onscreen action.

It would become the biggest selling home console of all time, with more than 150 million shipped.

Console and computer

- ■ **What?** Xbox
- ■ **Who?** Microsoft
- ■ **Where and when?** USA, 2001

After years of Japanese domination, the USA re-entered the market in a big way in 2001 with the launch of the powerful Xbox. The streaming service of its successor (Xbox One) allows gamers to play Xbox games remotely on their computer.

Xbox game played on a laptop

Motion control

- ■ **What?** Nintendo Wii
- ■ **Who?** Nintendo
- ■ **Where and when?** Japan, 2006

Despite intense competition from Sony and Microsoft, Nintendo enjoyed major success in the 2000s with its Wii console, which helped to popularize controlling the game using your motions. This technology allows gamers to use their remote control as virtual sporting equipment to play games such as tennis, golf, and boxing.

Player moves the controller to direct the action on screen.

The flushing toilet

By washing away disease-causing sewage, the flushing toilet has saved millions of lives. Surprisingly, it didn't immediately catch on when it was invented in the 16th century. The flushing mechanism wouldn't achieve mass popularity until someone came up with a way of removing not just the waste, but also the smells.

JOHN HARRINGTON

The English poet John Harrington invented the first flushing toilet in 1596. It had a cistern that released water into a toilet bowl, washing its contents into a pit below. Despite making a version for his godmother, Queen Elizabeth I, Harrington's toilet didn't prove popular.

THE S-BEND TOILET

The problem with early flushing toilets was that bad smells could travel up through the pipes that took away the waste. In 1775, the Scottish inventor Alexander Cummings came up with a solution in the form of an S-shaped water trap, which prevented bad smells from escaping.

S-bend water trap

S-bend toilet, 1870

Sir Joseph Bazalgette (below centre) inspects the progress of London's new sewerage system, 1860s

SEWERAGE SYSTEMS

The widespread use of flushing toilets in the mid-19th century prompted the construction of new sewerage systems to wash away the waste. An extensive system was built below London, UK, by the British engineer Sir Joseph Bazalgette. It made the city a cleaner and safer place, helping to end the spread of deadly diseases such as cholera.

The flush is activated by pulling a chain.

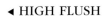

◀ **HIGH FLUSH**
This 1912 toilet has a raised cistern – gravity helped to increase the speed and power of the flush.

Water flushed from the cistern down the pipe into the toilet.

PORCELAIN TOILET

A major breakthrough in toilet technology was the one-piece ceramic toilet, designed by the British pottery manufacturer Thomas Twyford in the 1880s. Where previous models had been enclosed within wooden boxes, this new model, like the ornate example on the left, was free-standing, making it easier to clean.

The hinged wooden seat could be raised or lowered over the toilet.

HOW A TOILET WORKS

When you push the handle, it opens the flush valve, letting water from the tank flow into the bowl. Water and waste are then sucked out of the bowl down the siphon and away to the sewer. A U-bend traps water in the bottom of the bowl, stopping smells from the sewer escaping back into the toilet.

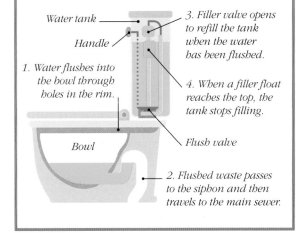

Water tank

Handle

1. Water flushes into the bowl through holes in the rim.

Bowl

3. Filler valve opens to refill the tank when the water has been flushed.

4. When a filler float reaches the top, the tank stops filling.

Flush valve

2. Flushed waste passes to the siphon and then travels to the main sewer.

TOILET PAPER

The Chinese were probably the first people to use toilet paper in around the 6th century. In the West, its invention is credited to the American inventor Joseph Gayetty, in 1857, although toilet paper on a roll was invented in 1890 by brothers Clarence and E Irvin Scott. It was not a success until the 20th century because people were embarrassed to buy it.

Nozzle shoots out warm water at the touch of a button.

The seat temperature can be controlled by the user.

SUPER TOILETS

Since the 1970s, Japan has specialized in creating technologically advanced toilets. These usually have additional features, such as seat warmers, automatic lids, deodorizers, and even speakers for playing music – all managed by a control panel. The high-tech toilets are sometimes known as "washlets", after one of the most popular Japanese brands.

Keeping up appearances

Not all inventions make big, revolutionary changes to the way we live. Some just offer us a bit of much-needed assistance as we go about our daily lives. From helping us to get bright white teeth and keeping our skin healthy to styling hair and painting our nails, here are some beauty-themed inventions that help us look and feel our best.

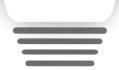

WOW!

Modern nail polishes were based on a type of car paint.

Sparkling teeth

- ■ **What?** Toothpaste in a tube
- ■ **Who?** Washington Sheffield
- ■ **Where and when?** USA, 1892

The practice of brushing teeth with a special cleaning paste became widespread in the 19th century, with the paste initially distributed in jars. In the 1890s, the British toothpaste manufacturer Colgate popularized an invention by the American dentist Washington Sheffield – toothpaste in a collapsible metal tube. Sheffield was said to have been inspired by paint that came in tubes. Colgate advertised it with the slogan: "Comes out a ribbon, lies flat on the brush".

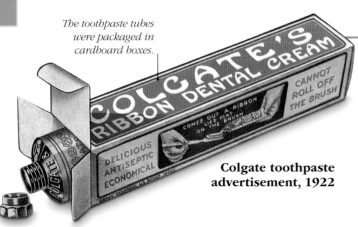

The toothpaste tubes were packaged in cardboard boxes.

Colgate toothpaste advertisement, 1922

Wet shaving

- ■ **What?** Safety razor
- ■ **Who?** King C Gillette
- ■ **Where and when?** USA, 1901

In the 19th century, men shaved using dangerous "cut-throat" razors with open blades. An American salesperson and inventor, King C Gillette, came up with the cheaper, safer alternative: disposable blades. Customers would buy a handle into which cheaply made individual blades could be placed. When the blade got blunt, it would be thrown away and replaced.

Gillette razor, 1930s

Painted nails

- ■ **What?** Liquid nail polish
- ■ **Who?** Cutex
- ■ **Where and when?** USA, 1917

The ancient Chinese were colouring nails as early as 3000 BCE. In the beginning of the 20th century, nail polish usually took the form of a paste or powder, before the American company Cutex introduced the first liquid nail polish in 1917.

The NEW Cutex Polish is usable to the last dr
Its Evaporation is less than half as much as ordinary Po.

TRY THESE NEW "SMOKY" SHAD

Nail polish advertisement, 1937

Coloured lips

- **What?** Swivel lipstick
- **Who?** James Bruce Mason Jr
- **Where and when?** USA, 1922

People have painted their lips since ancient times, but this was usually done with a brush. In the early 20th century, someone came up with the idea of putting solid lipstick in a sliding metal container. This was soon followed by the swivel-up tube, a device that continues to be used today.

Illustration of a woman applying lipstick, 1930

Dry shaving

- **What?** Electric razor
- **Who?** Jacob Schick
- **Where and when?** USA, 1928

In 1928, Colonel Jacob Schick of the US Army used the money he made from an earlier successful invention – a razor that stored blades in its handle – to come up with the first electrically powered dry shaver. Later innovations include the introduction of a protective foil covering over the blades by the British company Remington in 1937, and the development of the rotatory blade shaver by the Dutch company Philips in 1939.

Hairspray

- **What?** Aerosol spray can
- **Who?** Erik Rotheim
- **Where and when?** Norway, 1927

The Norwegian chemical engineer Erik Rotheim's invention – the aerosol can – didn't really catch on at first. It wasn't until World War II that it was adapted by the American chemist Lyle Goodhue into a device for dispensing insect repellent known as a "bug bomb" for US troops. People noticed the spray can's potential and, after the war, aerosol technology was adapted for a range of domestic uses, including for hairspray, as seen above in this 1955 advertisement.

Grooved body of this battery-powered razor made it easy to hold.

Schick Electric Shaver, c.1934

Sunscreen

- **What?** Ambre Solaire
- **Who?** Eugène Schueller
- **Where and when?** France, 1936

The French chemist Eugene Schueller's oil, Ambre Solaire, was the first mass-market sunscreen to protect skin against harmful ultraviolet (UV) radiation that can cause skin cancer. It was produced in the 1930s when sunbathing became popular in the south of France. The lotion was also used to protect soldiers from sunburn in World War II.

Fig. 1,

TIME TO RELAX

In the 19th century, water therapy was a popular treatment for all sorts of ailments and this US patent, registered in 1900 by Otto Hensel, shows his rocking bathtub, which moved up and down to gently splash water against the bather. A curtain from the tub to the bather's neck kept the water from spilling. Today, people may relax in hot tubs, whirlpool baths, and showers with varying jets of water.

No. 643,094.

O. A. HENSEL.

ROCKING OR OSCILLATING BATH TUB.

(Application filed Jan. 6, 1899.)

(No Model.)

Patented Feb. 6, 1900.

2 Sheets—Sheet 1.

In the wardrobe

Throughout history, clothes have inspired some major changes. Cloth-making inventions, such as the loom, were the main forces behind the Industrial Revolution of the 18th and 19th centuries. Clothes vary across the world, but sometimes an item of clothing is so useful it becomes popular everywhere.

A needle moves up and down, linking threads above and below the cloth.

KEEPING OUT THE RAIN

In 1824, the Scottish chemist Charles Macintosh invented a waterproof coat made from rubber-filled fabric. Named after their inventor, early "Mackintoshes" tended to melt in hot weather. The British engineer Thomas Hancock solved this by devising a process using heat and sulfur, called vulcanization, to make the rubber stronger.

Mackintosh coat, 1922

FAST STITCHING

In the mid-19th century, several American inventors came up with designs for a sewing machine, but from 1851 onwards it was Isaac Singer's machine that had the greatest success. However, his device was so similar to one made by another inventor, Elias Howe, that Howe sued Singer – and won. The two men would later go into business together.

Lightweight material lets air pass to the feet.

THE MODERN BRA

An American woman called Mary Jacob is said to have invented the first modern-style, lightweight brassiere, which was patented in 1914. According to the story, finding that her bulky corset poked out of a new dress, she designed a replacement piece of underwear using a couple of handkerchiefs and a few ribbons.

Rubber soles

SNEAKY SHOES

The American inventor Wait Webster patented an idea for making flexible shoes by attaching a rubber sole to a leather upper in 1832. But true sports shoes, called sneakers or trainers, did not appear until the invention of moulded rubber soles that gave a good grip. The first-ever sneakers, introduced in 1916, were so named because their rubber soles allowed the wearer to "sneak" up on someone.

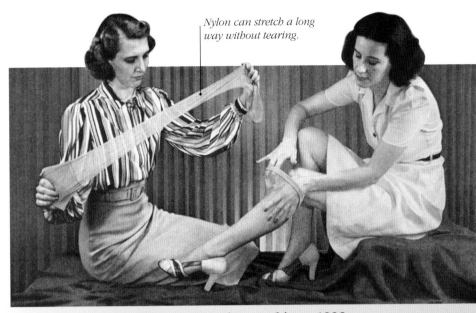

AFFORDABLE NYLON

With the invention of nylon in 1938 by the American chemist Wallace Carothers, stockings, which were previously made of expensive silk, suddenly became much cheaper. After World War II, the American company Glen Raving Knitting Mills created a new two-legged garment by joining nylon stockings together – now called tights or pantyhose.

Nylon can stretch a long way without tearing.

Women test nylon stockings, 1939

NON-SWEAT CLOTHING

Used for making outdoor clothing, Gore-Tex® was discovered in 1969 by the American engineer Robert W Gore. He found that rapidly expanding a substance called polytetrafluoroethylene, commonly known as Teflon™ (see p.195), produced a new material that is both waterproof and breathable, allowing sweat to escape.

▲ **ALL-WEATHER GEAR**
Gore-Tex® is now used to make a wide range of breathable, waterproof clothing, including skiing gear and other sportswear.

Fasteners

Making a successful garment is not just about getting the material, style, and size right. The item of clothing also needs to stay in place so that it doesn't fall open – or down – for as long as it's worn. Since ancient times, inventive minds have come up with a range of ingenious fasteners for clothes, from buckles and buttons to intricate locking arrangements of teeth, eyes, and hooks.

Button up!

- **What?** Buttons
- **Who?** Possibly Indus Valley Civilization
- **Where and when?** Mohenjo Daro, Pakistan, c.2500 BCE

The oldest-known button was produced by the Indus Valley Civilization of Pakistan and northern India about 5,000 years ago. Made of seashell, it would have fitted into a loop of cloth and was probably more ornamental than functional. Reinforced buttonholes, which allow rows of buttons to be made, were not invented until the 13th century.

Securing your sword

- **What?** Buckles
- **Who?** Possibly the Romans
- **Where and when?** Possibly Italy, c.100 BCE

It's not known when buckles first appeared, but they were certainly widely used by the Romans. They were mainly employed by soldiers to secure their body armour and weapons. Until the 15th century, when manufacturing

Bronze buckle, 7th century

methods improved, buckles in Europe were expensive and mainly worn by wealthy people.

Hook fastened through eye (loop)

Medieval ties

- **What?** Hook and eye fasteners
- **Who?** Unknown
- **Where and when?** England, 14th century

One of the simplest types of fastener for clothes consists of a small metal hook that fits snugly inside a loop or "eye". Widely used since medieval times, it is believed to have first appeared in England, where it was known as "crochet and loop" (crochet is a French term for "hook"). The fastener is still used today, particularly for bras.

Nappy fasteners

- **What?** Safety pin
- **Who?** Walter Hunt
- **Where and when?** USA, 1849

A safety pin uses a spring mechanism to keep the pin safely in place inside a clasp. As seen above, it is often used for holding together pieces of material, such

◄ **STEEL PINS**
Although Hunt's safety pin was made out of brass, modern safety pins are usually made from stainless steel and come in a variety of sizes.

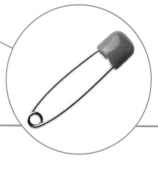

as a nappy. It was the brainchild of the American inventor Walter Hunt who sold his patent for just US$400 to a company that went on to make millions from the device.

The knob on one disc fits into the hole on the other.

Two discs fitted together

Hole

Snap and pop

- **What?** Snap fasteners
- **Who?** Heribert Bauer
- **Where and when?** Germany, 1885

Small interlocking discs were occasionally used as fasteners in ancient China, but the modern metal snap fastener was the work of the German inventor Heribert Bauer in the late 19th century. He called them *federknopf-verschluss*, which means "spring button closers". They are often used for securing children's clothes because they are very easy to open and close, but they also sometimes appear on adult clothing.

WOW!

The word "button" comes from an ancient Germanic word, *buttan*, meaning something that sticks out.

Modern Velcro®

Pull it together

- **What?** Zip
- **Who?** Gideon Sundback
- **Where and when?** Sweden, 1913

The first zip-like fastener was the work of the American inventor Whitcomb Judson, in 1893. It consisted of a row of metal eyes and hooks (rather than the metal teeth of modern zips), pressed together by a slider. Called the "C-curity", it was ingenious but it didn't work very well. So, Judson hired the Swedish scientist Gideon Sundback to make improvements. In 1913, Sundback came up with the zip we know today.

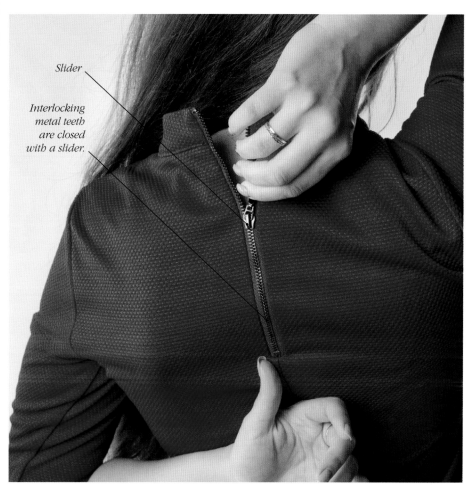

Slider

Interlocking metal teeth are closed with a slider.

Hooks and loops

- **What?** Velcro®
- **Who?** Georges de Mestrel
- **Where and when?** Switzerland, 1955

De Mestrel based his fastener on burrs – sticky seeds that are covered in tiny hooks to help them cling to rough surfaces, such as animal fur. He constructed it from two materials: one covered in tiny hooks and the other in tiny loops, which stick tight when pressed together. He got the name for his invention, Velcro®, from the French words *velours croché*, meaning "hooked velvet".

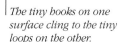

The tiny hooks on one surface cling to the tiny loops on the other.

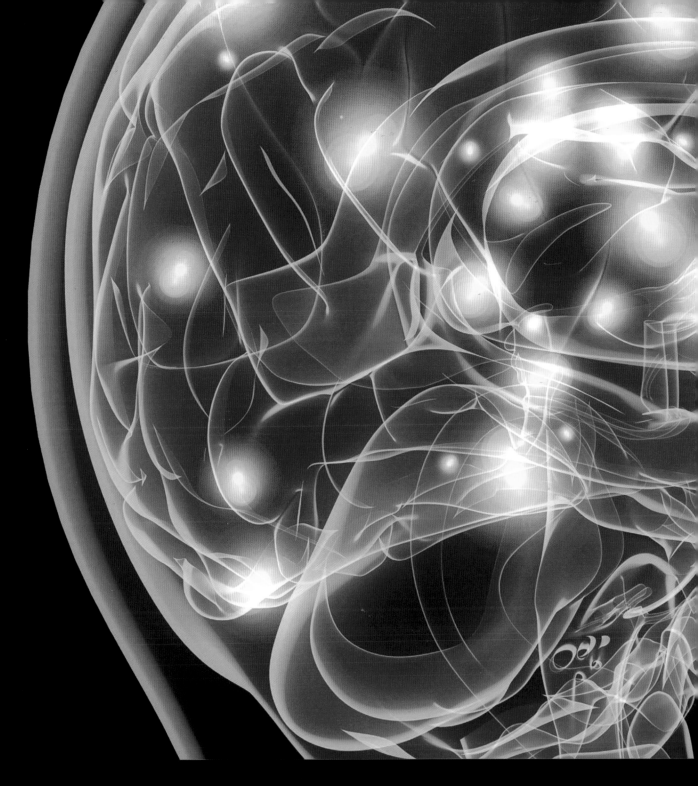

IN GOOD
HEALTH

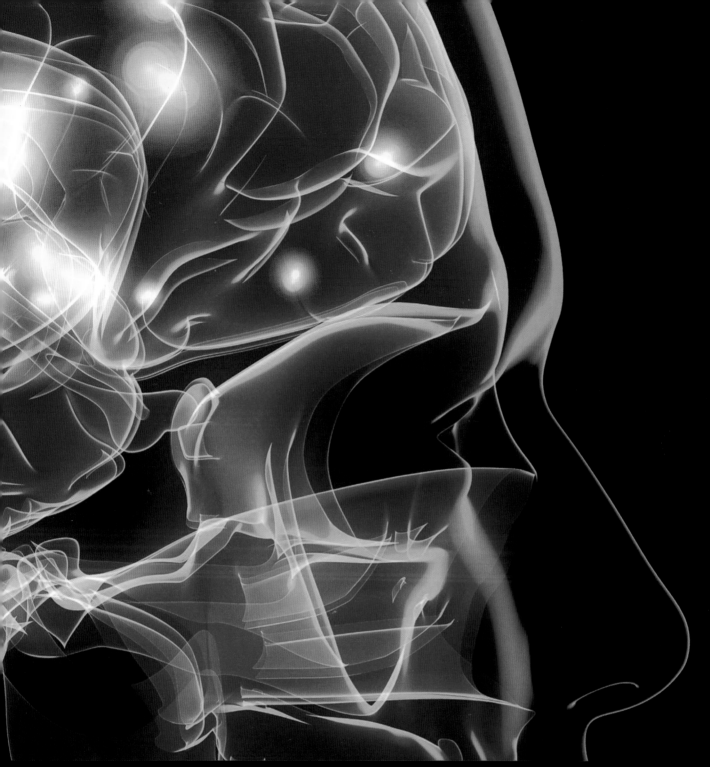

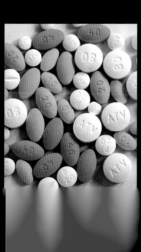

Medical technology has taken many leaps forward in the past 200 years. A range of inventions has enabled doctors to better explore the causes and cures of diseases.

Looking inside

Before 1895, looking inside a patient's body meant cutting it open. The discovery of X-rays by the German scientist Wilhelm Röntgen provided a new way. X-rays are a form of electromagnetic radiation (like light) that can pass through softer parts of the body, such as organs, but are absorbed by denser parts, such as bones, which then show up clearly on X-ray images. Many other methods have since been invented to look inside the body safely.

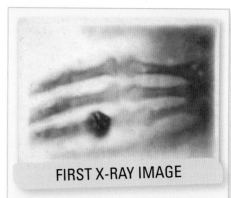

FIRST X-RAY IMAGE

While experimenting with a device called a cathode ray tube, Röntgen found that it was emitting mysterious rays, which seemed to pass through solid materials. He used the rays to take the first ever X-ray image in 1895 – a picture of his wife's ringed hand (above).

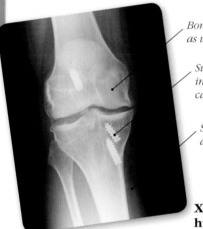

Bone shows up as white area.

Surgical screws inserted into bone can be seen clearly.

Soft tissue areas are blurry.

X-ray of a human knee

SHINING A LIGHT

The American doctors Basil Hirschowitz and Larry Curtiss invented the fibre-optic endoscope in 1957. It is a thin, flexible tube that is filled with glass or plastic fibres along which light signals can be transmitted. The device is inserted into the patient's body to relay images of its insides to the doctors.

NAMING THE UNKNOWN

Röntgen didn't know what the radiation was, so called it "X-ray" ("X" stands for "unknown"). His discovery won him a Nobel Prize in Physics in 1901. Today, X-rays are used by doctors to check for broken bones or foreign objects, including surgical implants, inside the body.

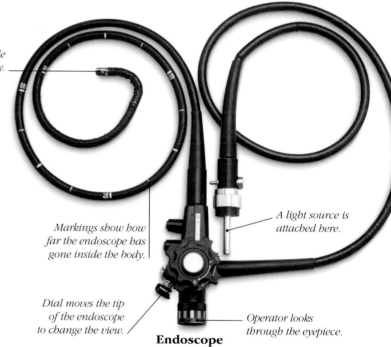

Tip goes inside the body.

Markings show how far the endoscope has gone inside the body.

A light source is attached here.

Dial moves the tip of the endoscope to change the view.

Operator looks through the eyepiece.

Endoscope

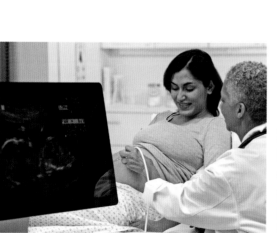

IMAGES FROM SOUND

First used in the 1950s, ultrasound scanners send high-pitched sounds into the body. Different tissues, such as bone or muscle, produce different echoes, creating a two-dimensional "sound picture", known as a sonogram. This process is harmless and is often used for scanning babies in the womb (left).

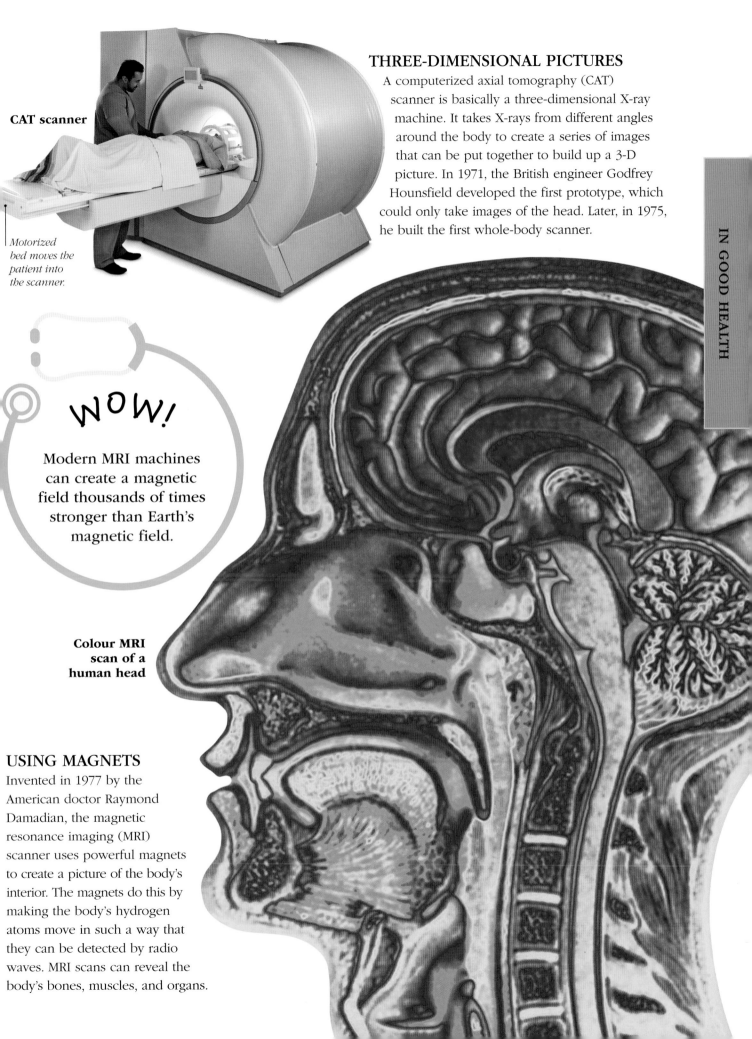

CAT scanner

Motorized bed moves the patient into the scanner.

THREE-DIMENSIONAL PICTURES

A computerized axial tomography (CAT) scanner is basically a three-dimensional X-ray machine. It takes X-rays from different angles around the body to create a series of images that can be put together to build up a 3-D picture. In 1971, the British engineer Godfrey Hounsfield developed the first prototype, which could only take images of the head. Later, in 1975, he built the first whole-body scanner.

WOW!

Modern MRI machines can create a magnetic field thousands of times stronger than Earth's magnetic field.

Colour MRI scan of a human head

USING MAGNETS

Invented in 1977 by the American doctor Raymond Damadian, the magnetic resonance imaging (MRI) scanner uses powerful magnets to create a picture of the body's interior. The magnets do this by making the body's hydrogen atoms move in such a way that they can be detected by radio waves. MRI scans can reveal the body's bones, muscles, and organs.

▲ IN HER LABORATORY
Marie Curie works in her laboratory at the Sorbonne University in Paris, France, in 1911.

LIFE STORY

1867	1891	1897	1903
Marie Sklodowska is born on 7 November in Warsaw, Poland. As a teenager, she studies science in secret at the Flying University.	She moves to Paris to study and meets Pierre Curie, a professor at the Sorbonne University. They later marry, in 1895.	Her first daughter, Irene, is born. She also becomes a scientist, winning a Nobel Prize in Chemistry in 1935. **Irene Curie**	The Curies are awarded the Nobel Prize in Physics, making Marie the first woman to achieve this honour.

Marie Curie

One of the great scientists of her age, the Polish-French physicist Marie Curie was a pioneer in the study of radioactivity – the stream of energetic particles produced when unstable atoms break up. Her work improved our understanding of radioactivity, leading to the treatment of cancers with radiation. For her discoveries of two radioactive elements, she became the first person to be awarded two Nobel Prizes.

Uranium ore, from which polonium and radium are extracted

NEW ELEMENTS

When Curie arrived in Paris, scientists had recently discovered that certain elements, such as uranium, were radioactive. Working with her husband, the scientist Pierre Curie, and alone, she discovered two more radioactive elements, polonium and radium, in 1898.

A WOMAN IN A MAN'S WORLD

In late 19th-century Europe, women were largely barred from the scientific world. In Curie's home country of Poland, women couldn't even attend university, forcing her to study in secret. Her career took off when she moved to Paris in France where she gained degrees in both physics and chemistry. Curie's extraordinary achievements paved the way for other female scientists.

Marie Curie's notebooks are still highly radioactive

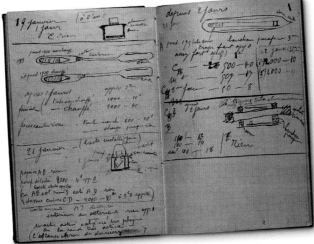

TREATING CANCER

Curie's discoveries led to the development of radiotherapy – a method of treating cancer with high bursts of radiation. Unfortunately, the dangers of radiation were not well understood at the time and Curie is believed to have died from a bone disease caused by long-term exposure to radiation.

LITTLE CURIES

In World War I, Curie arranged for 20 trucks to be equipped with X-ray machines, which could be used to scan wounded soldiers for bullets and broken bones. She even helped to drive the trucks to the war zone herself. By the end of the war, these trucks, known as "Little Curies" (left), had examined more than a million soldiers.

1906	1910	1934	1995
After Pierre's death in a street accident, Marie takes over his job as professor at Sorbonne University, becoming the first woman to hold such a position.	Marie wins her second Nobel Prize in Chemistry. She is the only woman to have won two Nobel Prizes, and the only person to have won for different sciences.	She dies at the age of 66, following a long period of illness believed to have been caused by prolonged exposure to radiation.	The remains of Pierre and Marie are moved to the Panthéon in Paris, where the most distinguished French citizens are buried.

Better diagnoses

Until around 200 years ago, the only tools doctors had for identifying illnesses were their own expertise and the patients' descriptions of their symptoms. Since then, a wide array of instruments for testing patients' health and working out what their symptoms mean has been developed. This has helped to turn diagnosis from a guessing game into something more scientific.

FAST FACTS

■ The ancient Greeks first came up with the term "diagnosis", meaning to identify an illness. They believed illnesses were caused by excess or lack of four body fluids called humours: blood, yellow bile, black bile, and phlegm.

■ In the 19th century, some scientists believed that someone's mental health could be diagnosed by phrenology – the study of the shape and size of a person's head.

Laënnec's stethoscope

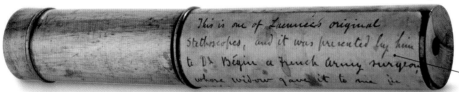

This is one of Laennec's original stethoscopes, and it was presented by him to Dr Bégin a French army surgeon whose widow gave it to me in

Single hollow tube made of wood and brass

Listening in

- ■ **What?** Stethoscope
- ■ **Who?** René Laënnec
- ■ **Where and when?** France, 1816

A stethoscope is used to listen to sounds made by the lungs and heart to detect any abnormal activity. The first stethoscope was a simple wooden tube that could be held against the chest of a patient. Modern versions with chest pieces, rubber tubing, and ear plugs (so a doctor can listen with both ears) were not developed until later in the 19th century.

Looking in

- ■ **What?** Ophthalmoscope
- ■ **Who?** Hermann von Helmholtz
- ■ **Where and when?** Germany, 1851

Invented by a German physician, the ophthalmoscope allows a doctor to peer through a patient's pupil to check on the health of the eye. In early ophthalmoscopes, light from a candle would reflect off the device's mirrored surface to illuminate the patient's eye. Over time, electric lights replaced candles.

French ophthalmoscope, produced after Helmholtz's version, mid-19th century

LÜER À PARIS

099000

Peephole to examine the inside of the eye

Doctor holds the device here.

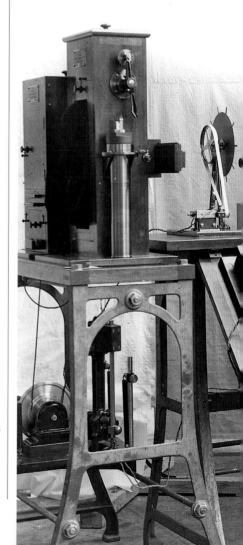

Taking temperature

- **What?** Clinical thermometer
- **Who?** Thomas Allbutt
- **Where and when?** UK, 1866

Medical thermometers had been invented by the mid-19th century – but they were more than 30 cm (12 in) long and could take up to 20 minutes to provide a reading. The British physician Thomas Allbutt improved their design by creating a thermometer that was half the size and gave a reading in just five minutes.

Allbutt's thermometer (left) and its case (right), c.1880

Measuring blood pressure

- **What?** Sphygmomanometer
- **Who?** Samuel Siegfried Karl von Basch
- **Where and when?** Austria, 1881

The sphygmomanometer is a simple device that measures blood pressure. Created by an Austrian doctor, it was improved upon by the Italian doctor Scipione Riva Rocci, who added an inflatable cuff that wraps around a patient's arm. Inflating the cuff squeezes the arm, stopping blood flow. The cuff is then slowly deflated until the doctor hears the blood flowing again, and the meter records its pressure.

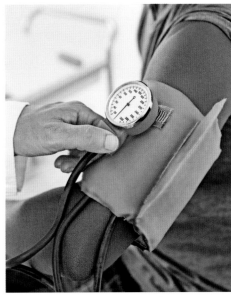

Modern sphygmomanometer

Measuring the heart's electrical activity

- **What?** Electrocardiograph (ECG or EKG)
- **Who?** Willem Einthoven
- **Where and when?** Netherlands, 1901

An electrocardiograph measures the small electric currents produced by the heart, which can help detect the presence of heart disease. Its inventor, the Dutch physician Willem Einthoven, was awarded the Nobel Prize in Medicine for his work, in 1924.

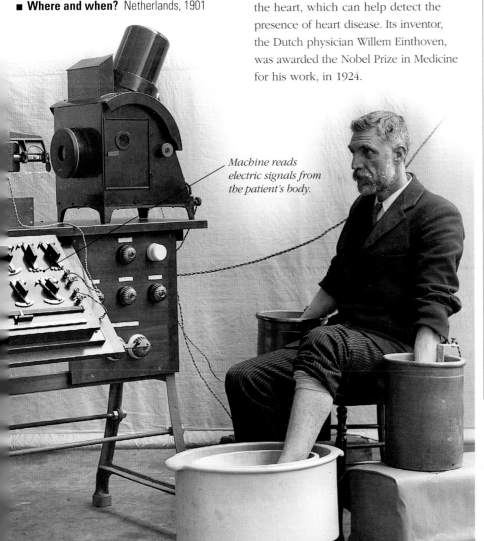

Machine reads electric signals from the patient's body.

Checking blood sugar

- **What?** Blood-Glucose Meter
- **Who?** Anton "Tom" Clemens
- **Where and when?** USA, 1966

People with diabetes (a disease in which blood sugar is not completely controlled) need to monitor their blood sugar levels. Until the 1960s, there was no easy way to do this. Then, an American engineer developed a device that could interpret the readings of glucose paper strips that change colour based on how much sugar a drop of blood contains.

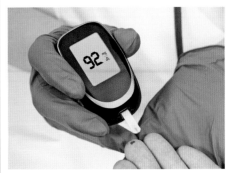

Modern blood sugar monitors can measure blood sugar digitally

◄ EARLY ECG
To use this ECG machine from 1911, patients had to put their limbs in buckets of salt water, which acted as electrodes, conducting the electricity.

229

Anaesthetics

Before the mid-19th century, surgery was very painful as it had to be carried out without effective painkillers. In the 1840s, the use of anaesthetics – medicines that cause temporary loss of sensation – began to become widespread. Today, a wide range of anaesthetics has made surgery largely pain free.

ANCIENT SURGERY

There is evidence of surgical operations from prehistoric times. One of the most widespread was trepanning – drilling holes in the head with sharp tools to relieve pain, in ritual ceremonies, or, as some believe, to let out "evil spirits". This trepanned skull from the Middle East is more than 4,000 years old.

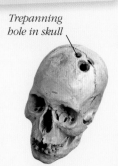

Trepanning hole in skull

A regulator controls the flow of ether fumes into the tube.

A rubber tube carries ether fumes from the jar to the mouthpiece.

SPEEDY SURGERY

This 17th-century painting shows a dentist pulling a tooth. Before anaesthetics, medical practitioners tried to make these procedures less painful by giving patients alcohol to drink, or sometimes even physically knocking them out, before operating on them as quickly as possible.

ETHER MIRACLE

The American dentist William Morton made a medical leap in 1846 when he used the chemical ether as an anaesthetic on a patient before performing a pain-free operation. Ether wasn't without its problems, as it was highly inflammable, but its use soon became widespread.

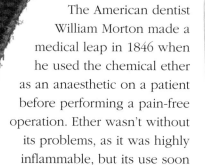

An early ether inhaler, based on Morton's original design

CHLOROFORM

Another anaesthetic drug to appear around the same time as ether was chloroform. It was first used by the Scottish doctor James Young Simpson in 1847 to relieve women's pain during childbirth. Some people objected to this use, believing it "unnatural". However, Britain's Queen Victoria allowed Simpson to use chloroform to soothe her birthing pains in 1853.

Bottle of chloroform from the late 19th century

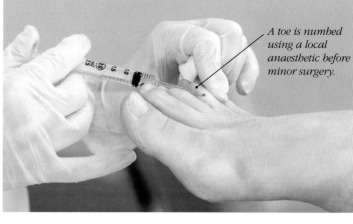

A toe is numbed using a local anaesthetic before minor surgery.

LOCAL ANAESTHETICS

The right dose of ether or chloroform knocked a patient out cold, but too large a dose could result in death. In 1903, the French chemist Ernest Fourneau developed Amylocaine, the first artificial local anaesthetic. It numbed the body part to be operated on but left the patient conscious. Many other local anaesthetics have since been created.

WOW!

Used to numb pain in the early 19th century, the gas nitrous oxide made people feel so happy that it was nicknamed "laughing gas".

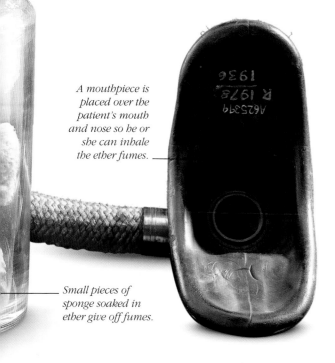

A mouthpiece is placed over the patient's mouth and nose so he or she can inhale the ether fumes.

Small pieces of sponge soaked in ether give off fumes.

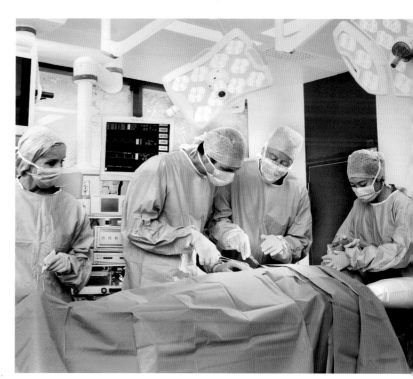

GENERAL ANAESTHETICS

Modern-day general anaesthetics are usually a combination of different drugs that make a patient lose consciousness during an operation. The dosages are controlled by an anaesthetic machine – also known as Boyle's machine, after the British doctor Henry Boyle who invented it in 1917. During surgery, an anaesthetist (the person on the far right, above) administers and monitors the anaesthetics.

Medical marvels

Major advances and breakthroughs in medical science have been made in the past few centuries. These have vastly increased the number of drugs and types of medical equipment available to us. While some offer life-saving treatments, others target minor aches and pains. Indeed, medicine has become specialized in a way that would have seemed unthinkable to doctors a few hundred years ago.

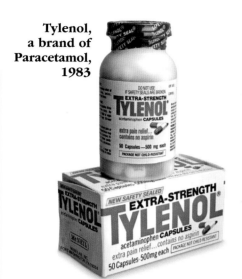

Tylenol, a brand of Paracetamol, 1983

Painkillers

- **What?** Paracetamol (acetaminophen)
- **Who?** Harmon Northrop Morse
- **Where and when?** USA, 1877

Sometimes it can take a while for a drug to catch on. In 1877, an American chemist developed the now popular drug Paracetamol, which is usually used as a mild painkiller and flu medication. But, unfounded doubts about its safety meant that it wasn't released to the public until 1950.

The miracle drug

- **What?** Aspirin
- **Who?** Felix Hoffman
- **Where and when?** Germany, 1897

Aspirin is used for treating such a wide range of ailments, including headaches, heart attacks, blood clots, and strokes, that it is sometimes known as the "miracle drug". It is a synthetic form of a natural substance called salicylic acid, which is found in willow bark and has been used to treat illnesses for centuries.

Carton of soluble aspirin powder, 1900

An iron lung helps a patient to breathe, 1940

Breathing easy

- **What?** Iron lung
- **Who?** Philip Drinker and Dr Louis Agassiz Shaw
- **Where and when?** USA, 1927

Patients whose breathing muscles were paralysed by an accident or disease could be helped to breathe again with the invention of the iron lung. It was a cumbersome machine – the patient had to be almost entirely enclosed within it – but it saved lives. It has since been replaced by smaller respirators and air ventilators.

Glass capsules of the sulfonamide Prontosil, 1936–1940

Fighting bacteria

- **What?** Sulfonamide drugs
- **Who?** Gerhard Domagk
- **Where and when?** Germany, 1932

Before antibiotics (bacteria-killing drugs) began to be widely used in the 1940s, another family of drugs – sulfonamides – was in use. Although some sulfonamides were effective against some bacterial infections, not all were safe, and one resulted in mass poisoning in 1937, causing more than 100 deaths in the USA. This led the US government to introduce safety testing for new drugs for the first time, in 1938.

Helping the heart

- **What?** Portable defibrillator
- **Who?** Frank Pantridge
- **Where and when?** UK, 1965

Defibrillators provide an electric shock to correct an abnormal heartbeat when someone is having a heart attack. Early machines were big and bulky, and they could be used only in hospitals. Frank Pantridge's invention was small enough to be carried in ambulances. Today, many public places have portable Public Access Defibrillators (PADs), which can be operated by anyone.

Electrode pads are placed on the patient's chest.

Public Access Defibrillator, 2006

The device plays recorded instructions telling the user what to do, simply and calmly.

Lowering cholesterol

- **What?** Statin drugs
- **Who?** Akira Endo
- **Where and when?** Japan, 1971

Statins are drugs used to lower cholesterol, a fatty substance that can build up in arteries and block them, sometimes causing heart attacks. The drugs were developed after research into fungi, and have become some of the world's best-selling medicines.

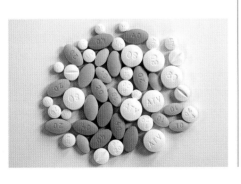

Preventing malaria

- **What?** Artemisinin
- **Who?** Tu Youyou
- **Where and when?** China, 1972

The problem with many early anti-malarial drugs, such as quinine, is that parasites eventually become immune to them. So, new drugs have to be invented – or old ones rediscovered. The Chinese chemist Tu Youyou produced artemisinin by retesting a 1,600-year-old treatment that used a plant called *Artemisia annua*. She was awarded the Nobel Prize in Medicine for her work.

Harvested *Artemisia annua* plants being prepared for sale in Uganda

Replica of one of Leeuwenhoek's microscopes

Screw to adjust the focus

Needle to hold a specimen

Lens held between two plates

EARLY STEPS

In the 1590s, the Dutch lens-makers Hans and Zacharias Jansen combined lenses in a tube to create the first microscopes. In the following century, the Dutch scientist Anton Van Leeuwenhoek built more powerful microscopes, becoming the first person to observe single-celled microorganisms. His device, which had just a single lens, could magnify specimens, or objects, up to 270 times.

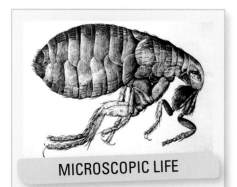

MICROSCOPIC LIFE

In the 17th century, scientists began to use microscopes more widely. In 1665, the British scientist Robert Hooke published a book, *Micrographia*, which contained the first illustrations of specimens, such as plants and tiny insects (including the flea above), as seen through a microscope.

Microscopes

Nobody used to know what causes diseases. In the 1860s, the French chemist Louis Pasteur (see pp.244–245) proved that diseases are caused by tiny organisms, called bacteria, which are too small to be seen with the unaided eye. The journey towards this "germ theory" began around 250 years earlier with the invention of the microscope, which let people see microorganisms for the first time.

► **COMPOUND MICROSCOPE**
This is a replica of Hooke's compound microscope – a microscope that uses two or more lenses.

Observer looked through the eyepiece.

Screw moves the device up and down to change the focus.

Metal pin to hold the specimen in place

Objective lens holder

TINY UNITS

The microscope used by the British scientist Robert Hooke in the 17th century was made mainly of wood. The focus was controlled by moving the whole device rather than the lenses or specimen. When observing a piece of cork close up, Hooke noticed that it was made up of tiny microscopic units, which he called "cells" – the word we now use to describe the small structures that make up all living organisms.

Louis Pasteur in his laboratory

GERM THEORY

The idea that infectious diseases are spread by germs, or microorganisms, is known as germ theory. Today, we take it for granted, but this view was highly controversial when Pasteur was studying it. With the help of the microscope, he demonstrated that tiny organisms called yeasts were responsible for contaminating beer and milk, and caused fermentation.

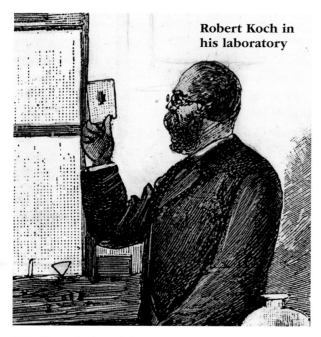

Robert Koch in his laboratory

FINDING BACTERIA

While Pasteur proved that diseases were caused by bacteria, the German scientist Robert Koch pinned down the specific culprits. Microscopes enabled him to identify the bacteria that cause diseases such as anthrax (1876), tuberculosis (1882), and cholera (1883). For these discoveries, Koch is known as the "father of bacteriology" (the study of bacteria).

COMPOUND MICROSCOPE

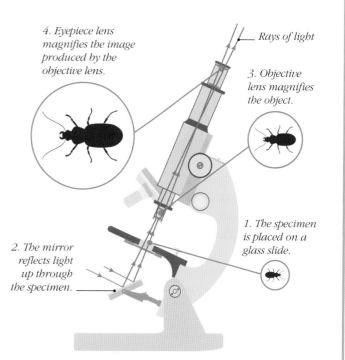

4. Eyepiece lens magnifies the image produced by the objective lens.

Rays of light

3. Objective lens magnifies the object.

2. The mirror reflects light up through the specimen.

1. The specimen is placed on a glass slide.

A compound microscope operates in roughly the opposite way to a telescope. Rather than having a large lens for gathering faint light from far away, a microscope has a small lens for focusing light on small objects that are close up. Microscopes usually have a light source, an objective lens that can be focused, and a fixed eyepiece. The lenses focus by bending light to make the image appear larger.

ELECTRON MICROSCOPES

In the 1930s, the German physicist Ernst Ruska developed a microscope that could magnify up to 500,000 times. Instead of using light, the device used a beam of electrons. It would eventually be possible to produce images of molecules and atoms. Today's most powerful microscopes can magnify up to 30 million times.

Image of bacteria (yellow) on the tip of a household pin, taken by an electron microscope

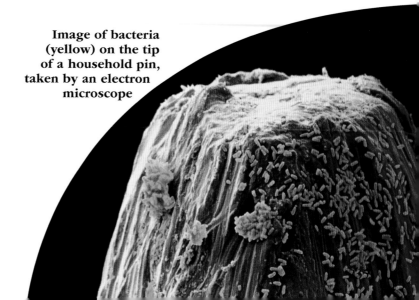

War on germs

In the early 1800s, many patients died in hospitals from infections picked up during surgery or childbirth. By the middle of the century, scientists had begun to understand that infections were caused by invisible germs. They campaigned to improve the cleanliness of hospitals, but faced opposition from doctors who refused to accept the new theories.

THE FIRST ANTISEPTIC

In the 1860s, the British surgeon Joseph Lister took the first practical steps to prevent airborne infections during surgery. He cleaned wounds with carbolic acid – the first antiseptic (a chemical that kills disease-causing germs). Lister also set up a machine that sprayed a fine mist of carbolic acid while he operated. This greatly reduced infection rates.

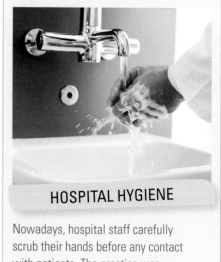

HOSPITAL HYGIENE

Nowadays, hospital staff carefully scrub their hands before any contact with patients. The practice was pioneered by the Hungarian doctor Ignaz Semmelweis in 1847 at a hospital in Vienna, Austria. He discovered that if doctors washed their hands in mildly chlorinated water before surgery, the death rate of patients dropped.

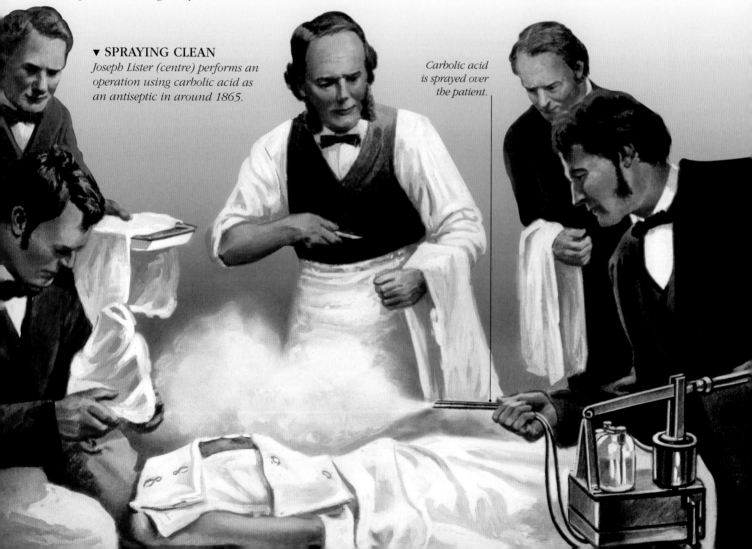

▼ SPRAYING CLEAN
Joseph Lister (centre) performs an operation using carbolic acid as an antiseptic in around 1865.

Carbolic acid is sprayed over the patient.

STERILE MEDICAL KITS

Influenced by Lister's ideas, doctors began boiling their surgical instruments to sterilize them (get rid of germs) before operations. In 1886, the American industrialist Robert Wood Johnson and his brothers founded a pharmaceutical company, called Johnson & Johnson, to make sterile bandages and surgical equipment. After two years, they began manufacturing the world's first commercial first-aid kits, bringing sterile medical care to the masses.

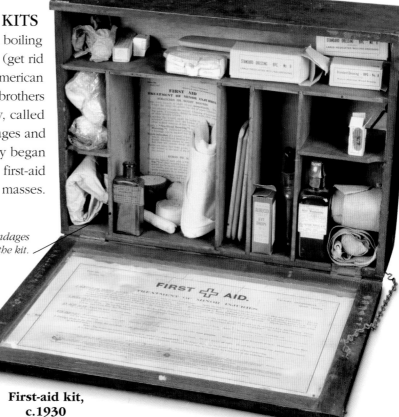

Medicines and sterile bandages are stored in compartments in the kit.

First-aid kit, c.1930

Carbolic soap, 1894

GERM-KILLING SOAP

In 1834, the German chemist Friedlieb Ferdinand Runge discovered carbolic acid (or phenol) – the substance Lister used as an antiseptic. By the end of the 19th century, this antiseptic was widely available to the general public in the form of mass-produced soap bars.

Sterile padding absorbs blood.

STICKING PLASTERS

Until the early 20th century, applying a bandage to a small cut was a fiddly business that usually required two people. In 1920, Earl Dickson (an American inventor and employee of Johnson & Johnson) came up with a solution – sticking plasters. These were small squares of bandage attached to a strip of sticky tape. Manufactured under the name Band-Aid, they are now used all over the world.

WOW!

The mouthwash Listerine was named after Joseph Lister to highlight its antibacterial properties.

Face masks prevent doctors from spreading respiratory infections.

SAFE SURGERY

Modern surgeons take numerous precautions to protect against infections. These include wearing face masks, surgical caps, scrub suits (sanitary clothing), and latex gloves. Using antiseptics alongside these continues to help sanitize modern surgical spaces.

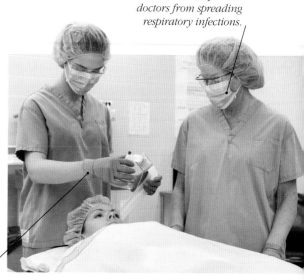

Sterile gloves are thrown away after one use.

237

Developing treatments

Advances in medical science in the past 250 years have led to the development of a wide range of effective treatments for controlling or even eliminating diseases. Many have come about through trial and error, with innovation often racing ahead of scientific understanding.

20th-century painting of James Lind giving a lemon to a scurvy patient

PREVENTING SCURVY

Until the 18th century, sailors on long journeys often came down with a mysterious illness, which we now know to be scurvy. This is caused by a lack of vitamin C, which is present in citrus fruits. In 1747, the British surgeon James Lind demonstrated that sailors who regularly ate citrus fruits, such as lemons, didn't suffer from this illness. When the British navy finally took his advice, it cured scurvy in sailors almost overnight.

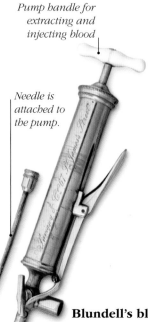

Pump handle for extracting and injecting blood

Needle is attached to the pump.

BLOOD TRANSFUSION

The British doctor James Blundell performed the world's first human blood transfusion in 1818. He injected a woman who had lost blood during childbirth with blood drawn from her husband. Although Blundell's procedure was successful, transfusions at the time didn't always work – blood types weren't fully understood and mixing different blood types could prove fatal.

Blundell's blood transfusion apparatus, 19th century

Early dialysis machine, 1949

KIDNEY DIALYSIS

In 1944, the Dutch doctor Willem Kolff invented a dialysis machine, which treats patients whose kidneys have failed. This first "artificial kidney" was a bulky device that cleaned the patient's blood of waste products by taking it out of the body, filtering it through a membrane, and then returning it. Today, this procedure – kidney dialysis – is fairly commonplace.

LASER EYE SURGERY

Using a scalpel to reshape a patient's cornea (the outer transparent part of the eye) and correct their vision was pioneered by the Spanish ophthalmologist José Barraquer in the 1950s. Following years of research and practice, the first reshaping procedure using an ultraviolet laser as the cutting tool was performed in 1988 by the American doctor Marguerite McDonald.

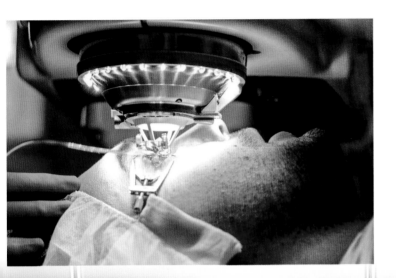

WOW!

In 1665, the British doctor Richard Lower carried out the first ever blood transfusion procedure – between two dogs.

ROBOTIC SURGERY

Although a robot that can perform operations independently has yet to be invented, robots have been assisting with operations since the early 1980s. The first was the Arthrobot, developed in 1983 by a team of Canadian researchers led by Dr James McEwen. The robot moved a patient's leg during surgery by following a surgeon's voice commands.

IN GOOD HEALTH

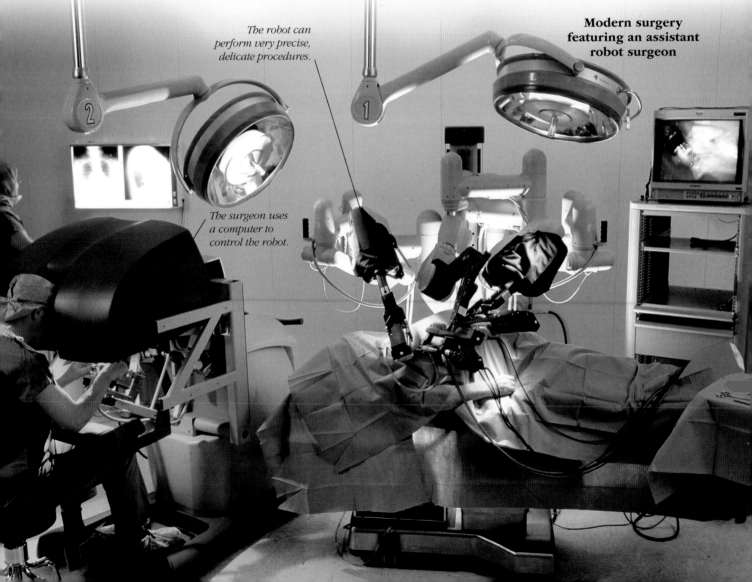

The robot can perform very precise, delicate procedures.

The surgeon uses a computer to control the robot.

Modern surgery featuring an assistant robot surgeon

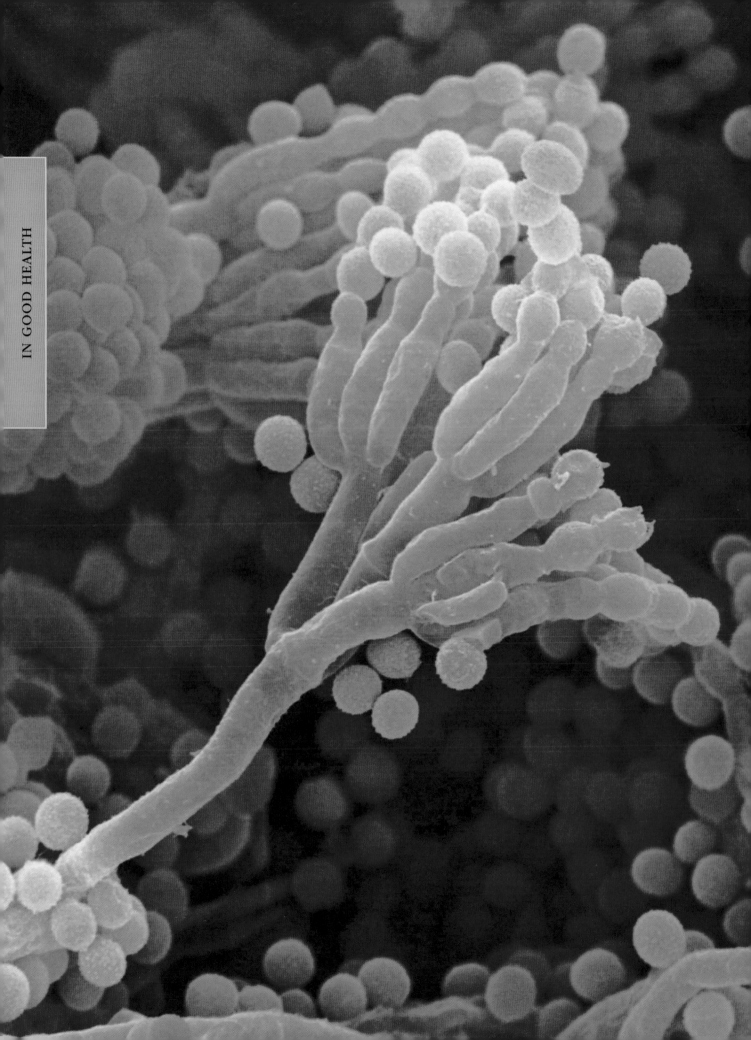

SUPER MOULD

This close-up image taken by a scanning electron microscope (see p.235) shows penicillium mould, which is used to create penicillin, the world's first antibiotic. Its bacteria-killing properties were discovered by accident in 1928 by the Scottish doctor Sir Alexander Fleming. Penicillin and other antibiotics have since saved millions of lives.

Vaccinations

A vaccine is made of weakened forms of the microbes that cause a disease. This is then given to someone (usually as an injection) so their body can prepare itself against the full disease. The first effective vaccine was developed by the British doctor Edward Jenner in the late 18th century to combat smallpox. Since then, scientists have created vaccines for many other diseases.

THE FIRST VACCINE

Jenner noticed that milkmaids infected with cowpox – a similar disease to smallpox, but much milder – didn't catch smallpox. So, he infected a boy with cowpox, and then tried to infect him with smallpox. The boy didn't catch the disease, confirming Jenner's belief that the boy was now immune to smallpox. Seen above is an illustration of Jenner vaccinating his son.

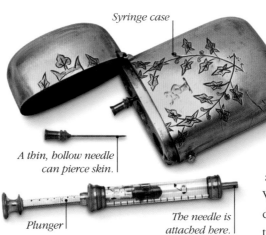

Syringe case

A thin, hollow needle can pierce skin.

Plunger

The needle is attached here.

Syringe with a spare needle and metal case, late 19th century

THE SYRINGE

The invention of the hypodermic syringe in 1853 made it easier for doctors to give vaccinations. It was the work of three men: the Irishman Francis Rynd who invented the hollow needle; and the French surgeon Charles Pravaz and the Scottish physician Alexander Wood who, working independently, devised a way of attaching the needle to a plunger device.

Rabies vaccine being injected into a patient's stomach

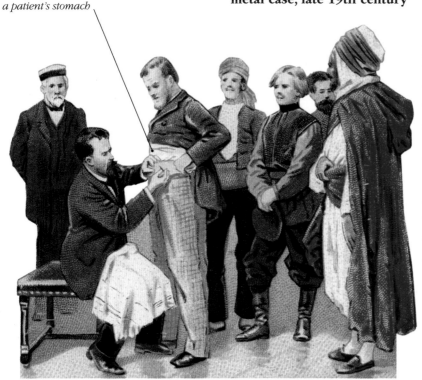

PASTEUR'S WORK

For a while, smallpox was the only disease that people could be vaccinated against. In the early 19th century, scientists didn't know of any other disease with a naturally weak strain of the disease-causing microbe. A breakthrough was made when the French scientist Louis Pasteur (see pp.244–245) discovered how to artificially weaken bacteria, using heat and chemicals, in 1862. This enabled him to produce the first vaccines for rabies in 1885.

◀ TAKING PRECAUTIONS
Here, Pasteur is shown vaccinating people against rabies. He also created a vaccine against anthrax.

THE JET INJECTOR

Invented in 1936 by the American engineer Marshall Lockhart, the jet injector delivers medicine as a thin, high-pressure jet of liquid that can pierce skin. It can be operated very quickly, which has led to it being used in mass vaccination programmes. But, because of the risk of infection, it has been replaced in recent times by disposable, single-use versions.

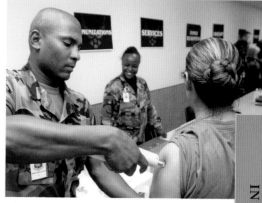

Flu vaccine being injected using a jet injector

WOW!

Although vaccines are available now for many diseases, there is still no vaccine for the common cold.

Flu virus particles (shown in white, below) attack red blood cells

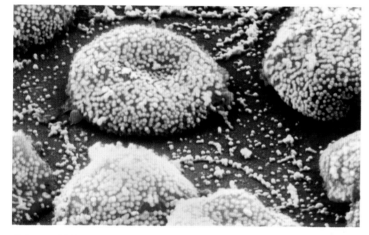

MODERN VACCINES

In the 20th century, more vaccines were developed, including those against tuberculosis (1921), measles (1963), and rubella (1966). In the 1950s, the American physician Jonas Salk created a polio vaccine but refused to patent it so as to make it freely available to everyone.

▼ ORAL VACCINATIONS
The oral polio vaccine, being given here to a girl in Yemen, was invented by the American physician Albert Sabin in the 1960s.

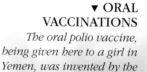

DEFEATING DISEASES

The search for new vaccines is ongoing. In the 1940s, the first flu vaccines appeared, followed by vaccines against hepatitis A in the 1990s, and malaria in 2018. However, there are still many deadly diseases, such as Ebola and AIDS, that cannot be vaccinated against.

FAST FACTS

■ Once one of the world's deadliest diseases, smallpox killed around 400,000 people a year in Europe in the late 18th century.

■ In 1980, the World Health Organization (WHO) declared that smallpox had been successfully wiped out by vaccination; so far, it is the only infectious disease to have been eradicated.

Louis Pasteur

The French biologist and chemist Louis Pasteur was one of the giant figures of 19th-century medicine. His many discoveries, particularly in the fields of germ theory and vaccination (see pp.242–243), revolutionized the scientific thinking of the day. They also saved millions of lives by providing great leaps forward in the treatment of deadly diseases, such as anthrax and rabies.

Workers examine the pasteurization tanks in a milk treatment depot in London, UK, 1935

PASTEURIZATION

In the 1860s, Pasteur developed a way of preventing liquids, such as wine and milk, from spoiling because of contamination by bacteria. His technique involves steadily heating the liquid, which kills the bacteria without changing the liquid's taste. This process is known as pasteurization.

Microscope that Pasteur used to study silkworms

Silkworm cocoon from which silk is made

THE SILK INDUSTRY

Pasteur saved France's silk industry when it was being ravaged by a silkworm disease. He discovered that the disease could be passed from adult silkworms to the young, so he recommended destroying the eggs of infected moths. This made sure that only the healthy silkworms survived and the disease was wiped out.

LIFE STORY

1822	1859	1860s
Born on 27 December in Dole, France, Pasteur grows up to study chemistry. In 1848, he becomes a professor at the University of Strasbourg, France.	He uses special sealed flasks (right) to demonstrate that food rots because of microbes in the air.	Having invented pasteurization in 1863, Pasteur suffers a stroke in 1868 that partially paralyses his left side. He recovers over time and is able to continue his work.

VACCINE DISCOVERY

In 1879, when Pasteur was researching a poultry disease called chicken cholera, he realized that weakened strains of a disease could be used to create a vaccine against the full-strength disease. This discovery helped him to develop vaccines against anthrax and rabies.

Doctor giving rabies vaccination

FIGHTING RABIES

Pasteur produced a vaccine for rabies (an infectious disease that affects humans and animals) in 1885. His first rabies patient was nine-year-old Joseph Meister, who had been bitten by an infected dog. Pasteur became a national hero after the boy made a full recovery.

Louis Pasteur in his laboratory

1881	1885	1887	1895
Pasteur creates a vaccine for the deadly disease anthrax, which he uses to successfully immunize animals, such as sheep, goats, and cows.	He vaccinates a human for the first time, helping to cure a boy with rabies.	He establishes the Pasteur Institute in Paris, which is dedicated to the research of infectious diseases.	Pasteur suffers another stroke, but fails to recover this time. He dies on 28 September 1895.

Dental health

Dentistry wasn't recognized as a separate form of medicine until the early 18th century, when the French surgeon Pierre Fauchard wrote an influential book about caring for and treating teeth. Since then, scientists have made many advances in dental technology, helping to keep our teeth clean, healthy, and looking their best.

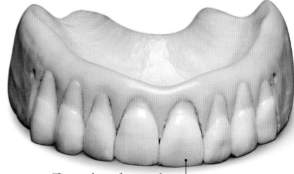

Dentures made from hippopotamus teeth, c.1795

The two large front teeth are recycled human teeth.

FALSE TEETH

Dentures (false teeth) – made from both human and animal teeth – have been around since prehistoric times. As people ate more sugar in the 18th century and teeth rotted, the demand for dentures grew. Making dentures from an artificial material – porcelain – was pioneered by the Frenchman Alexis Duchâteau in 1774, and improved then patented in the UK in 1791 by the French dentist Nicholas Dubois de Chémont. Modern dentures are usually made of plastic.

THE DENTIST'S CHAIR

The American dentist Milton Hanchett invented the first adjustable dentist's chair in 1848. It had a headrest, a back that could be tilted, and a seat that could be moved up and down. Another American dentist, Basil Manly Wilkerson, came up with the first hydraulic chair, in 1877, which could be raised and lowered using a pedal.

Headrest

Curved leather seat for patient's comfort

Pedal for adjusting the height of the chair

High-tech hydraulic chair, c.1925

BRUSHING TEETH

The oldest known toothbrush was found in China and dates back to c.750 CE. It has a brush made of pig bristles (thick hair) attached to a bone handle. Modern toothbrushes have nylon bristles attached to a plastic handle. The above image shows British children brushing their teeth in around 1920.

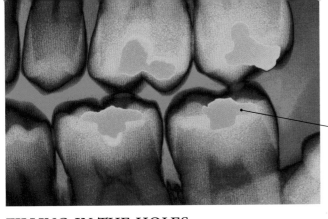

Coloured X-ray
of teeth

Amalgam filling

FILLING IN THE HOLES

In the 1820s, several dentists, including Auguste Taveau
in France and Thomas Bell in the UK, started using a new
dental filling called amalgam. Made from silver and mercury,
it could be easily moulded to fit a cavity in a tooth. In the
20th century, more natural-looking white fillings made
of powdered glass, ceramic, and plastic were developed.

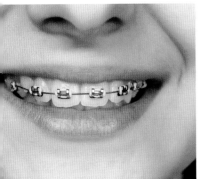

DENTAL BRACES

The first wire braces for pulling
the teeth into position were made
by the French dentist Christophe-
François Delabarre in 1819. Various
improvements have been made
since then, including the addition
of elastic bands in the 1840s and the
development of dental adhesives in
the 1970s to keep the braces in place.

Modern dental braces

WOW!

Before the invention
of amalgam fillings,
dental fillings were made
of hot, melted metal,
which could be
very painful.

Drill head

*Flexible arm for
moving the drill*

REMOVING DECAY

Dental drills are mainly used
for removing decayed parts of
teeth. They underwent a major
evolution from the mid-19th
century onwards, beginning
with the introduction of the
clockwork drill in 1864, followed
by the electric drill in 1875.
But these were surpassed by
the compressed air-powered
turbine drill in 1949. Invented
by the New Zealand dentist
John Patrick Walsh, its drill
head could spin at the rate
of 400,000 rpm (rotations per
minute) – compared to just
3,000 rpm for an electric drill.

*Rope and pulley system
operates the drill head.*

◄ SPEEDING IT UP
*Invented by the American dentist
James Beall Morrison in 1871,
the foot-powered "treadle" drill
sped up dental treatment.*

*Adjustable
footrest*

*Foot pedal
is pushed up
and down to
turn the drill.*

**Treadle drill,
1871**

New body parts

Today, there are many different artificial body parts, known as prostheses, available. These include devices to help people hear and see better, prosthetic limbs that can move naturally, and even artificial hearts. The oldest known prosthetic body part is a wood and leather toe that was found on an Egyptian mummy dating back to around 800 BCE.

X-ray shows the position of an implanted pacemaker.

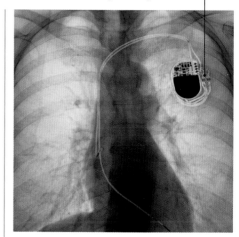

Spectacles appear in this 14th-century German painting

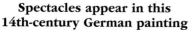

Seeing clearly

- **What?** Spectacles
- **Who?** Roger Bacon; Alessandro di Spina
- **Where and when?** UK, 13th century; Italy, 14th century

The origin of spectacles is not at all clear. In the 13th century, the English friar Roger Bacon described using lenses to aid sight. The Italian monks Alessandro di Spina and Salvino degli Armati also developed the idea, with spectacles appearing early in the 14th century. The earliest spectacles had thick lenses made of quartz.

Hearing better

- **What?** Electric hearing aid
- **Who?** Miller Reese Hutchison
- **Where and when?** USA, 1898

The first electrical hearing aid came out in 1898, but was quite bulky and had a separate battery pack. The introduction of transistors in the 1950s led to their size being reduced to a device small enough to fit around the ear. Hearing aids got even smaller following the arrival of digital technology in the 1980s.

Hearing aid, 1929

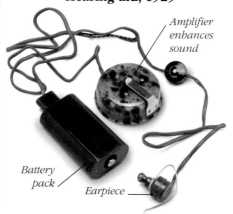
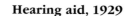

Amplifier enhances sound

Battery pack

Earpiece

Beating hearts

- **What?** Implantable pacemaker
- **Who?** Rune Elmqvist
- **Where and when?** Sweden, 1958

Pacemakers are devices that send small electrical signals to the heart to keep it beating properly. The first pacemakers sat outside the body and greatly limited the patient's movements. Invented in 1958, a pacemaker that is placed inside the body (above) allows patients to live a more normal life.

Contact lenses

- **What?** Soft contact lenses
- **Who?** Otto Wichterle
- **Where and when?** Czechoslovakia, 1961

The first contact lenses were created by the German ophthalmologist Adolf Gaston Eugen Fick in 1888. Made of blown glass, they could be worn for just a couple of hours. Lighter plastic versions were introduced in 1936 by the American scientist William Feinbloom. Soft contact lenses made of flexible plastics called hydrogels followed in the 1960s. These were created by the Czech chemist Otto Wichterle. A durable material called silicone-hydrogel is often used in contact lenses today.

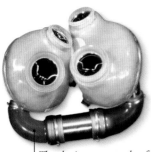
The device was made of aluminium and plastic.

Artificial heart

- **What?** Jarvik 7
- **Who?** Robert Jarvik
- **Where and when?** USA, 1982

In 1982, an American dentist suffering from heart failure became the first person to be fitted with an artificial heart – allowing him to live for another 112 days. Named after its inventor, the Jarvik 7 heart was the first of many to be created over the following decades. In some cases, an artificial heart may buy time for a patient until a real heart becomes available for transplant.

Spikes on the bottom of the blade help to grip the track.

Prosthetic legs

- **What?** Flex-Foot
- **Who?** Van Philipps
- **Where and when?** USA, 1996

Lightweight and flexible, modern artificial or prosthetic limbs enhance the mobility of the user. The American bioengineer Van Philipps, who had lost a leg below the knee at the age of 21, invented a range of prosthesis called Flex-Foot. Among these is the "Flex-Foot Cheetah", which is made of a carbon-fibre "blade", and is aimed at athletes. It flexes on impact with the ground, helping an athlete move quickly.

▶ **BLADE RUNNERS**
A long jumper competes in the 2011 World Para Athletics Championship. Athletes' prosthetic legs act like springs, allowing them to run and jump at high speeds.

Bionic hand

- **What?** I-Limb
- **Who?** David Gow
- **Where and when?** UK, 2007

Invented at a Scottish hospital, the I-Limb was the world's first fully functioning bionic (electronically controlled) hand. Its fingers can move independently according to muscle signals sent from the patient's arm. Patrick Kane (right) was the first person to be fitted with the device, aged 13.

>> **FAST FACTS** >>

- Around the 10th century, the Chinese were using magnifying lenses to read.
- Hearing aids evolved out of telephone technology – transmitters that amplified the sound in telephones were adapted for use in early hearing aids.
- The British surgeon Sir John Charnley performed the first successful hip replacement operations in the early 1960s.

SPACE

Astronauts now live and work in space, robotic probes explore other planets, and telescopes reveal distant galaxies. Where will our inventions take us next?

Studying the stars

People have been fascinated by stars and planets since prehistoric times, but for thousands of years they could only study them with their unaided eyes. In the 17th century, telescopes opened up new ways of seeing the Universe, and astronomers have been building bigger and better instruments ever since.

Reflector telescope, 1724

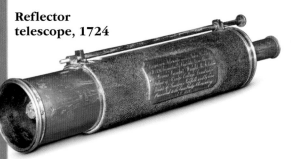

Photo of Orion nebula, 1883

Infrared camera view, 2010

WHAT IS A TELESCOPE?

Telescopes use a large lens or mirror to collect light, and a smaller lens called the eyepiece to create images of distant objects that are brighter and larger than those formed by our normal eyesight. The principle was discovered by the Dutch lens maker Hans Lippershey around 1608.

ASTROPHOTOGRAPHY

After the invention of photography in the 19th century, astronomers soon attached cameras to telescopes. Cameras can collect light over long periods, creating bright images that reveal much more detail than human eyesight can detect. Modern electronic cameras can detect types of light, such as infrared, that are invisible to human eyes.

TYPES OF TELESCOPE

Refractor telescopes were the first telescopes to be invented. They use large lenses to bend light rays so they cross at a focal point. Reflector telescopes use curved mirrors to bounce light rays to a focus. As the light rays spread apart again, one or more lenses in the eyepiece alter their paths to create a magnified, or enlarged, image.

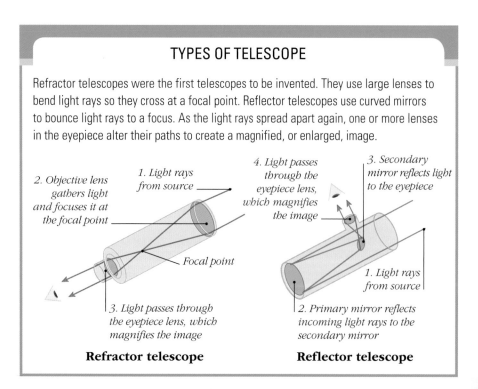

2. Objective lens gathers light and focuses it at the focal point

1. Light rays from source

Focal point

3. Light passes through the eyepiece lens, which magnifies the image

Refractor telescope

4. Light passes through the eyepiece lens, which magnifies the image

3. Secondary mirror reflects light to the eyepiece

1. Light rays from source

2. Primary mirror reflects incoming light rays to the secondary mirror

Reflector telescope

► **THE VERY LARGE TELESCOPE (VLT)**
This is one of four huge telescopes built by the European Southern Observatory in Chile's high desert. Each telescope contains a mirror that is 8 m (26 ft) wide and weighs 22 tonnes. Using the VLT reveals images that are four billion times fainter than the unaided eye can detect.

SPLITTING LIGHT

The spectroscope was invented in 1814 by the German physicist Joseph von Fraunhofer. It spreads light rays from stars onto different paths depending on their colour or energy. Fraunhofer discovered dark, narrow lines in the Sun's spectrum, which later scientists linked to light being absorbed by particular chemicals. Astronomers today use spectroscopy to study what celestial objects are made of.

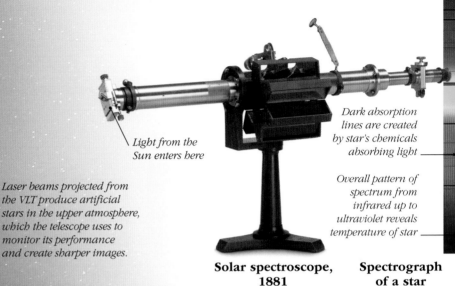

Light from the Sun enters here

Laser beams projected from the VLT produce artificial stars in the upper atmosphere, which the telescope uses to monitor its performance and create sharper images.

Dark absorption lines are created by star's chemicals absorbing light

Overall pattern of spectrum from infrared up to ultraviolet reveals temperature of star

Solar spectroscope, 1881

Spectrograph of a star

SPACE TELESCOPES

Visible light is just one part of the electromagnetic radiation emitted by cosmic objects. Things too cool to shine visibly still emit infrared radiation (heat), while very hot objects and violent events release high-energy ultraviolet, X-rays, and gamma rays. Earth's atmosphere blocks most of this radiation, so astronomers use space-based telescopes to map the sky.

Chandra X-ray Observatory

Nested mirrors deflect and focus X-rays from distant exploding stars.

SMART TELESCOPES

All modern large telescopes are reflectors. Some have huge one-piece mirrors made of thin, lightweight materials, but most use interlocking honeycomb grids of smaller mirrors to reduce their weight. Computer-controlled motors behind the mirrors can adjust their overall shape to correct distortions and ensure perfect focus for whichever direction the telescope is pointing.

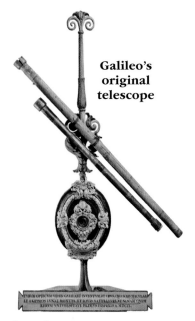

Galileo's original telescope

Telescopes

Telescopes have come a long way in the four centuries since the lens maker Hans Lippershey assembled two lenses at either end of a long tube around 1608. Today, they have become huge machines capable of detecting galaxies at the edge of the Universe and invisible radiation from gas and dust between the stars.

Early telescope

- **What?** Galileo's telescope
- **Who?** Galileo Galilei
- **Where and when?** Italy, 1609

Several astronomers built their own telescopes after hearing of Lippershey's invention, but the most successful was the Italian Galileo Galilei (see pp.258–259). Through careful study, he increased the power of his telescopes from three times magnification (×3) to 20 times (×20), which allowed him to make important discoveries about the Universe.

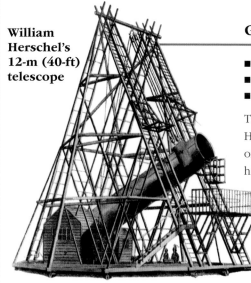

William Herschel's 12-m (40-ft) telescope

Giant reflectors

- **What?** The first giant telescope
- **Who?** William Herschel
- **Where and when?** UK, 1789

The German-born astronomer William Herschel built the best reflecting telescopes of the time after settling in the UK. After his 1781 discovery of Uranus, he was financed by King George III and built an enormous telescope with a 1.2-m (4-ft) mirror, mounted on a huge turntable that allowed it to point in different directions.

Mirrors for magnification

- **What?** Newton's reflector
- **Who?** Isaac Newton
- **Where and when?** UK, 1668

While studying the properties of light in the 1660s, the English scientist Isaac Newton realized that a curved mirror could bend light to a focus just as well as a lens. His "Newtonian" telescope avoided the distortions that plagued early lens-based designs.

Eyepiece

Replica of Newton's telescope

Radio telescope

- **What?** The Lovell Telescope
- **Who?** Bernard Lovell and Charles Husband
- **Where and when?** UK, 1957

The science of radio astronomy began in the 1930s, when astronomers discovered radio waves coming from celestial objects other than the Sun. Because radio waves are longer than visible light waves, they need much larger telescopes to capture

Reflecting metal dish 76.2 m (250 ft) across gathers radio waves →

Antenna is focal point for radio waves, which then generate electrical signals

and focus them. In the 1950s, the British astronomer Bernard Lovell built the first large "dish" telescope at Jodrell Bank near Manchester.

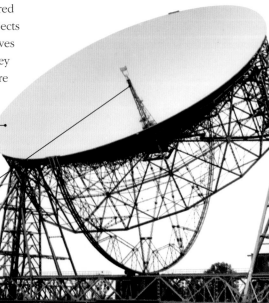

Lovell Telescope near Macclesfield, Cheshire, UK

Observing from orbit

- **What?** Infrared Astronomical Satellite (IRAS)
- **Who?** NASA
- **Where and when?** Low Earth Orbit, 1983

From the late 1940s, rocket-borne radiation detectors revealed that space was filled with invisible rays that are absorbed by Earth's atmosphere. Ultraviolet satellite observatories launched since the 1960s study some of these rays, while infrared satellites, pioneered by IRAS, use specially cooled telescopes to detect weak heat radiation and map the night sky.

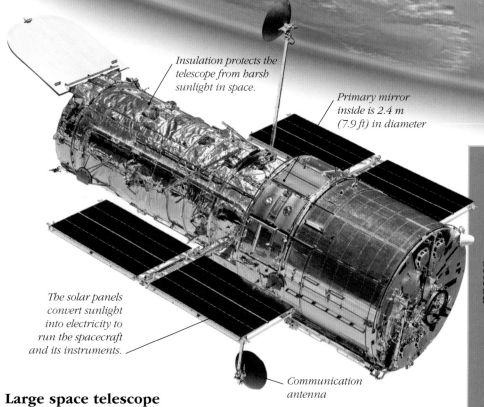

Insulation protects the telescope from harsh sunlight in space.

Primary mirror inside is 2.4 m (7.9 ft) in diameter

Sunshade helps protect and cool IRAS telescope

The solar panels convert sunlight into electricity to run the spacecraft and its instruments.

Communication antenna

Large space telescope

- **What?** Hubble Space Telescope
- **Who?** NASA
- **Where and when?** Low Earth Orbit, launched 1990

In 1946, the American astrophysicist Lyman Spitzer was the first to suggest putting a telescope in space to orbit above the distortions of Earth's atmosphere. The Hubble Space Telescope was finally launched in 1990 and has a crystal-clear view of deep space. Named in honour of the American astronomer Edwin Hubble, it has delivered some of the sharpest pictures of celestial objects and made discoveries ranging from previously unknown moons in our Solar System to distant galaxies at the edge of the Universe.

Future telescope

- **What?** European Extremely Large Telescope (E-ELT)
- **Who?** European Southern Observatory
- **Where and when?** Chile, c.2024

Currently under construction, the next generation of telescopes will be even larger and more powerful. The European Extremely Large Telescope (E-ELT) in the Atacama Desert in Chile will use a honeycomb network of mirrors whose positions are constantly adjusted by computer. With a total diameter of 39.3 m (129 ft), the telescope will gather 100 million times more light than a human eye. This will enable astronomers to see planets that orbit other stars and study the most distant galaxies in the Universe.

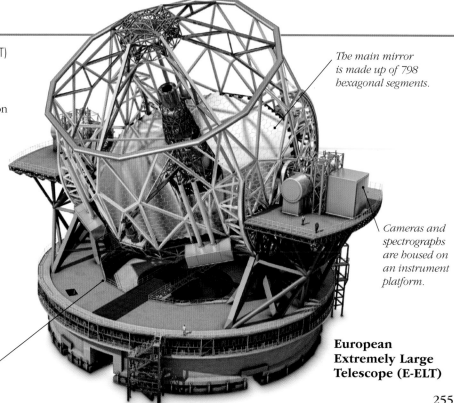

The main mirror is made up of 798 hexagonal segments.

Cameras and spectrographs are housed on an instrument platform.

The main deck supports the telescope's weight and can rotate to turn it around.

European Extremely Large Telescope (E-ELT)

ATACAMA OBSERVATORY

The world's largest observatories are linked "arrays" of radio telescopes such as the Atacama Large Millimeter Array (ALMA) in Chile's Atacama Desert. Here, some 66 movable radio antennae have their signals combined together to generate the same detail as a single 16-km (10-mile) telescope.

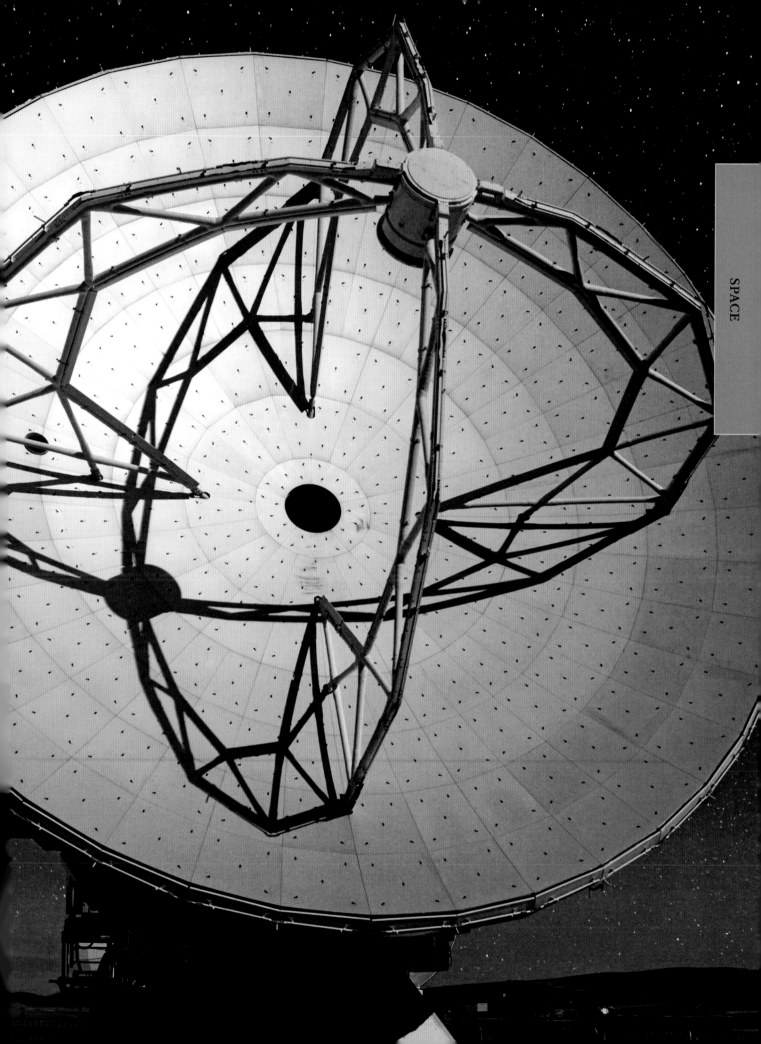

Galileo Galilei

Born in Pisa, Italy, in 1564, Galileo Galilei is best known for discovering evidence that planets orbit the Sun, not the Earth, but he was also a polymath – a scientist and inventor in many fields. Having first trained in medicine at the University of Pisa, Galileo is said to have become fascinated by physics after watching the pendulum-like motion of a swinging chandelier.

THROUGH THE TELESCOPE

After hearing reports of the newly invented telescope, Galileo built his own, much improved versions around 1609. His telescope revealed the phases of the planet Venus and a family of moons orbiting Jupiter. These features convinced him that the heliocentric (Sun-centred) model of the Universe put forward in 1543 by Polish astronomer Nicolaus Copernicus must be correct.

Large, heavy objects only fall more quickly than small, light ones because their ratio of weight to surface area is greater.

Galileo's sketches of the Moon

TESTING GRAVITY

Galileo studied the properties of falling objects and realized that, if it weren't for air resistance, bodies with different masses would fall towards the ground at the same rate. He is said to have demonstrated this to pupils around 1590 by dropping two things with different masses from the top of the Leaning Tower of Pisa.

▶ **THE ITALIAN POLYMATH**
This Italian portrait of Galileo shows him with the tools of his trade, including his telescope and a celestial globe on the table.

LIFE STORY

1564	c.1581	1592	1609
Galileo is born in Pisa, to parents Vincenzo (a noted musician) and Giulia.	At the University of Pisa, he studies medicine but also takes up mathematics and natural philosophy, and applies mathematical analysis to the study of physics.	Galileo becomes professor of mathematics at Padua. While there, he invents the thermoscope and a military compass.	He builds his first telescopes and uses them to make observations of the skies.

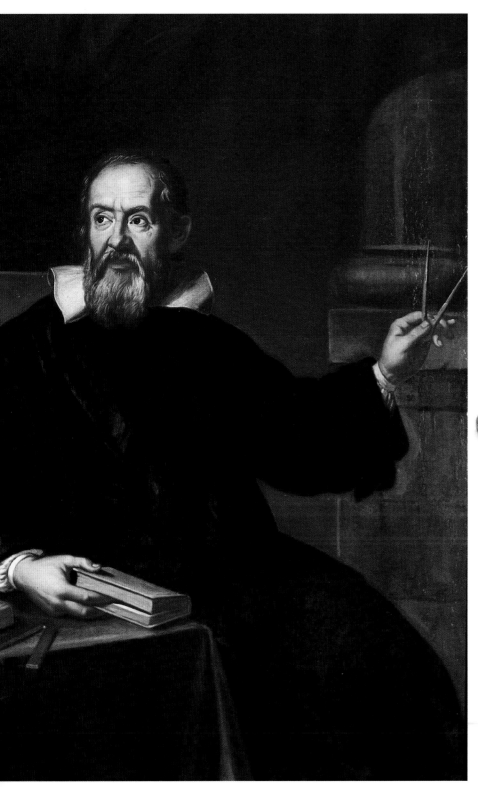

GALILEO'S THERMOMETERS

Around 1600, Galileo invented a "thermoscope". This temperature-measuring device relied on his discovery that fluids change their density when they grow warmer or colder. His followers later used the principle to design a thermometer in which weighted glass balls rose or sank to reveal the temperature.

Replica of Galilean thermometer

CLASH WITH AUTHORITY

Galileo's teaching of a Sun-centred Universe put him in conflict with the powerful Catholic Church, which insisted on Biblical teachings that Earth was the centre of everything. In his later years, Galileo was forced to defend his teachings when he was put on trial by the Inquisition (a church court). Found guilty of heresy, he spent the last nine years of his life under house arrest near Florence, and died in 1642. In 1992, the Church formally recognized that Galileo was right.

1610	1615	1633	1642
Galileo publishes *The Starry Messenger*, a book outlining his discoveries with the telescope. He argues for Copernicus's heliocentric (Sun-centred) system rather than a geocentric (Earth-centred) one.	At a Church inquisition (trial) in Rome, Galileo is ordered to stop teaching the Copernican theory of the Universe.	After publishing his *Dialogue Concerning the Two Chief World Systems*, Galileo is tried at another inquisition, and is sentenced for heresy.	Galileo dies near Florence. Despite suffering blindness for the last four years of his life, he had continued to write and invent until his final year.

Satellites

A satellite is a natural or artificial object that orbits another. Just as the Moon orbits Earth, so do man-made satellites that are launched into space on a trajectory where they move at high speed but are held on more or less circular paths by the tug of Earth's gravity. Since the 1950s, satellites have revolutionized many aspects of our everyday lives and improved our knowledge of Earth and the wider Universe.

FIRST SATELLITE

Although some earlier rockets had briefly reached space before falling back to Earth, the first object to stay in orbit was Sputnik 1, launched by Russia in October 1957. A simple, football-sized sphere equipped with antennae and a battery-powered radio transmitter, it heralded the start of the space age.

REACHING ORBIT

Putting a satellite into orbit required new, more powerful rockets, such as the R-7 missile. Today, satellites such as the Insat 3 weather satellite are launched by towering multi-stage rockets. After the lower stages of the rocket have placed the satellite in an initial orbit, an upper stage motor fires to boost it to its final trajectory.

Streamlined cover called a "fairing" is lowered over satellite prior to launch

Loading the Insat 3D satellite, 2013

ANIMALS IN ORBIT

Some early satellites carried animals on board to test how spaceflight might affect humans. Launched in 1957, Sputnik 2 carried a small dog called Laika. She was sent into space with no hope of return, but most later animal astronauts wore specially made spacesuits and returned safely – including two chimpanzees sent into space by NASA in 1961.

POWERING SATELLITES

Early satellites relied on batteries that drained rapidly in the cold of space, giving them a limited lifetime. The USA's second satellite, Vanguard 1, was launched in 1958 and tested the idea of using solar panels to generate electricity from the Sun. Today, almost all satellites rely on solar power.

Solar "wing" is a 7.1-sq-m (76-sq-ft) array of three solar panels, generating up to 2,300 watts of power

Camera gathers information about Earth from above, in an activity known as "remote sensing"

Illustration of a Sentinel-2 remote-sensing satellite

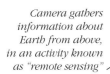

NASA's Phonesat 2.5 uses smartphone components powered by solar cells.

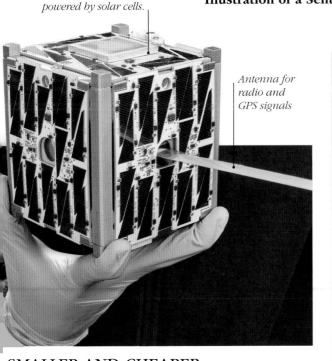

Antenna for radio and GPS signals

SMALLER AND CHEAPER

Advances in electronics have made satellites smaller, cheaper, and more robust. Miniature "cubesats" are built from standardized units that slot together, and weigh far less than conventional satellites but have many of the same abilities. They can be quickly built and their small size means they can be launched cheaply, "hitching a lift" on a larger satellite's launch.

SATELLITE ORBITS

Satellites follow different orbits depending on their function. Those that simply need to be above Earth's atmosphere – such as communication satellites (comsats) for satellite phones – use a low Earth orbit (LEO), 200–2,000 km (120–1,200 miles) up. Other comsats often use geostationary orbits, which means that they stay fixed above a point on the equator, while some specialized satellites use highly elliptical (elongated) orbits. Satellites observing Earth use polar orbits, which allow them to cover large areas of the rotating globe in close-up.

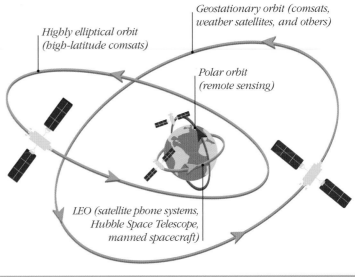

Highly elliptical orbit (high-latitude comsats)

Geostationary orbit (comsats, weather satellites, and others)

Polar orbit (remote sensing)

LEO (satellite phone systems, Hubble Space Telescope, manned spacecraft)

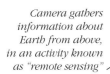

Watching over Earth

From their orbits high above Earth, dozens of satellites keep watch over our planet. They range from surveillance satellites photographing enemy territory to weather satellites providing accurate forecasts and remote-sensing satellites that use advanced technology to map Earth's geology, land use, and changing climate.

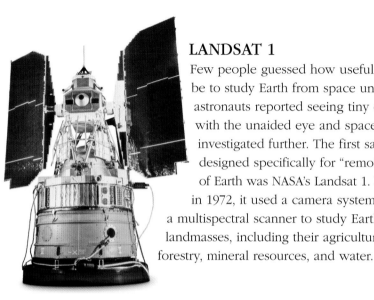

LANDSAT 1

Few people guessed how useful it would be to study Earth from space until early astronauts reported seeing tiny details with the unaided eye and space agencies investigated further. The first satellite designed specifically for "remote sensing" of Earth was NASA's Landsat 1. Launched in 1972, it used a camera system and a multispectral scanner to study Earth's landmasses, including their agriculture, forestry, mineral resources, and water.

WOW!

In 1967, American spy satellites monitoring nuclear tests discovered blasts of gamma rays from galaxies billions of light years away.

▼ **MONITORING GLACIERS**
False-colour and infrared imaging highlights ice-free ground (red) around the Petermann Glacier (blue) in Greenland.

SPIES IN THE SKY

Spy satellites from the late 1950s onwards paved the way for remote sensing. They used cameras with telephoto lenses to photograph enemy territory, returning reels of film in capsules that were parachuted back to Earth and snatched from mid-air by retrieval aircraft. When digital imaging improved to match the quality of film images, pictures could be sent by radio waves.

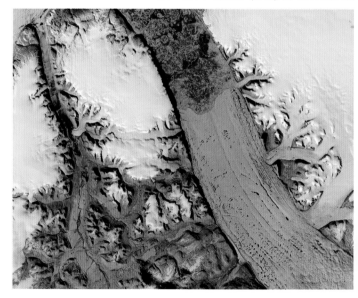

MULTISPECTRAL IMAGING

One of the most useful forms of remote sensing involves photographing the landscape through different coloured filters, known as multispectral imaging. The brightness of the ground at different wavelengths can reveal information ranging from soil conditions and crop growth to the location of mineral resources and underground water.

WEATHER WATCHERS

The first weather satellite, TIROS-1, was launched in 1960, and by the 1970s, satellites were placed in high orbits where they could photograph weather patterns across large areas of Earth. Today, remote-sensing instruments can monitor wind speeds, temperature, and other conditions in the atmosphere and oceans, measuring large-scale patterns and changes to Earth's overall climate.

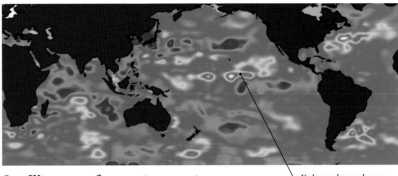

Satellite map of ocean temperatures during the 2017 El Niño climate event

False colour shows central Pacific Ocean waters are warmer than usual.

▼ RADAR COMPOSITE
Satellite radar can help map details of features in inaccessible areas, such as these Russian volcanoes, in any weather, day or night.

Colour-coding reveals elevation of the peaks: green is lowest, rising through yellow, red, and pink to white, the highest.

RADAR MAPPING

Modern radar satellites map Earth's surface with high precision by firing beams of radio waves at the surface and measuring their reflections. The time the signal takes to return indicates the distance to the reflecting surface, while changes to the reflected waves reveal other details such as surface texture and mineral composition. The German space agency's TanDEM-X mission used two satellites to create the most detailed three-dimensional map of Earth so far.

Twin TerraSAR-X and TanDEM-X satellites in polar orbit

Communication

Two everyday uses of satellite technology are telecommunications and navigation. The location of satellites high above Earth makes them ideal for sending and receiving radio signals between widely separated regions. Signals from a network of satellites also allow navigation systems to pinpoint our position on the ground and show us the best route to our destination.

BOUNCING RADIO SIGNALS

The simplest way of communicating via satellite is to use a reflector that simply bounces a beam of radio waves back to Earth. NASA's Echo 1A satellite of 1960 was an early test of this principle – a huge metallic balloon that orbited at heights of up to 1,600 km (994 miles) and provided a target for bouncing radio signals.

Total mass of satellite is just 180 kg (400 lb)

Inflated satellite is 30.4 m (100 ft) in diameter

Curved antennae receive satellite commands from Earth.

Solar cells generate 14 watts of power – less than a light bulb, but enough to run the satellite.

Equatorial antennae relay signals and keep Earth in view as the satellite spins.

SATELLITE NAVIGATION

Scientists quickly realized that radio signals from orbiting satellites could be used to pinpoint locations on Earth. An early test was the US Navy's TRANSIT system, launched in 1960. This used five separate satellites in low orbits that could provide a receiver on board a ship or submarine with their location once per hour.

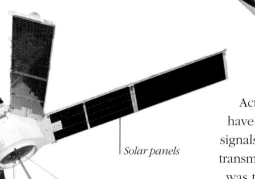

Solar panels

Antenna

Transit 5 satellite, part of the first satellite navigation system

COMMUNICATIONS SATELLITE

Active communications satellites have electronics on board to receive signals from one antenna on Earth and transmit them towards another. Telstar 1 was the first of these "comsats" to be launched. It entered low orbit a few hundred kilometres above Earth in July 1962, and carried the first television broadcasts across the Atlantic Ocean.

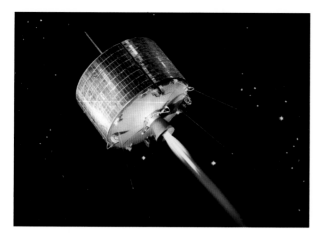

SYNCOM

Science-fiction author Arthur C Clarke realized in 1945 that satellites in high "geostationary" orbits would be able to relay global communication signals. They would hang in a fixed position over the equator, so antennae could bounce signals over a large area via a satellite without having to track it. The first satellite to put Clarke's idea into practice was Syncom 3, which relayed live television coverage of the 1964 Tokyo Olympics.

HOW GPS WORKS

The Global Positioning System (GPS) and similar navigation systems rely on networks of satellites in precisely known orbits. Each satellite carries a super-accurate atomic clock and transmits a time signal continuously. A computerized receiver measures how long it takes signals from different satellites to arrive, and uses that information to calculate the distance between itself and each of the satellites. Together, the measurements pinpoint the receiver's exact location.

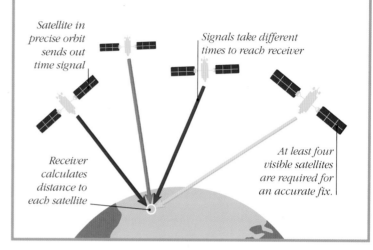

Satellite in precise orbit sends out time signal

Signals take different times to reach receiver

Receiver calculates distance to each satellite

At least four visible satellites are required for an accurate fix.

CALLS TO ORBIT

Most international telephone calls travel under the sea in optical fibre cables, avoiding the time delays introduced when relaying signals over a long distance through ground stations via comsats in high orbit. But what if you are in a remote location with no link to a mobile or landline network? Satellite telephones send signals directly to a satellite in low orbit, enabling communication from almost everywhere. They were originally designed for ships at sea, by the Inmarsat organization in the 1980s.

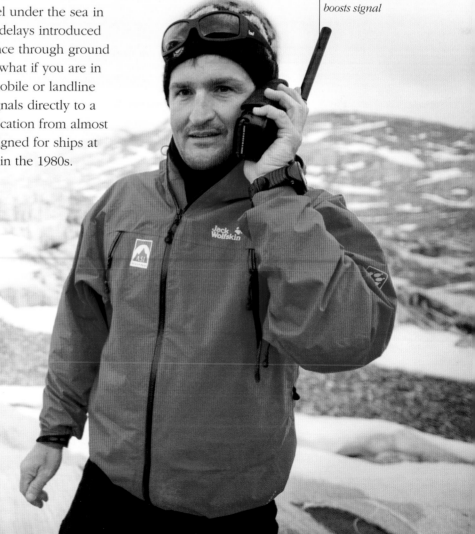

External antenna boosts signal

WOW!

GPS navigation receivers can pinpoint your location to within 5 m (16 ft) – Europe's Galileo system can do it to the nearest centimetre!

▶ **SATELLITE HANDSET**
Today, satellite phones are widely used by explorers and rescuers in isolated regions.

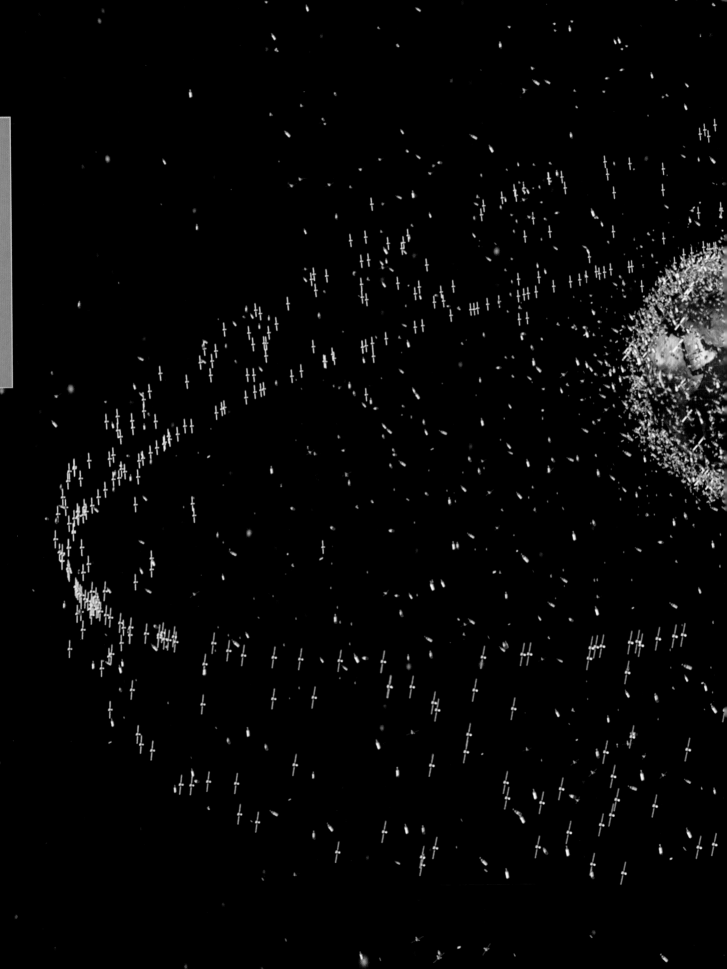

SPACE DEBRIS

Orbits around Earth have become crowded with space junk ranging from old rocket stages to tiny chips of paint. Travelling at high speed, this debris could be a major hazard for new satellites and spacecraft, so engineers are looking at how to remove the clutter before space becomes too dangerous to explore.

Rockets

A rocket is a propulsion device that works through the principle of action and reaction. It burns fuel to create expanding gases. As the gases escape at one end, the rest of the rocket is thrust forward in the opposite direction. First used as fireworks in China in the 13th century, rockets now produce enough thrust to launch satellites and spacecraft into orbit high above Earth.

PIONEER OF ROCKETRY

The Russian schoolteacher Konstantin Tsiolkovsky laid much of the groundwork for 20th-century rocketry in a series of books and scientific articles. He was the first to suggest using liquid fuel for increased thrust, and building rockets in stages. Although he built models to demonstrate his ideas, he was never able to put them into practice.

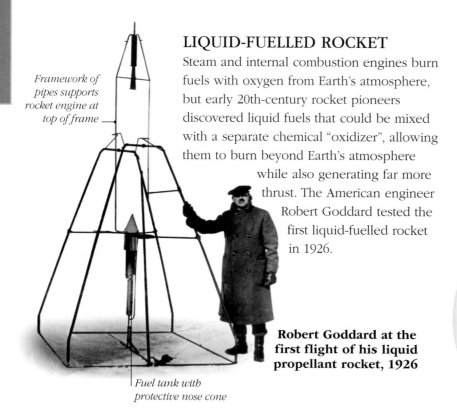

Framework of pipes supports rocket engine at top of frame

LIQUID-FUELLED ROCKET

Steam and internal combustion engines burn fuels with oxygen from Earth's atmosphere, but early 20th-century rocket pioneers discovered liquid fuels that could be mixed with a separate chemical "oxidizer", allowing them to burn beyond Earth's atmosphere while also generating far more thrust. The American engineer Robert Goddard tested the first liquid-fuelled rocket in 1926.

Robert Goddard at the first flight of his liquid propellant rocket, 1926

Fuel tank with protective nose cone

WOW!

The first object launched into space by a rocket was a small missile fired from the top of an adapted V-2 rocket by American engineers in 1949.

SPACE RACE

After World War II, Russia and the USA raced to develop powerful ballistic missiles – rockets that could carry weapons to high altitude and then drop back to Earth, delivering weapons across thousands of kilometres. Space scientists on both sides realized that missiles could also be used peacefully to launch satellites. The launch of the first satellite, Sputnik 1, on a converted Russian R-7 missile named *Semyorka* in 1957 began the "space race" that lasted almost two decades.

R-7 rocket carrying Sputnik 1, 1957

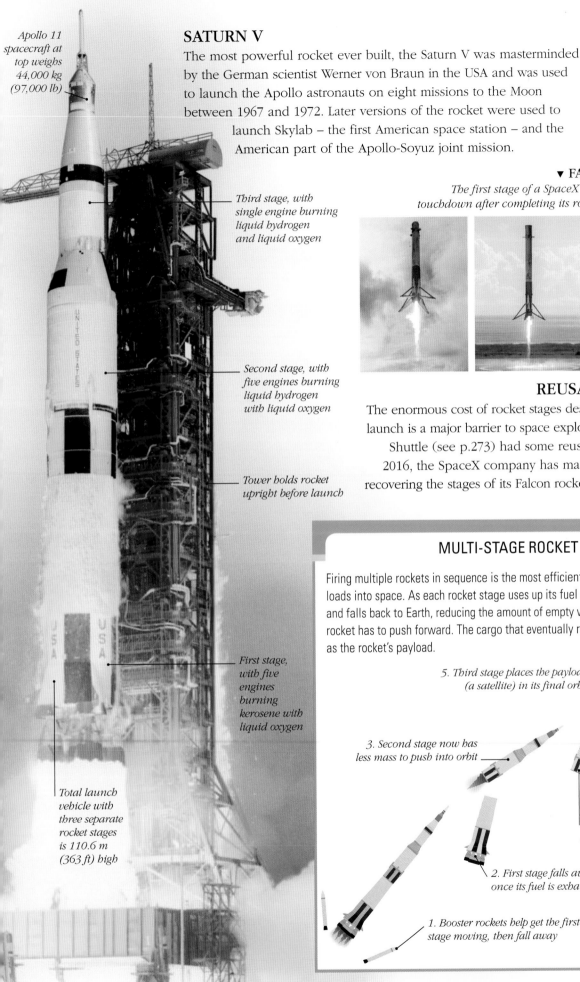

Apollo 11 spacecraft at top weighs 44,000 kg (97,000 lb)

SATURN V

The most powerful rocket ever built, the Saturn V was masterminded by the German scientist Werner von Braun in the USA and was used to launch the Apollo astronauts on eight missions to the Moon between 1967 and 1972. Later versions of the rocket were used to launch Skylab – the first American space station – and the American part of the Apollo-Soyuz joint mission.

Third stage, with single engine burning liquid hydrogen and liquid oxygen

Second stage, with five engines burning liquid hydrogen with liquid oxygen

Tower holds rocket upright before launch

First stage, with five engines burning kerosene with liquid oxygen

Total launch vehicle with three separate rocket stages is 110.6 m (363 ft) high

▼ FALCON 9 LANDING

The first stage of a SpaceX rocket makes a vertical touchdown after completing its role in a satellite launch.

REUSABLE ROCKETS

The enormous cost of rocket stages destroyed or lost during launch is a major barrier to space exploration. NASA's Space Shuttle (see p.273) had some reusable elements. Since 2016, the SpaceX company has made huge advances in recovering the stages of its Falcon rocket for future missions.

MULTI-STAGE ROCKET

Firing multiple rockets in sequence is the most efficient way to get heavy loads into space. As each rocket stage uses up its fuel supply, it detaches and falls back to Earth, reducing the amount of empty weight the rest of the rocket has to push forward. The cargo that eventually reaches orbit is known as the rocket's payload.

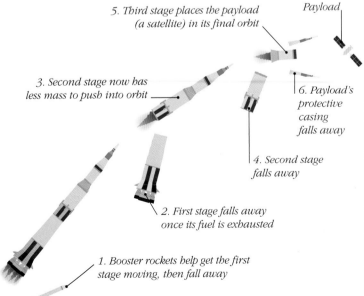

5. Third stage places the payload (a satellite) in its final orbit

Payload

3. Second stage now has less mass to push into orbit

6. Payload's protective casing falls away

4. Second stage falls away

2. First stage falls away once its fuel is exhausted

1. Booster rockets help get the first stage moving, then fall away

Rocket race

Rockets come in a wide variety of shapes and sizes, from fireworks to battlefield weapons and long-range missiles. However, the largest and most powerful rockets are those used to launch satellites and manned spacecraft into orbit and beyond. Although the first experiments with liquid-fuel rockets took place in the 1920s, it took military interest in rockets to make spaceflight a reality.

Military rockets

- **What?** V-2 rocket
- **Who?** Werner von Braun
- **Where and when?** Germany, 1942

In the 1930s, the development of rockets was mostly confined to amateur engineers. In Germany, however, a team led by Werner von Braun was ordered to develop them for the Nazi war effort. The result was the V-2 long-range missile. Its steering and guidance systems were a huge technical advance for rocketry, and in 1942, it became the first man-made object to enter space – but the V-2 was also a terrible weapon of war, responsible for an estimated 9,000 deaths by the end of World War II in 1945.

Launch of the Explorer satellite on Juno 1

Satellite launchers

- **What?** Juno I
- **Who?** Werner von Braun
- **Where and when?** USA, 1958

After the Russians' launch of Sputnik 1 into orbit in 1957, American scientists were further demoralized by the explosion of their Vanguard rocket. Anxious to catch up, they turned to Werner von Braun, who was now working for the US Army. Within a month, his team launched the Explorer 1 satellite on a missile adapted into a four-stage rocket called Juno 1.

Space workhorse

- **What?** Soyuz rocket
- **Who?** OKB-1 design bureau
- **Where and when?**
  Russia, 1966

The most successful rocket in the world today is the Soyuz. In use since 1966 for manned and unmanned launches, Soyuz has flown more than 1,700 times, with relatively few failures. Since the retirement of the Space Shuttle, Soyuz has been the only means of sending astronauts to the International Space Station.

▶ **SOYUZ TMA-15**
Blasting off in 2009, this Soyuz rocket took three astronauts to the International Space Station to begin a six-month stay in space.

The lower stage consists of four booster rockets clustered around the core rocket.

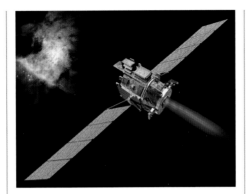

Ion engines

- **What?** Deep Space 1
- **Who?** NASA
- **Where and when?** USA, 1998

Most rockets burn fuel explosively to generate thrust and overcome gravity. Ion engines use electricity from solar cells to eject a stream of charged particles (ions). The thrust from an ion engine is tiny, but operating over months rather than seconds they can achieve tremendous speeds. NASA first trialled ion propulsion on its robotic space probe, Deep Space 1.

Future rockets

- **What?** SLS "Block 1"
- **Who?** NASA
- **Where and when?** USA, 2019 (planned)

Since its decision to retire the Space Shuttle in 2011, NASA has been developing the most powerful rocket ever built. The Space Launch System (SLS) should pave the way for new crewed missions to the Moon, Mars, and beyond. Commercial companies such as SpaceX and Blue Origin have equally ambitious plans.

SLS will be taller than the Statue of Liberty and produce 30 times more thrust than a 747 jet.

Illustration of Space Launch System in flight

Orion crew vehicle

Rocket-powered aircraft

- **What?** SpaceShipOne
- **Who?** Burt Rutan, Scaled Composites LLC
- **Where and when?** USA, 2004

Carrier aircraft have transported small rocket-powered vehicles for release at high altitude since the 1950s. The American engineer Burt Rutan's SpaceShipOne was the world's first private, rocket-powered, manned spaceship. Adopted by Virgin Galactic, its wing design allows it to float slowly back to Earth after briefly reaching space without going into orbit around Earth.

SpaceShipOne, carried by twin-hulled plane

Manned spaceflight

Putting humans into space and bringing them back alive is the ultimate spaceflight challenge. Crewed spacecraft are heavier and more complex than most satellites, since they must carry equipment to keep astronauts alive for the duration of their missions, and protect them during the potentially hazardous return to Earth.

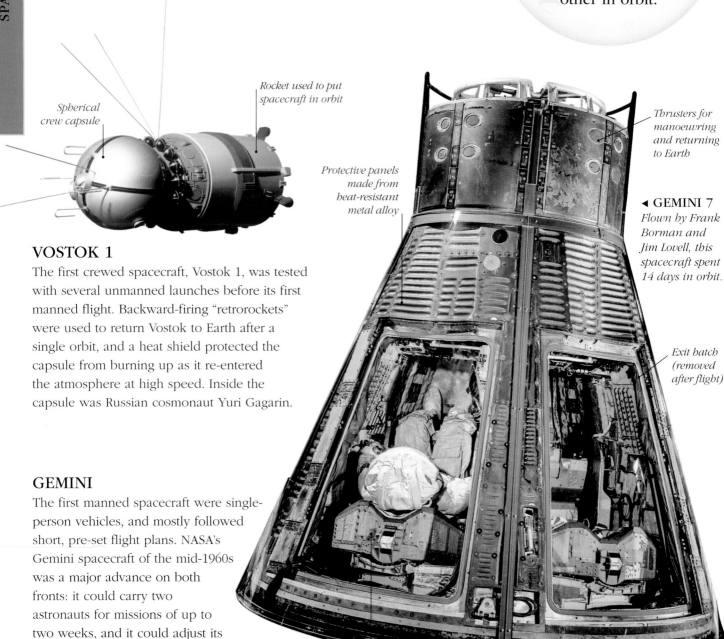

WOW!

The crews of Gemini 6A and Gemini 7 steered their spacecraft to within 30 cm (12 in) of each other in orbit.

Rocket used to put spacecraft in orbit

Spherical crew capsule

Thrusters for manoeuvring and returning to Earth

Protective panels made from heat-resistant metal alloy

◄ **GEMINI 7**
Flown by Frank Borman and Jim Lovell, this spacecraft spent 14 days in orbit.

Exit hatch (removed after flight)

VOSTOK 1

The first crewed spacecraft, Vostok 1, was tested with several unmanned launches before its first manned flight. Backward-firing "retrorockets" were used to return Vostok to Earth after a single orbit, and a heat shield protected the capsule from burning up as it re-entered the atmosphere at high speed. Inside the capsule was Russian cosmonaut Yuri Gagarin.

GEMINI

The first manned spacecraft were single-person vehicles, and mostly followed short, pre-set flight plans. NASA's Gemini spacecraft of the mid-1960s was a major advance on both fronts: it could carry two astronauts for missions of up to two weeks, and it could adjust its orbit with a system of thrusters – small rockets capable of pushing the spacecraft in various directions.

Ejector seats for use in emergencies

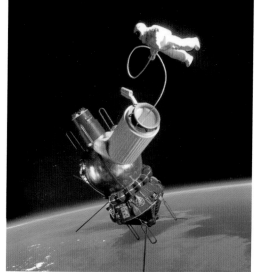

Illustration of Leonov's first spacewalk

◄ LAUNCH OF SPACE SHUTTLE ATLANTIS ON STS-129 MISSION
One of five operational orbiters, Atlantis flew 33 missions, including this one to the International Space Station in 2009.

SPACEPLANE TO ORBIT

The Space Shuttle, flown by NASA from 1981 to 2011, took a totally new approach to spaceflight. Crews of up to seven flew aboard a plane-like orbiter spacecraft, with a large cabin and cargo hold. Its engines drew fuel from a huge tank during launch. On reaching orbit, the fuel tank fell away and the spacecraft continued on its journey. At the end of its mission, it glided back to Earth like a giant paper plane and could then be reused on other missions.

SPACE WALKERS

Early astronauts wore flight suits and helmets for emergencies, but did not expect to leave their capsules. In March 1965, Voskhod 2 cosmonaut Alexei Leonov wore a specially designed suit to carry out the first walk in space. A few months later, astronaut Ed White made the first American spacewalk, steering himself with a gun-like personal thruster.

The crew module is 5 m (16.4 ft) in diameter and 3 m (10 ft) long.

Orion capsule

Solar panels provide power during a mission.

Buzz Aldrin's footprint on the Moon, photographed on the Apollo 11 mission

MISSION TO THE MOON

The Apollo Moon missions of the late 1960s used a complex three-part spacecraft. An orbiting command module carrying three astronauts was attached to a service module that carried supplies for missions of up to 12 days, while a lunar module carried two of the astronauts from the command module to the Moon's surface and back. In July 1969, Apollo 11's Neil Armstrong and Buzz Aldrin became the first men to set foot on the Moon.

FUTURE MISSIONS

Scheduled to fly in the 2020s, NASA's Orion spacecraft features an Apollo-like craft with a conical crew module attached to a cylindrical service module. However, Orion is far larger, and the reusable crew module will be able to carry crews of four to six on missions of up to six months in order to explore Mars and asteroids, conduct experiments, and service the International Space Station.

Manned missions

In the course of six decades, the idea of human spaceflight has gone from the unthinkable to the almost routine (though still inevitably risky). So far more than 550 people have flown into space, the vast majority of them aboard either the USA's Space Shuttle or Russia's Soyuz spacecraft. In future decades, tourism may see at least brief trips into space become commonplace.

WOW!

In 1961, when President Kennedy committed the USA to reaching the Moon by the end of the decade, NASA had just 15 minutes of human spaceflight experience.

Americans into orbit

- **What?** Mercury program
- **Who?** Seven US astronauts (six of whom flew on Mercury missions)
- **Where and when?** USA, 1958–1963

Hampered by less powerful rockets, NASA's Mercury programme lagged behind the Russians. The first American in space, Alan Shepard, could only make a "hop" into space that failed to reach orbit in May 1961. In February 1962, the Atlas rocket was ready to take John Glenn into orbit aboard the Mercury capsule Friendship 7.

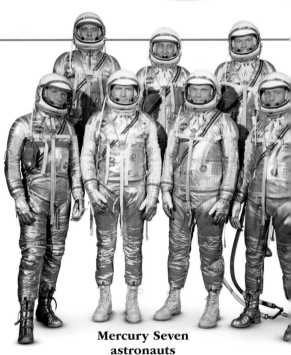

Mercury Seven astronauts

The first man in space

- **What?** Vostok 1
- **Who?** Yuri Gagarin
- **Where and when?** Russia, 1961

Until the 1950s, no one knew what effect spaceflight might have on a human being. Before risking a cosmonaut, Russia had to prove that it was possible to survive by launching several spacecraft with dogs on board. Yuri Gagarin's first record-breaking flight was limited to a single orbit of the Earth lasting 108 minutes. In 1963, the first woman in space, Valentina Tereshkova, orbited Earth 48 times for more than 70 hours in Vostok 6.

A Soyuz capsule in 2015, docked to the International Space Station

Soyuz modules

- **What?** Soyuz spacecraft
- **Who?** OKB-1 design bureau/Energia Corp.
- **Where and when?** Russia, 1967–present

First launched in 1967 (on a disastrous mission that killed its pilot), the Soyuz spacecraft was nevertheless a major advance. It was the first with three modules, including specialized capsules for working in orbit and returning to Earth. Thanks to several generations of updates, it has been the backbone of the Russian space programme.

▼ MOON BUGGY
NASA's lunar rover could carry two astronauts and their rock samples at speeds of up to 18.6 km/h (11.5 mph).

Exploring the Moon

- **What?** Apollo program
- **Who?** NASA
- **Where and when?** USA, 1968–1972

In July 1969, Apollo 11 was the first of eight historic missions that landed astronauts on the Moon. The Apollo Moon landings presented many new challenges for NASA. The 12 astronauts who walked on the Moon wore special spacesuits designed to supply them with oxygen, protect them from the hazards of the lunar surface, and allow them to set up scientific instruments and collect rock samples. Later Apollo missions carried Lunar Roving Vehicles (LRVs) so that astronauts could explore a far greater area.

Historic handshake

- **What?** Apollo-Soyuz Test Project
- **Who?** Apollo/Soyuz 19
- **Where and when?** USA/Russia, 1975

In July 1975, Apollo and Soyuz spacecraft met in orbit and used a special docking module to link the two incompatible systems. This marked the end of the space race between the USA and Russia, but it was not until the 1990s that rendezvous between the Space Shuttle and the Mir space station became regular events.

Commanders of Apollo and Soyuz spacecraft shake hands in space

The first space tourist

- **What?** ISS EP-1 mission
- **Who?** Dennis Tito
- **Where and when?** Russia, 2001

Faced with a cash shortage in the late 1990s, the Russian space agency offered to take paying passengers to orbit. The first, American millionaire Dennis Tito, visited the International Space Station in 2001. Several other tourists flew in the 2000s, but plans for widespread space travel have now been left to commercial promoters.

Dennis Tito (middle)

Space stations

Space stations allow astronauts to live and work in orbit for long periods of time. From simple laboratories made from adapted rocket casings, they have grown into permanent communities of scientists who carry out experiments, manufacture materials, observe Earth, and study the effects of long-duration spaceflight on the human body.

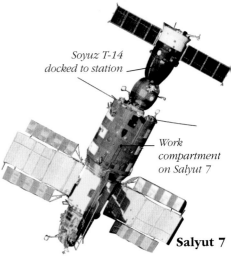

Soyuz T-14 docked to station

Work compartment on Salyut 7

Salyut 7

Advanced Salyuts

- **What?** Salyut 6 and 7
- **Who?** Soviet Space Agency
- **Where and when?** Russia, 1982–1991

The Salyut 6 and 7 space stations had a docking port at both ends, allowing a new crew to arrive before the old one departed. Salyut 7 also tested the idea of "hard docking" – extending the working area of the station by permanently attaching an unmanned tug spacecraft to one end.

Salyut 1

- **What?** Salyut 1
- **Who?** Soviet Space Agency
- **Where and when?** Russia, 1971

The first space station, Salyut 1, was launched by Russia in 1971. This simple cylindrical laboratory had a docking port for a Soyuz spacecraft, and was visited by the three-man crew of Soyuz 11 for 23 days in June 1971 – the longest spaceflight up to that time. However, the station was abandoned after the Soyuz 11 crew died in an accident during their return to Earth.

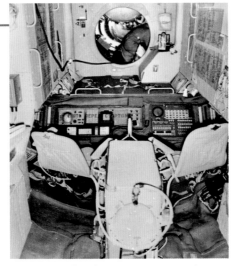

Interior of Salyut 1 space station

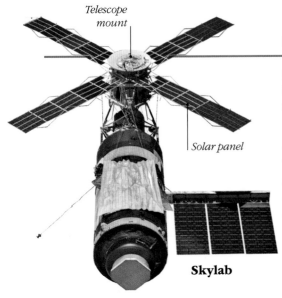

Telescope mount

Solar panel

Skylab

Skylab

- **What?** Skylab
- **Who?** NASA
- **Where and when?** USA, crewed 1973–1974

Skylab, the first American space station, was constructed from an empty Saturn rocket stage and hosted three crews during nine months of operation. It carried an ultraviolet telescope for observing the Sun, as well as equipment modules for carrying out a range of experiments into life and chemistry in the weightless environment of space.

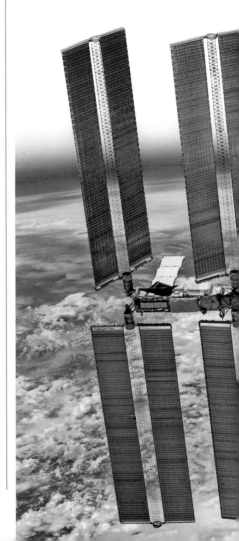

Modular space station

- **What?** Mir
- **Who?** Energia
- **Where and when?** Russia, 1986–2001

A significant advance, Russia's Mir station was built in orbit by "hard docking" several distinct units. The core was launched in February 1986, followed by modules for scientific research and power generation, and a new docking port to allow visits by NASA's Space Shuttle. In 1995, Valeri Polyakov completed 437 days on board Mir – the longest continuous stay in space.

Core module with five others attached

Mir space station as viewed from the Space Shuttle Endeavour

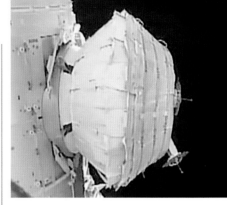

Inflatable modules

- **What?** BEAM
- **Who?** Bigelow Aerospace
- **Where and when?** USA, 2016

The Bigelow Expandable Activity Module (BEAM) is an inflatable, lightweight habitat that was attached to the ISS in 2016. It keeps its shape because of air pressure inside it. Experiments are being carried out to test conditions on board, and engineers hope BEAM could pave the way for other inflatable modules in the future.

The International Space Station

- **What?** International Space Station
- **Who?** NASA, Roskosmos, ESA
- **Where and when?** International, launched 1998

Built in segments since 1998 and continuously manned since 2000, the International Space Station (ISS) is an ambitious collaboration with contributions from the USA, Russia, Europe, Brazil, Japan, and elsewhere. Finally completed in 2011, it is expected to remain in operation until at least 2028.

Solar panels

▼ ISS MODULES
The ISS's typical crew of six astronauts live and work in a series of connected modules with a total volume similar to that of a Boeing 747 airliner.

*Backpack containing
life-support systems*

*Pressure
helmet with
protective visor*

Living in space

Keeping astronauts fit and healthy as spaceflights have become longer and more complex is a huge challenge, and has required considerable inventiveness. And not only do astronauts have to live and work in cramped conditions, they also have to be kept safe when they leave their spacecraft.

*Controls for
life-support systems*

*Gloves lock
onto suit
at wrists*

*Main suit in
two parts
that join
at waist*

*White material
reflects sunlight
and heat*

*Layered fabrics
trap air and
protect wearer*

SPACE CLOTHES

The first astronauts wore protective spacesuits throughout their missions but, by the mid-1960s, safety improvements and larger spacecraft allowed them to spend most of their time in more comfortable flight suits. By the 1990s, the spacesuits worn by NASA astronauts for working outside the Space Shuttle (left) had developed into self-contained personal spacecraft.

WOW!

All waste water on the ISS is recycled by passing through a series of filters and chemical reactions. It ends up cleaner than our drinking water on Earth.

*Astronaut Cady Coleman
washes her hair with a
water-saving shampoo.*

KEEPING FIT

As missions have lengthened from mere days to months, it's become more important to keep astronauts in shape for their return to Earth. Weightless conditions in zero-gravity space weaken muscles and bones, so astronauts take a variety of supplements and exercise regularly, often using elastic straps to mimic the pull of gravity.

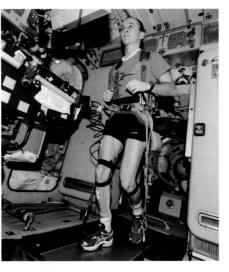

KEEPING CLEAN

Personal hygiene in space can be a problem – water is too precious to waste and, if it is sprayed around, it forms weightless drops that interfere with delicate electronic systems on board. Instead of showers, astronauts use small pouches of liquid soap, water, and "no rinse" shampoos.

GROWING PLANTS

Long missions beyond Earth orbit will need to be self-sufficient, so space agencies are carrying out experiments to understand how exposure to space conditions affects plants and their seeds. Crops grown in water and nutrients (hydroponics) or in the soil of other planets could one day provide food and help to refresh air supplies.

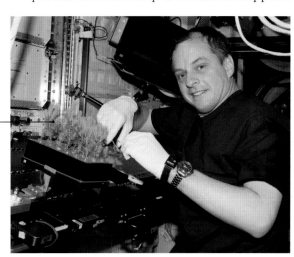

Seedlings can grow well even with very little gravity in space.

Astronaut T J Creamer tends tree seedlings on the ISS

EATING DINNER

Food arrives at the ISS on unmanned cargo spacecraft, usually in sealed packs that can be rehydrated from water valves in the station's service module. Ovens reheat canned or packet food, but their temperature is limited for safety reasons.

SPACE

LIFE ON MARS

Future explorers on Mars will face unique challenges, and engineers are already trialling solutions on Earth. Astronauts will need lightweight, flexible spacesuits to work in Martian gravity. They will also have to be protected from dangerous radiation, perhaps by living and working mostly in underground habitats.

FAST FACTS

■ The changing alignments of the planets as they orbit the Sun mean that crewed missions to Mars would have to wait for about three years before Earth was close enough for them to return home.

■ Russian cosmonauts set an unbroken series of records for long-duration spaceflight aboard the Mir space station in the 1990s.

▲ SIMULATING LIFE ON MARS
American researchers in the Utah desert wear prototype spacesuits and practise procedures for a future exploration mission on the surface of Mars.

Space agencies

Space agencies have been at the forefront of space exploration and technological innovation since the dawn of the space age in the 1950s. These government or internationally funded organizations set long-term goals, develop the equipment needed (often alongside commercial businesses), train astronauts, manage the missions, and encourage new ways of using space and space technology.

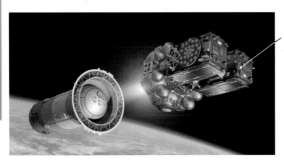

Illustration of ESA's two Galileo navigation satellites detaching from Soyuz upper stage in 2014

EUROPE'S SPACE AGENCY

The European Space Agency (ESA) was founded in 1975 from a merger of two earlier organizations. Its Ariane rocket series is now on its sixth generation, and the agency has launched increasingly ambitious space probes and satellites, as well as contributing to the International Space Station.

WHAT IS NASA?

The US National Aeronautics and Space Administration (NASA) was founded in 1958 and given overarching control of many different laboratories and facilities working on the American space programme. Its success in putting Apollo astronauts on the Moon by 1969 encouraged other countries to create their own agencies.

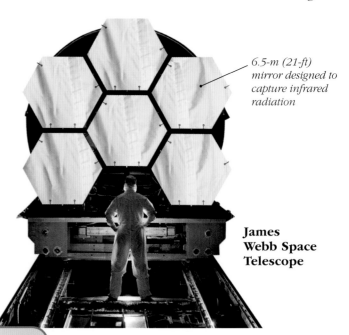

6.5-m (21-ft) mirror designed to capture infrared radiation

James Webb Space Telescope

WORKING TOGETHER

Space agencies frequently collaborate to pool funding and expertise for major projects. ESA has contributed to the NASA-led Hubble and James Webb Space Telescopes, while Japan's JAXA and Russia's Roskosmos agencies are also frequent NASA partners.

SPACE AGENCIES TIMELINE

1958	1959	1961	
NASA is established in order to counter the Russian lead in satellite and space technology.	NASA launches its first Pioneer space probes into near-Earth space. Throughout the 1960s, space probe missions become more ambitious.	US president John F Kennedy (right) tasks NASA with landing a crewed mission on the Moon, a goal which is achieved in July 1969.	

▲ **TRAINING FOR SPACE**
Since the 1960s, NASA has used huge water tanks to mimic the weightlessness of space, mostly at the agency's Johnson Space Center in Texas.

1979	1992	2003	2014
ESA debuts its Ariane 1 rocket, and soon becomes a major launch provider for the commercial satellite industry.	Russia establishes Roskosmos, an agency that unites the many different design bureaus of the former Soviet space programme.	Japan's space agencies unite as the Japanese Aerospace Exploration Agency (JAXA). Other national space agencies exist in India (1969), Canada (1989), and China (1993).	The Indian Space Research Organization (ISRO) reaches Mars on its first attempt, with its Mangalyaan space probe.

Space technology for Earth

Although some people see space exploration as purely scientific research or even a waste of money, in reality space technology has transformed all our lives. Aside from the many benefits brought by satellites, the challenge of getting humans into space and returning them safely to Earth has inspired countless engineers to make advances that have later found applications on Earth.

Remains of old stone fort at Shisr, Oman.

SATELLITE ARCHAEOLOGY

Remote sensing has found a huge range of uses (see pp.262–263), but one of the most surprising is in archaeology. Researchers using satellite photos can identify ancient tracks and disturbances that reveal the presence of buried ruins such as a lost city, nicknamed the Atlantis of the Sands, at Shisr in Oman.

CMOS sensor

DIGITAL IMAGING

Early spaceprobes and satellites used either television cameras or photographic film to capture images. In the early 1990s, NASA scientist Eric Fossum invented an improved sensor to capture images as digital electronic data. These CMOS sensors are now widely used in mobile phones, digital cameras, and other imaging systems.

Digital camera with lens removed

SPACE BLANKETS

The insulating foil blankets that are provided after endurance races and to keep people warm in disaster areas originated from insulation used on the Apollo lunar landing module. Made by applying a thin aluminium coating to a plastic film, they reflect infrared radiation and trap heat close to the wearer's body.

FREEZE-DRIED FOOD

Although the process of freeze-drying to preserve food was invented in the 1930s, its unique benefits were discovered by NASA scientists looking at methods for storing food on long-duration Apollo spaceflights. Freeze-drying removes water but preserves vitamins, minerals, and other nutrients that are restored when the meal is rehydrated.

Fruit retains its appetizing colour and flavour

Freeze-dried strawberries

WOW!

According to some estimates, each dollar invested in the US space programme results in up to US$10 of wider long-term benefits.

FIRE SAFETY

Fire is one of the deadliest hazards for spacecraft and their crews, and space agencies such as NASA have made some important breakthroughs in fire safety. Firefighters use air bottles, face masks, and other equipment made from a heat-resistant aluminium composite that was first developed for use in rocket casings, and materials based on Apollo spacecraft heat shields are used to insulate structural steel supports in high-rise buildings.

Lightweight, heat-resistant alloys reduce weight of equipment.

Heat-resistant textiles based on astronaut flight suits

Robotic probes

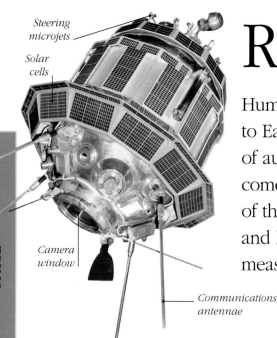

Steering
microjets

Solar
cells

SPACE

Camera
window

Communications
antennae

Human exploration of space has so far been limited
to Earth orbit, but space agencies have sent dozens
of automated space probes to explore planets, moons,
comets, and asteroids. Flyby missions offer a brief glimpse
of these objects, orbiters carry out more detailed surveys,
and landers and rovers touch down on the surface to
measure conditions and analyse rocks.

LUNA 3

Our closest neighbour in space, the Moon
was an obvious target for early exploration.
The first successful probe, the Russian-built
Luna 3, flew past in October 1959 and sent
back the first pictures of the far side of the
Moon, which permanently faces away from
Earth. Throughout the 1960s, both the USA
and Russia sent a variety of orbiters and
landers to investigate further.

**Illustration of
Venera 9 on Venus**

THE VENERA MISSIONS

Venus is the nearest planet to Earth,
but it proved a huge challenge to
space probes. Several American and
Russian probes made fleeting flybys
or entered orbit, but early Russian
landers were destroyed in Venus's
hostile atmosphere. In 1975, Russia's
heavily armoured Venera 9 finally
sent back the first picture of the
volcanic landscape.

VOYAGER GRAVITY ASSIST

Even at high speeds, reaching the distant outer planets takes
years. Fortunately, NASA engineers discovered a way of
shortening journey times by using the gravity of other planets
as a "slingshot" in a manoeuvre known as gravity assist. This
enabled them to send two Voyager space probes on a tour of
the outer Solar System in the 1970s and 1980s.

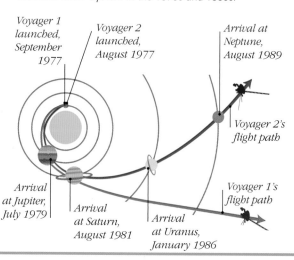

Voyager 1
launched,
September
1977

Voyager 2
launched,
August 1977

Arrival at
Neptune,
August 1989

Voyager 2's
flight path

Arrival
at Jupiter,
July 1979

Arrival
at Saturn,
August 1981

Arrival
at Uranus,
January 1986

Voyager 1's
flight path

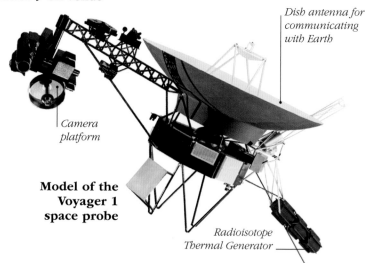

Dish antenna for
communicating
with Earth

Camera
platform

**Model of the
Voyager 1
space probe**

Radioisotope
Thermal Generator

POWER WITHOUT THE SUN

Probes in the inner Solar System can use solar panels to
make electricity, but missions venturing any further out from
the Sun than Mars need an alternative power supply. To
solve the problem, NASA developed Radioisotope Thermal
Generators (RTGs). These nuclear power supplies can
produce electricity by harnessing the gentle heat emitted
by small amounts of radioactive plutonium.

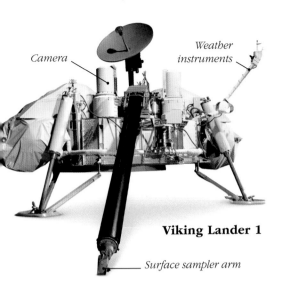

Camera

Weather instruments

Viking Lander 1

Surface sampler arm

MARTIAN ROVERS

Since 1997, NASA has sent a series of increasingly ambitious robot rovers to explore Mars, investigating its atmosphere and geology and looking for signs of ancient life and water. Driving conditions on the rocky, dusty surface can be treacherous, and the limited speed of radio signals makes it difficult to direct the vehicles from mission control on Earth. So, recent rovers use artificial intelligence systems to make basic decisions – such as avoiding obstacles and recognizing which types of rock to study – without human intervention.

LANDERS ON MARS

Mars is easier to reach than most other planets, but landing in its thin atmosphere is difficult. In 1976, NASA's pair of Viking orbiters put two landers on the surface, using parachutes and precisely fired retrorockets to control their descent. While the orbiters mapped Mars from space, the landers relayed the first images and data from the ground.

Illustration of Galileo and Jupiter

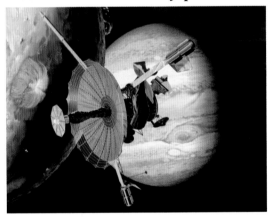

PROBING THE GIANTS

Following its first brief flybys of the giant outer planets, NASA has sent two orbiters to investigate Jupiter, and one to Saturn. Arriving at Jupiter in 1995, Galileo released a smaller probe that parachuted into the giant planet's atmosphere. The Cassini mission carried a European-built lander that touched down on Saturn's giant moon Titan in 2005.

▶ **CURIOSITY ON MARS**

NASA's car-sized, solar-powered Curiosity rover touched down on Mars in August 2012 and has since driven more than 18 km (11.2 miles).

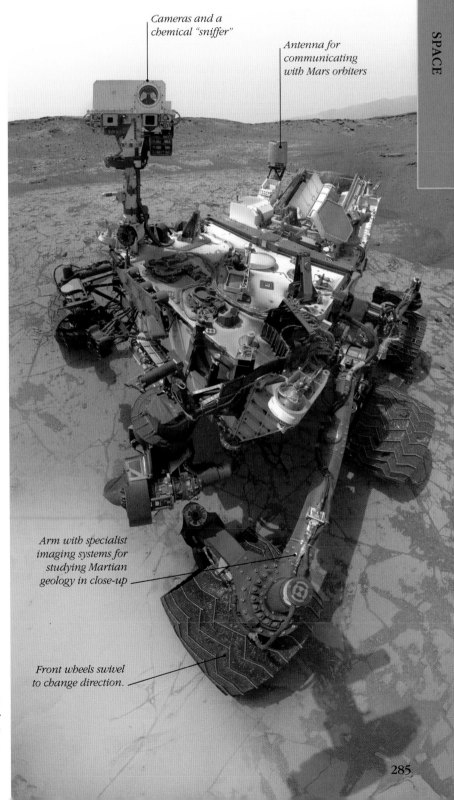

Cameras and a chemical "sniffer"

Antenna for communicating with Mars orbiters

Arm with specialist imaging systems for studying Martian geology in close-up

Front wheels swivel to change direction.

Pushing the boundaries

Since the late 1950s, dozens of robot probes have ventured to all parts of the Solar System. Early missions concentrated on our Moon in preparation for the manned Apollo landings. Our first survey of the major planets was completed by the late 1980s, and since then probes have become ever more complex and ambitious.

Orbiting Mars

- **What?** Mariner 9
- **Who?** NASA
- **Where and when?** USA, launched 1971

After early flybys of both Venus and Mars in the 1960s, Mariner 9 became the first spacecraft to orbit another planet when it arrived at Mars in November 1971. When the probe arrived, a planet-wide dust storm was in progress, but after that cleared, the images sent back transformed our understanding of the Red Planet.

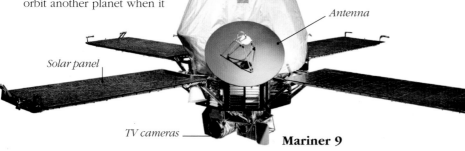

Solar panel

Antenna

TV cameras

Mariner 9

Asteroid explorers

- **What?** NEAR Shoemaker
- **Who?** NASA
- **Where and when?** USA, launched 1996

After several early flybys of small asteroids, NASA's Near Earth Asteroid Rendezvous Shoemaker (NEAR Shoemaker) probe spent a year orbiting the near-Earth asteroid Eros in 2000–2001, before eventually touching down on the asteroid's surface. More recently, a NASA mission called Dawn has investigated the Solar System's two largest asteroids, Ceres and Vesta.

Illustration of NEAR Shoemaker orbiting Eros

Illustration of Giotto and Halley's Comet

Studying Halley's Comet

- **What?** Giotto
- **Who?** ESA
- **Where and when?** Europe, launched 1985

In the mid-1980s, space agencies launched probes to intercept Halley's Comet as it flew past the Sun for the first time in 76 years. Russia, Japan, and Europe all took part. Launched in French Guiana, the European Space Agency's Giotto probe flew within 596 km (370 miles) of the comet's icy nucleus.

WOW!

Currently travelling through space at a distance of 20.9 billion km (13 billion miles) from Earth, Voyager 1 is the most distant man-made object ever launched.

Orbiting Saturn

- **What?** Cassini/Huygens
- **Who?** NASA/ESA
- **Where and when?** USA/Europe, launched 1997

Following its early flybys, NASA launched orbiter probes to the giant planets Jupiter and Saturn. The bus-sized Cassini reached Saturn in 2004. It spent more than a decade investigating the planet and its rings and moons. It also released a European-built lander called Huygens that touched down on Saturn's mysterious giant moon, Titan.

Illustration of Philae on Comet 67P

Landing on a comet

- **What?** Rosetta/Philae
- **Who?** ESA
- **Where and when?** Europe, launched 2004

The European Rosetta probe took more than a decade to reach its target, a comet known as 67P, before orbiting it for some two years. Shortly after arrival, Rosetta released a small lander called Philae, which unfortunately bounced into a deeply shadowed area where it could not charge its solar cells. However, at the end of the mission, Rosetta itself was steered to a successful landing.

Racing to Pluto

- **What?** New Horizons
- **Who?** NASA
- **Where and when?** USA, launched 2006

Beyond the planets, the outer Solar System is encircled by a ring of small icy objects, known as the Kuiper Belt. In 2006, NASA launched a high-speed probe to Pluto, one of the largest and closest of these worlds. It became the fastest object to leave Earth orbit, and after a slingshot (see p.284) at Jupiter, it flew past Pluto in July 2015, before continuing onwards to new targets.

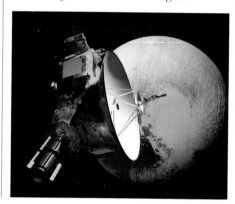

Close-up on Jupiter

- **What?** Juno
- **Who?** NASA
- **Where and when?** USA, launched 2011

Juno is NASA's latest Jupiter orbiter. Part of NASA's New Frontiers programme, it is designed to study the giant planet in greater detail than ever before. On arrival in 2016, Juno entered a polar orbit that delivers views of Jupiter's high latitudes for the first time. Unlike previous Jupiter missions, the probe is solar powered, with three huge "wings" to harvest sunlight.

FAST FACTS

- Unlike satellites, space probes need sufficient speed to escape Earth's gravity entirely – launch must achieve an "escape velocity" of 11.2 km/s (7 miles per second).
- Voyagers 1 and 2 both carry a "golden record" containing greetings in various languages, music, birdsong, and other sounds from life on Earth for future spacefaring civilizations to play.

Bands of clouds and storms swirl across Jupiter's southern hemisphere in this view from Juno.

Ingenious inventors

The background to how inventors came up with their ingenious ideas is often fascinating and unexpected. Here are the stories of some very well-known inventors, alongside others whose names are less familiar – though you may well know their inventions!

ANDERSON, MARY (1866–1953)

In 1903, a snowy journey on a streetcar (tram) inspired American inventor Anderson to sketch out an idea for a windscreen wiper. At the time, drivers had to lean out of the window and clear their windscreens by hand. Her device, made from wood with rubber blades, was controlled by a handle inside the vehicle. Anderson never found a backer for her invention, but in later decades others copied the idea and wipers became a standard feature on most vehicles.

BABBAGE, CHARLES (1791–1871)

This English mathematician and mechanical engineer is often called the "father of the computer". Babbage worked on various prototypes of his mathematical machines, including the Difference Engine of 1821, used for compiling mathematical tables, and later, the Analytical Engine, which even had a form of memory. His machines were not completed in his lifetime, but his contribution to computer science is never forgotten.

BERNERS-LEE, TIM (1955–)

Berners-Lee is recognized as the inventor of the World Wide Web. The British software engineer and computer scientist first came up with the idea of people around the world sharing information in 1980, and by 1989, he had developed the global information system, or Web. As director of the Web standards agency, the World Wide Web Foundation, Berners-Lee says: "It has taken all of us to build the Web we have, and now it is up to all of us to build the Web we want – for everyone."

BRUNEL, ISAMBARD KINGDOM (1806–1859)

Brunel is credited as one of the most significant Britons of all time for his contribution to civil and mechanical engineering. The network of tracks and bridges he built for the Great Western Railway and pioneering work on steamships such as the SS *Great Britain*, launched in 1843 (see p.106), are testament to his genius.

COOPER, MARTIN (1928–)

The first public demonstration of a portable cellular phone, or mobile, was made by the American engineer Martin Cooper in April 1973. At that time, Cooper was employed by Motorola and the call was made on the Dyna-Tac, a handheld device on which Cooper and his team had worked. Cooper's other inventions include the first radio-controlled traffic light system and handheld police radios.

DA VINCI, LEONARDO (1452–1519)

The Italian painter and sculptor is best known for his paintings "Mona Lisa" and "The Last Supper". But he also had a passionate interest in science, architecture, mathematics, engineering, and human anatomy, filling notebooks with sketches of inventions way ahead of the times. He wrote most of his accompanying notes backwards, in mirror writing, possibly to protect his ideas from being stolen by others. A flying machine, armoured vehicle, helicopter, parachute, and SCUBA gear are amongst his many designs.

FLEMING, SANDFORD (1827–1915)

In 1876, the Scottish Canadian railway engineer was travelling through Ireland when he missed his train. The timetable, or Fleming's own timing, may have been wrong, but it made him consider the need for standardized time. So, he came up with the concept of worldwide standard time. In 1879, Fleming proposed dividing the world into 24 time zones and, in 1884, clocks were reset in line with his ideas.

FRANKLIN, BENJAMIN (1706–1790)

Franklin is a key historical figure and one of the Founding Fathers of the USA. He also had an avid interest in science and invention. Franklin began investigating electricity and, in 1756, by means of a kite and a key, demonstrated that lightning is electricity – a discovery that led to his invention of the lightning rod. Later inventions included bifocal glasses, a cast-iron stove, and a glass musical instrument called an armonica.

GOODE, SARAH E (1855–1905)

This American inventor and entrepreneur is believed to be the first African American women to be granted a US patent. Not much is known about her life, but she was freed from slavery and moved to Chicago where she ran a furniture shop with her carpenter husband. In 1885, she was awarded the patent for her folding, hide-away bed. Her nifty invention could double as a bed or a folding writing desk thanks to a clever design that incorporated hinged sections that could be raised or lowered into place.

GUTENBERG, JOHANNES (c.1395–c.1468)

The German printer, whose "Forty-Two-Line" Bible (also known as the Gutenberg Bible) was the first book in Europe to be printed using movable type, perfected his printing press around 1439. Until Gutenberg invented his metal type, printing had been a laborious task using carved wooden blocks. Although his invention revolutionized printing, Gutenberg died a poor man.

HANNAH, MARC (1956–)

Special effects in films such as *Jurassic Park* and *Beauty and the Beast* are partly thanks to electrical engineer and computer graphics designer Marc Hannah. The African American co-founded the company Silicon Graphics Inc (SGI) in 1982 and helped pioneer the 3-D graphics technology used in many Hollywood blockbusters. More recently, Hannah has worked on multimedia plug-ins for listening to music on MP3 players and handheld video-game players.

HUYGENS, CHRISTIAAN (1629–1695)

The 17th-century Dutchman is regarded as one of the most important scientists and astronomers of all time. In the 1650s, he made improvements to telescopes that enabled him to see the rings and a moon orbiting Saturn. Huygens put forward groundbreaking theories about light waves and calculations for centrifugal force. He also excelled at invention, constructing the first pendulum clock (1657), prototypes for a small wristwatch, various telescopes, and a combustion engine that ran off gunpowder.

JONES, ELDORADO (1860–1932)

The American Eldorado Jones earned the nickname "the Iron Woman". This is because she invented a small portable iron, but it could equally have been for her tough attitude to both work and men (she refused to employ them). She also invented a travel ironing board, an anti-damp salt shaker, and a collapsible hat stand. The airplane muffler, patented in 1923, was her most famous invention. It muffled the tremendous sound of an aircraft without causing loss of power.

KNIGHT, MARGARET (1838–1914)

Knight invented a machine to make flat-bottomed paper bags. The patent was awarded to Knight in 1871, after a lengthy legal dispute with a man who tried to steal her idea. A prolific inventor, she also created a machine for cutting shoe soles, a safety device for cotton looms, a window frame, and various devices for engines.

KWOLEK, STEPHANIE (1923–2014)

This US chemist and polymer scientist nearly had a career in fashion, but opted for chemistry. Hired by the chemicals company DuPont – one of only a few female chemists employed there – in 1965, she discovered a new synthetic fibre called Kevlar. Strong yet lightweight, this fibre is used to make body armour for the police and military, and is also used in aeroplanes, boats, and ropes.

LAKE, SIMON (1866–1945)

American marine engineer Simon Lake is remembered as the "Father of the Modern Submarine". In 1894, he built his first submarine with a pressurized compartment, a vessel built for shallow waters that he named *Argonaut Jr.* Lake went on to create *Argonaut I*, which could be used at sea and moved on wheels along the ocean floor. In 1901, Lake produced a military sub called the *Protector*, but it wasn't until 1912 that he first had a submarine accepted by the US Navy.

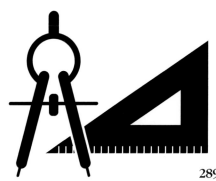

LAMARR, HEDY (1914–2000)

Best known as a Hollywood actor, the Austrian-American Lamarr is now recognized as an important inventor. In 1941, with her business partner George Antheil, she received the patent for a wireless communication system (a forerunner of Wi-Fi and Bluetooth technology) to be used by the military. "Inventions are easy for me to do," she later claimed. "I suppose I just came from a different planet."

LEIZU OR XI LING SHI (2ND MILLENNIUM BCE)

The Chinese teacher Confucius told the story of how the ancient empress Leizu became the first person to discover silk. Around 2640 BCE, the young wife of Emperor Huangdi was sitting under a mulberry tree when the cocoon of a silkworm fell in her teacup and she saw how it was formed of tiny threads. This revelation inspired her to rear silkworms and experiment with the fibres to create silk fabric using a loom – a process that became known as sericulture.

MANGANO, JOY (1956–)

American inventor Mangano has patents for hundreds of everyday products, from wheeled luggage and jewellery boxes to rubber platform shoes and reading glasses. In 1990, she invented the Miracle Mop, a self-wringing plastic floor mop with a self-rinsing cotton head. Now a multi-millionaire, she heads her own company, Ingenious Designs Inc. In 2015, her story was made into the film *Joy*, starring Jennifer Lawrence.

MARCONI, GUGLIELMO (1874–1937)

The "father of radio" was a young Italian scientist called Guglielmo Marconi. He was fascinated by radio waves and, through tireless experimentation, pioneered long-distance radio transmission and radio telegraphy. In 1896, Marconi demonstrated the first wireless transmission between buildings in London, UK. The following year, his equipment could transmit across the English Channel and, by 1901, across the Atlantic Ocean to the USA. He shared the Nobel Prize for Physics in 1909.

MASON, STANLEY (1921–2006)

The American businessman and inventor worked on a multitude of consumer items, including microwave cookware, plastic dental floss, baby wipes, support bras, and surgical masks. The squeezable ketchup bottle and fitted disposable nappy are his most famous creations. The nappy came about when he had his own children: "I held up the cloth diaper, and it was square. I looked at the baby, and it was round. I knew there was a engineering problem."

IBUKA, MASARU (1908–1997)

The Japanese industrialist started his career in a photochemical laboratory, where he showed early promise as an inventor with his modulated light transmission system – a kind of neon. He founded the company that would become Sony in 1949, developing the first Japanese tape recorder, a transistor radio, and the Trinitron TV system. The Walkman of 1979 was inspired by Ibuka's love of listening to opera on long flights and the need for a streamlined, lightweight, portable, personal player.

MATZELIGER, JAN ERNST (1852–1889)

Born to a Dutch father and an enslaved mother, the Surinamese inventor developed an early interest in machinery at his father's shipyard. By 1877, employed in a shoe factory in Massachusetts, USA, he began working out how to attach a shoe sole to its upper by machine. This job was done by hand and even a skilled worker could complete only 50 pairs a day. Matzeliger's machine, patented in 1883, raised shoe production to between 150 and 700 pairs a day.

MONTAGU, JOHN (1718–1792)

In 1762, the British statesman and 4th Earl of Sandwich ordered a chef to make him something he could eat with his hands so he could snack without going to the dinner table. The result was the sandwich – meat, for instance, between slices of bread.

OTIS, ELISHA (1811–1861)

The American inventor of the safety device for lifts and hoists was a self-taught mechanic. Developed in the 1850s, his safety device was simple, employing springs to bring a falling hoist or lift to a standstill if the cables broke. Otis also patented an automatic turner for making wooden

bedsteads, a steam plough, and a railway safety brake. In 1861, he patented his steam engine for lifts, but died the same year.

RAUSING, RUBEN (1895–1983)

At lunch one day at home in Sweden, Rausing's wife Elizabeth suggested a clever way to fill and seal a container with a liquid such as milk. Head of a struggling food packaging company, Ruben rose to the challenge. In 1944, he patented the sterile, tetrahedron-shaped, plastic-coated carton he developed with Swedish engineer Erik Wallenberg. The company moved to the square design a few years later. Today, Tetra Pak is one of the most successful packaging companies in the world.

RITTY, JAMES (1836–1918)

The cash register was the cunning idea of Ritty, the proprietor of an American bar. He came up against the problem of his takings disappearing without any record. He got together with his mechanic brother John and invented a machine with keys that could be pressed to record the amount of money taken at each transaction. In 1879, he patented his machine "Ritty's Incorruptible Cashier" and opened a factory in Dayton, Ohio, USA, to produce his invention.

TALBOT, WILLIAM HENRY FOX (1800–1877)

In 1835, Talbot made a photographic negative of the window of his home, Lacock Abbey, UK – it is the earliest surviving negative in the world. Talbot's love of drawing inspired him to find a different way of capturing images on paper. In 1841, he perfected his technique of creating a calotype (early photograph) using a camera and paper treated with silver nitrate and potassium iodide.

TOYODA, SAKICHI (1867–1930)

The Japanese industrialist and founder of the group that would become Toyota was also the inventor of the automatic power loom. Toyoda was 18 years old when he decided to become an inventor. In 1891, he patented his first invention – the wooden handloom, which required just one hand rather than two. By 1896, he had developed Japan's first steam-powered loom. Throughout his life, Toyoda made improvements to his original design, with patents granted all over the world.

SIKORSKY, IGOR (1889–1972)

The Russian-American inventor of the helicopter had an early fascination with flight. He believed the best way to fly was to go straight up with a horizontal rotor. In Russia, Sikorsky came up with early unsuccessful prototypes for the helicopter. In 1919, he emigrated to the USA, formed an aircraft company, and developed the first four-engine plane. Then in 1939, he developed the first helicopter, the VS-300, which was taken up by the US military.

WAKEFIELD, RUTH GRAVES (1903–1977)

Many inventions are a happy accident, and that is what happened when Wakefield baked cookies for the customers at her Massachusetts roadside inn around 1938. Wakefield claimed the chocolate chip cookies she created were like that by design, but other stories suggest that she expected the broken bits of chocolate in her cookie mix to melt. Whichever story is true, Wakefield's "Toll House Chocolate Crunch Cookie" is the basis of America's favourite cookie.

WELLESLEY, ARTHUR (1769–1852)

The famous Wellington boot takes its name from the British statesman and military leader Arthur Wellesley, the 1st Duke of Wellington. The war hero was often seen wearing his favourite leather boots. In the early 1800s, he was given a pair of Hessian boots by a group of German soldiers. Wellington asked his bootmaker to copy the design, but remove the tassel and extend the front over the knee for added protection. The style was copied by aristocrats everywhere and nicknamed the "Wellington". The rubber version was patented in 1852.

WOODS, GRANVILLE (1856–1910)

Woods was an African American engineer who was granted more than 50 patents in his lifetime, many of his inventions being for the safety and improvement of the railways. In 1887, he invented the Synchronous Multiplex Railway Telegraph, which enabled contact between a moving train and a station. Thomas Edison took him to court, claiming he had invented it first, but Woods won the case. He also helped improve inventions like the safety circuit, telephone, and phonograph, and invented an egg incubator and an automatic brake.

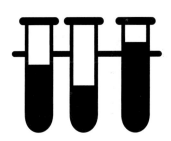

Glossary

Air resistance A force that pushes against an object that is moving through the air, slowing it down. This is also called drag.

Alloy A mixture of two or more metals.

Alternating current (AC) An electrical current that changes its direction of flow many times every second to allow the efficient use of electricity.

Altitude The height of an object relative to sea or ground level.

Ammonia A colourless gas with a strong odour made up of nitrogen and hydrogen. It is often used to make fertilizers that aid plant growth.

Anaesthetic A pain-relieving drug or gas given to a patient before an operation. It can be "local", which affects just one part of the body, or "general", so the person is made temporarily unconscious before and during major surgery.

Ancestor A person – usually one more remote than a grandparent – from whom a human is descended. An ancestor can also refer to animals and plants.

Anode The positively charged electrode in a cell, such as a battery.

Antenna This device is used to transmit or receive radio or television signals. It is also known as an aerial.

Antibiotic A medicine that kills – or limits the spread of – bacterial infections in humans or animals.

Antiseptic A substance that is put on cuts to prevent an infection.

Archaeology The study of things that show how people lived in the distant past.

Astronomy The study of objects in space, including planets, stars, and galaxies.

Atom The smallest part of a chemical element, made up of particles called protons, neutrons, and electrons.

Bacteria (singular: bacterium) These are tiny, single-celled organisms. Some bacteria cause disease, while others help and protect the human body.

Battery A portable container of chemicals that stores and supplies electricity to a range of devices, from toys to cars.

Bellows A device that expands to draw in air through a valve, then contracts to force the air through a tube.

Bipedal A human, animal, or something else – for example, a robot – that uses two legs for walking.

Bitumen This sticky, black substance made from tar or petrol is used mainly to surface roads.

Bronze A yellow-brown metal alloy made up mostly of copper and tin. It is a popular choice of material for sculptures because it is strong, hard-wearing, and rust-resistant.

▲ *MID-19TH CENTURY CHINESE OCEAN COMPASS*

Bronze Age A historical period, between the Stone Age and Iron Age, that is defined by the use of bronze as the most important material for making weapons and tools. It began around 3000 BCE in the Middle East and spread around the world over about 2,500 years.

Carbon An important chemical element that comes in a variety of forms, from coal to diamond. Carbon can also be combined with itself and other elements to produce millions of different compounds, from plastics to DNA.

Cathode The negatively charged electrode in a cell, such as a battery.

Celestial A way of describing an object or event that occurs in the sky or outer space, such as a comet or an eclipse.

Charcoal This grey-black porous solid, made by heating wood in the absence of oxygen, is mostly carbon. It has several uses, such as burning to generate heat for warmth or to cook. It can also be used as a material for drawing.

Circuit A complete and closed path that electricity flows around. All electric and electronic things have circuits inside them.

Combustion A chemical reaction in which a fuel, such as wood or coal, burns with oxygen from the air to release heat energy.

Conductor A substance that lets heat or electricity flow easily through it.

Contamination The process of polluting or poisoning – for example, an oil spill polluting the ocean, or harmful bacteria poisoning the human body.

Coolant A substance, usually a liquid, used to reduce the temperature of something, such as a car engine or factory machine.

Copper One of the chemical elements, copper is a soft, red metal that is an excellent conductor of electricity and heat.

Cosmic Something that belongs, or relates to, the Universe.

Crankshaft A metal shaft in an engine that changes the up-and-down motion of pistons into rotary motion to drive wheels.

Density The amount of matter stored within a known volume of a material.

Differential A set of gears that revolve at different speeds, allowing a vehicle to go around corners smoothly.

Direct current (DC) An electrical current, such as that from a battery, that flows in one direction to generate electricity.

Displace The action of moving something out of its normal position – for example, an object in a glass of water can displace the water, causing a spillage.

Domesticate The process of improving farming methods (of animals or plants) or living styles (such as dogs in houses) to help and develop the way humans live.

Efficient A machine or system that reaches a high level of productivity.

Elasticity A property of a material that allows it to stretch and bend when you push or pull it, and then returns to its original shape.

Electricity A type of energy caused by electrons inside an atom. Static electricity is made by electrons building up in one place, while current electricity happens when electrons move around.

Electrode An electrical contact in a circuit. Electrodes can have a positive or negative charge.

Electromagnet A coil of wire that generates temporary magnetism when electricity flows through it.

Electron This is a particle inside an atom with a negative charge. Electrons orbit the atom's nucleus (or core) in layers called shells.

▲ *THOMAS EDISON AND HIS ASSOCIATES TESTING A LAMP*

Electronic ignition A system that needs an electronic circuit to start a machine, such as in a car.

Element A pure substance that cannot be broken down into any simpler substances. Elements are the building blocks of all matter. There are 118 elements, most of which occur naturally.

Energy The capacity to do work. It may come from a source such as coal or the Sun, and can be used to generate electricity.

Engine A device that burns fuel and oxygen to release stored heat energy that can power a machine.

Equator An imaginary line that goes around the middle of Earth to divide the northern and southern halves of the planet. The equator is often drawn onto maps and globes.

Force A pushing or pulling action that changes an object's speed, direction of movement, or shape.

Fossil fuel A substance that burns easily, releasing heat that has formed from the remains of ancient plants and other organisms. Fossil fuels include coal, natural gas, and oil.

Friction This type of force occurs between two objects, where their surfaces rub against each other to slow down movement.

Fuse A safety device for electrical machines that stops the current flowing if it is too strong.

Gasoline The North American term for petrol – a flammable liquid that is mainly used to fuel different forms of transport, from cars to boats.

Gearbox The set of gears that connect the engine of a vehicle to its wheels.

Generator A device that converts energy from rotational motion into electricity.

Geocentric A way of viewing or measuring Earth by putting it at the centre.

Germ A microscopic plant or animal, especially one that can cause illness.

Gravity The force of attraction that exists between all objects, and is what pulls objects down towards Earth. In space, gravitational forces are much smaller, which is why astronauts float.

Harpoon A barbed, spear-like missile that is used for hunting large fish and whales.

Heliocentric A way of viewing or measuring by putting the Sun at the centre.

Hieroglyphics An ancient form of writing that uses pictures to represent sounds and words. The ancient Egyptians, and some other civilizations, used this system.

Hull The main body of a ship or boat, not including the masts, yards, sails, or rigging.

Hydrogen The simplest, lightest, and most abundant of all chemical elements. This gas is one component of water and can be used as a sustainable fuel.

Ignition The system in a petrol engine that makes the mixture of petrol and air in the cylinders catch fire.

Incandescent A way of describing something that is very hot and glowing, such as the filament in a light bulb.

Infrared A type of electromagnetic radiation that carries energy in invisible waves from hot objects.

Insulator A material that does not let heat or electricity flow easily through it.

Intake The amount of food, water, air, or another substance taken into the body or a machine.

Iron Age A historical period after the Bronze Age that is defined by the use of iron as the most important material for making weapons and tools. It began around 1200 BCE in the Middle East, and spread around the world over about 1,500 years.

Laser The acronym for Light Amplification by Stimulated Emission of Radiation. A laser can produce a very powerful beam of light by exciting atoms inside a tube.

LED An acronym for light-emitting diode. An LED is a device that produces light when an electric current passes through it. The colour of its light depends on the compounds used in it.

Lever A tool that increases a small force into a large force – for example, a person exerts a small force on a nutcracker by squeezing it and breaking a nut.

Levitation The act of rising up or hovering in the air.

Magnet A piece of iron that attracts metals with iron or steel in them.

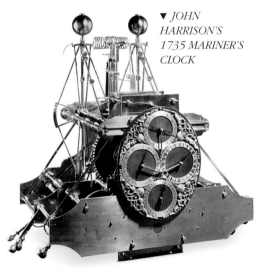

▼ *JOHN HARRISON'S 1735 MARINER'S CLOCK*

▲ *LASER SHOW AT A CONCERT*

Magnetic field The area surrounding a magnet that is able to attract objects to itself.

Mesopotamia Present-day Iraq and its surrounding areas, between the Tigris and Euphrates rivers.

Medieval A term that describes something, such as a painting or building, made during a period of European history from about 600–1500.

Mezzotint An engraving technique that involves scraping and polishing a copper plate.

Microbe A living organism too small to be seen with the unaided eye. There are three main types of microbe: bacteria, viruses, and fungi. They can be beneficial or harmful to plants and animals.

Microwave A very short, electromagnetic wave used for radar, cooking food in a microwave oven, or for sending information by radio.

Module (space) A self-contained part of a spacecraft.

Mould A soft growth that develops on rotting food or on some items that are left for a long time in humid conditions.

NASA An acronym for National Aeronautics and Space Administration. NASA is a US government agency that studies space and controls space travel.

Navigation The process of finding the position of a car, ship, or aircraft, or the best route from there to somewhere else.

Neutron A particle inside an atom that has no charge.

Nuclear reactor A device designed to maintain and control nuclear reactions. They are used mainly for electricity generation in nuclear power plants.

Nucleus The centre of an atom that is made up of protons (positively charged particles) and neutrons (particles with no charge).

Nutrient A food or any nourishing substance that plants or animals need to live and grow.

Orbit The path that an object takes in space when it moves around a star, planet, or moon.

Ore A rock or mineral from which a useful element can be purified and isolated.

Oscillate The act of moving in a back-and-forth fashion, like that of a pendulum.

Patent A legal application to protect an invention and the way it is made from being copied by another person or company.

Payload The amount of objects or people on an aircraft or a spacecraft.

Pendulum A weight suspended from a fixed point that swings freely back and forth under the force of gravity. A pendulum is commonly used to regulate movements, for example in clocks.

Pesticide A chemical substance that is used for destroying insects or other organisms that are harmful to plants or animals.

Phonetic The use of written language to represent different sounds made in speech.

Pollution The introduction of a substance into an environment that has harmful or poisonous effects.

Polymer An organic molecule made from many identical units joined together. Plastics are an example of polymers.

Prehistoric A way of describing a time before there were written records.

Probe An unmanned, robotic spacecraft controlled and monitored from Earth. A space probe may approach a moon or star, land on a planet or comet, or travel out of the Solar System.

Propeller A mechanical device with blades that is attached to a boat or an aircraft. The engine makes the propeller spin round and causes the boat or aircraft to move.

Proton A particle inside an atom that has a positive electric charge. The number of protons in an atom determines its chemical properties.

Prow The front part of a ship.

Radiation The process by which heat transfers through air or an empty space.

Radioactive A material in which the nucleus of each atom is unstable and breaks apart, releasing high-energy particles in the form of nuclear radiation.

Renewable energy A type of energy that will not run out, and is generated from sources such as the Sun, wind, and water.

Resistor An electronic component that reduces the electric current flowing through a circuit.

Saltpetre This is another name for the compound potassium nitrate. Saltpetre is an active ingredient in many things, from fertilizers to fireworks.

Satellite An object in space that travels around another object in a path called an orbit. Scientists have sent artificial satellites into Earth's orbit to take photographs, transmit data, and help people navigate on Earth.

Semaphore An early system of signalling that is used to communicate information from a distance. The position of two pivoting arms or blades represents different letters or numbers.

Semiconductor A substance used in electronics that has the ability to switch from being an insulator that blocks electricity to a conductor that carries it.

Smelting The process of extracting metal from its ore.

Solar A way of describing something that is related to, or caused by, the Sun.

Solar System The Sun and all the planets, moons, and other celestial bodies that go around the Sun.

Spacecraft Vehicles used to explore the Solar System.

Steel A hard, strong metal made from iron and small amounts of carbon. Steel is widely used in construction, from making skyscrapers to bridges.

Sumerian A way of describing something that relates to the ancient Mesopotamian (present-day Iraq) civilization of Sumer, or the Sumerian language.

Synthetic Another word for artificial.

Thrust A push or a force. When something pushes or accelerates in one direction there is a force (thrust) just as large in the opposite direction.

Torque A force that makes an object turn.

Transistor A semiconductor device made of crystals of silicon mixed with tiny amounts of other elements that alter its electrical properties. The result is a device that can control the flow of electrical current very precisely.

Turbine A machine designed to produce continuous power. It includes a wheel or rotor that turns fast due to the flow of water, steam, or gas that goes over it.

Vacuum An empty space that contains no air or material of any kind.

Virus An infectious particle that is much smaller than bacteria and is responsible for lots of different diseases.

▼ FOUR STAR-TRACKING LASER BEAMS EMERGE FROM A TELESCOPE AT THE PARANAL OBSERVATORY IN CHILE

Index

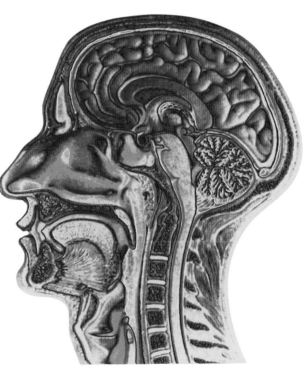

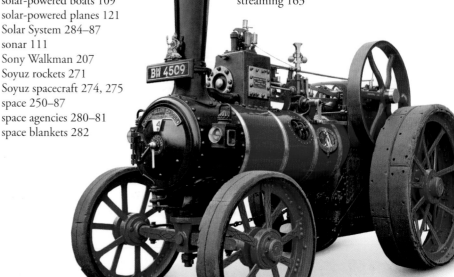

Acknowledgments

Smithsonian Institution:
Tricia Edwards, Lemelson Center, National Museum of American History, Smithsonian

Dorling Kindersley would like to thank:
Ellen Nanney from the Smithsonian Institution; Square Egg Studio for illustrations; Liz Gogerly for writing pp.288–291 Ingenious Inventors; Helen Peters for the index; Victoria Pyke for proofreading; Charvi Arora, Bharti Bedi, Aadithyan Mohan, Laura Sandford, and Janashree Singha for editorial assistance; Revati Anand and Baibhav Parida for design assistance; Surya Sarangi and Sakshi Saluja for picture research; Vishal Bhatia for CTS assistance; and Nityanand Kumar for technical assistance.

The publisher would like to thank the following for their kind permission to reproduce their photographs:

(Key: a-above; b-below/bottom; c-centre; f-far; l-left; r-right; t-top)

1 Getty Images: Science & Society Picture Library. **2–3 Alamy Stock Photo:** dpa picture alliance archive. **4 Alamy Stock Photo:** Akademie (crb); Nick Fox (cra); Science History Images (cr); Christopher Jones (cr/ketchup). **Bridgeman Images:** Archives Charmet (tr). **Getty Images:** Saro17 (crb/bike); Time Life Pictures (cra/Vinci). **iStockphoto.com:** crokogen (br). **5 123RF.com:** Roy Pedersen (ca); Shutterbas (ca/flight); Andriy Popov (cra). **Alamy Stock Photo:** Sergio Azenha (c); Phanie (cra/laser). **Depositphotos Inc:** Prykhodov (c/phone). **Dreamstime.com:** Tamas Bedecs (tr). **ESA:** ESA / ATG medialab (crb/sentinel). **Getty Images:** De Agostini Picture Library (cb/engine); Bloomberg (tc); DAJ (cr/port); Heritage Images (cr). **Mary Evans Picture Library:** Illustrated London News Ltd (bc). **NASA:** (cr/EVA); JPL-Caltech / MSSS (br). **Science Photo Library:** NASA (crb). **6–7 Getty Images:** DEA / G. DAGLI ORTI (t). **7 Getty Images:** Print Collector (clb); Jacqui Hurst (cb); Science & Society Picture Library (cb/compass). **8 Alamy Stock Photo:** PjrStudio (tr). **Getty Images:** CM Dixon / Print Collector (c); PHAS (ftr). **8–9 akg-images:** Erich Lessing (b). **9 Bridgeman Images:** (4th millennium BC) / South Tyrol Museum of Archaeology, Bolzano, Italy (fcr). **Dorling Kindersley:** Museum of London (cr). **10–11 Getty Images:** Florilegius (b). **11 Bridgeman Images:** Granger (crb). **12 Getty Images:** Print Collector (bc). **12–13 Getty Images:** SSPL (b). **13 Alamy Stock Photo:** Nick Fox (cr). **Getty Images:** SSPL (tr). **14 Alamy Stock Photo:** age fotostock (b). **Getty Images:** Leemage (cr). **15 Alamy Stock Photo:** Science History Images (clb). **Bridgeman Images:** Prehistoric / Ashmolean Museum, University of Oxford, UK (tc). **Getty Images:** Archiv Gerstenberg / ullstein bild (br); Science & Society Picture Library (c). **16 Alamy Stock Photo:** Lebrecht Music and Arts Photo Library (bl). **Mary Evans Picture Library:** The Mullan Collection (cl). **17 Alamy Stock Photo:** Granger Historical Picture Archive (c). **Getty Images:** Science & Society Picture Library (tc). **18 Alamy Stock Photo:** Steve Hamblin (cla). **Getty Images:** Science & Society Picture Library (bl). **18–19 Getty Images:** SSPL (b). **19 123RF.com:** Henner Damke (bc). **John Hamill:** (cr). **Imaginechina:** Wang Jinmiao (tc). **20 Bridgeman Images:** Galleria degli Uffizi, Florence, Tuscany, Italy (clb). **Getty Images:** Popperfoto (tl). **21 Alamy Stock Photo:** Science History Images (bc); World History Archive (t). **22 Collection and Archive of Museum of Kotsanas Museum of Ancient Greek Technology:** (clb). **22–23 Alamy Stock Photo:** Johnny Greig Int (b). **23 Getty Images:** Ann Ronan Pictures / Print Collector (tr); SSPL (cla). **24 akg-images:** Erich Lessing (c). **Alamy Stock Photo:** Antiqua Print Gallery (bl); Tim Gainey (br). **24–25 akg-images:** GandhiServe e.K. (t). **25 Alamy Stock Photo:** imageBROKER (br). **Getty Images:** SSPL (tr). **26–27 Getty Images:** Time Life Pictures. **28 Bridgeman Images:** Archives Charmet (cr). **Getty Images:** View Stock (l). **29 Getty Images:** Fine Art Images / Heritage Images (br); Ullstein bild Dtl. (t). **The Metropolitan Museum of Art:** Purchase, Arthur Ochs Sulzberger Gift, 2002 (bc). **30 Bridgeman Images:** Pictures from History (cl). **Dorling Kindersley:** © The Board of Trustees of the Armouries (cra, cr); **Tomek Mrugalski:** (bc). **31 Dorling Kindersley:** © The Board of Trustees of the Armouries (bl); Wallace Collection, London (t). **Getty Images:** DeAgostini (br). **32 Alamy Stock Photo:** HD SIGNATURE CO.,LTD (clb). **32–33 Alamy Stock Photo:** Josse Christophel. **33 akg-images:** Science Source (tc). **Dorling Kindersley:** Andy Crawford / Ray Smith (bc). **Getty Images:** Universal History Archive / UIG (cr). **34 Alamy Stock Photo:** Berenike (bc). **The Metropolitan Museum of Art:** Purchase, Raymond and Beverly Sackler Gift, 1988 (clb). **34–35 Getty Images:** Heritage Images (t). **35 Alamy Stock Photo:** PBL Collection (bl). **Getty Images:** De Agostini Picture Library (ca). **Science Photo Library:** British Library (cb) **36 Alamy Stock Photo:** Dennis Cox (c); kpzfoto (bc). **Getty Images:** Science & Society Picture Library (crb); SSPL (cra). **37 Rex Shutterstock:** Roger-Viollet. **38–39 iStockphoto.com:** pr3m-5ingh. **39 Depositphotos Inc:** Mimadeo (cb). **Getty Images:** Bettmann (clb); Bloomberg (cb/SUVs). **40 Getty Images:** Historical (b); Science & Society Picture Library (cra). **41 Alamy Stock Photo:** Age Fotostock (crb). **Depositphotos Inc:** Hayatikayhan (bl). **Getty Images:** Photo 12 (tl). **42 123RF.com:** Anton Samsonov (br); Maxim Sergeenkov (cl). **43 Alamy Stock Photo:** Peter Llewellyn RF (cra); Erik Tham (cl); Geoff Vermont (bc). **Getty Images:** Fertnig (bl). **44 Getty Images:** Science & Society Picture Library (tl, cl). **44–45 Getty Images:** Kerry Sherck (b). **45 Alamy Stock Photo:** Photofusion Picture Library (tl). **Avalon:** Woody Ochnio (cra). **Science Photo Library:** Martyn F. Chillmaid (crb). **46 Alamy Stock Photo:** The Print Collector (cr). **Dorling Kindersley:** Ernie Eagle (bc). **Getty Images:** Science & Society Picture Library (cr). **47 123RF.com:** Winai Tepsuttinun (t). **Alamy Stock Photo:** Islandstock (crb). **Dorling Kindersley:** Doubleday Swineshead Depot (clb); Happy Old Iron, Marc Geerkens (cra). **Getty Images:** STR (br). **SGC:** (ca). **48 Getty Images:** Neale Clark / robertharding (cl). **48–49 Getty Images:** The Print Collector. **49 Alamy Stock Photo:** Granger Historical Picture Archive (c). **Getty Images:** Bettmann (tr); Gregor Schuster (br). **50 Alamy Stock Photo:** Akademie (crb); Chronicle (cl). **Getty Images:** Heritage Images (tl). **51 Dreamstime.com:** Penywise (bl). **Getty Images:** Print Collector. **52 Getty Images:** Science & Society Picture Library (clb). **52–53 Dorling Kindersley:** Dave King / The Science Museum, London. **53 Alamy Stock Photo:** croftsphoto (br). **Bridgeman Images:** Hand-powered hydraulic press. Engraving, 1887. / Universal History Archive / UIG (cr); Power loom weaving, 1834 (engraving), Allom, Thomas (1804-72) (after) / Private Collection (tc). **54–55 Science Photo Library:** Lewis Houghton. **56 Getty Images:** Hulton Deutsch (cla); Science & Society Picture Library (cra). **56–57 Getty Images:** Bloomberg (b). **57 Alamy Stock Photo:** Bildagentur-online / McPhoto-Kerpa (br). **Bridgeman Images:** Granger (cla). **Getty Images:** Science & Society Picture Library (c). **58 Alamy Stock Photo:** Paul Fearn (bl). **Dreamstime.com:** Mikael Damkier / Mikdam (tr). **Getty Images:** Mark Newman (c); Universal Images Group (crb). **59 Alamy Stock Photo:** Michael Roper (cl). **Dreamstime.com:** Neacsu Razvan Chirnoaga (tr). **Getty Images:** Iain Masterton (br). **60 Getty Images:** Bettmann. **61 Alamy Stock Photo:** Science History Images (clb). **Getty Images:** Science & Society Picture Library (cra); Roger Viollet (bl). **62 Science Photo Library:** Gregory Tobias / Chemical Heritage Foundation. **63 123RF.com:** Pauliene Wessel (bc). **Alamy Stock Photo:** Martyn Evans (ca); Christopher Jones (crb). **Rex Shutterstock:** AP (tr). **64 Alamy Stock Photo:** Anton Starikov (tr). **Science Photo Library:** Hagley Museum And Archive (bl); Patrick Landmann (cr). **65 Alamy Stock Photo:** dpa Picture Alliance Archive (bl); Image Source (c). **Depositphotos Inc:** Fotokostic (tr). **iStockphoto.com:** Marekuliasz (cla). **66 Alamy Stock Photo:** Paul Fearn (clb); LJSphotography (br). **Getty Images:** Science & Society Picture Library (cra). **67 Alamy Stock Photo:** Matthew Chattle (tc); Andriy Popov (cl). **Getty Images:** Ulrich Baumgarten (bl); Bloomberg (cr). **68 Alamy Stock Photo:** STOCKFOLIO ® (cr). **Dreamstime.com:** Andrew Vernon (bc). **Library of Congress, Washington, D.C.:** Library of Congress (136.04.00) [Digital ID# us0136_04] (cl). **69 Alamy Stock Photo:** David Izquierdo Roger (cra); MIKA Images (br). **Dreamstime.com:** Anurak Anachai (tr); Igor Golubov (cb). **70–71 Getty Images:** Bloomberg. **72 akg-images:** Interfoto (cl). **Alamy Stock Photo:** Joseph Clemson 1 (c); Granger Historical Picture Archive (crb). **73 Alamy Stock Photo:** Chris Willson (cr). **Dreamstime.com:** Alla Ordatiy (clb); Wittayayut Seethong (tl); Chee Siong Teh (br). **74–75 iStockphoto.com:** Dreamnikon. **76 National Museum of American History / Smithsonian Institution:** (cra). **Rex Shutterstock:** Sipa USA (b). **77 Getty Images:** VCG (r). **Rex Shutterstock:** Ray Stubblebine (c); Seth Wenig / AP (clb). **Science Photo Library:** Peter Menzel (tl). **78 Depositphotos Inc:** Ilterriorm (bc). **NASA:** (br). **Science Photo Library:** Sam Ogden (tr). **79 Getty Images:** Bloomberg (cl); Chip Somodevilla (tr, bc). **Starship Technologies:** (cr). **80–81 Getty Images:** Chung Sung-Jun. **82–83 Getty Images:** Blackstation. **83 Alamy Stock Photo:** ITAR-TASS News Agency (cb). **Getty Images:** (cb/ship). **Rex Shutterstock:** TESLA HANDOUT / EPA-EFE (clb). **84 Alamy Stock Photo:** dumbandmad.com (bc). **Getty Images:** Culture Club (tr); Science & Society Picture Library (c). **84–85 Getty Images:** NurPhoto (b). **85 Bryton Inc.:** (c). **Getty Images:** Andrew Bret Wallis (tr). **Lumos**

Helmet: (tl). **86 Alamy Stock Photo:** Alex Ramsay (cb). **Dorling Kindersley:** Bicycle Museum Of America (bl); National Cycle Collection (cla); Gary Ombler / Jonathan Sneath (cra). **87 Dorling Kindersley:** Bicycle Museum Of America (ca). **Getty Images:** Saro17 (bl). **88–89 iStockphoto.com:** Homydesign. **90–91 Alamy Stock Photo:** SuperStock (tc). **90 Getty Images:** Science & Society Picture Library (clb). **91 BMW Group UK:** BMW Motorrad (br). **Dorling Kindersley:** Motorcycle Heritage Museum, Westerville, Ohio (cra). **Dreamstime.com:** Austincolle (c). **Getty Images:** Science & Society Picture Library (tc). **Lightning Motorcycle/Worlds Fastest Production Electric Motorcycles:** (clb). **92 Getty Images:** Bettmann (cl). **92–93 Getty Images:** Joseph Sohm (c). **93 Getty Images:** fStop Images - Caspar Benson (crb). **magiccarpics.co.uk:** John Colley (bc). **94 Foundation Museum Autovision/Museum AUTOVISION:** (cb). **Dorling Kindersley:** Simon Clay / National Motor Museum, Beaulieu (cra). **Rex Shutterstock:** Gianni Dagli Orti (cla). **94–95 Alamy Stock Photo:** Drive Images (b). **95 Audi AG:** (cra). **Getty Images:** Owaki / Kulla (t). **96 Alamy Stock Photo:** Granger Historical Picture Archive (cr). **Image from the Collection of The Henry Ford:** (cl). **Getty Images:** Bettmann (tl). **97 Alamy Stock Photo:** Granger Historical Picture Archive. **Getty Images:** Heritage Images (bl). **98–99 Alamy Stock Photo:** Fabian Bimmer. **100 Alamy Stock Photo:** Oldtimer (tr). **Getty Images:** Rolls Press / Popperfoto (bc); Ullstein Bild Dtl. (cl). **100–101 Getty Images:** Paul Kane (b). **101 Alamy Stock Photo:** Viennaslide (cra). **Getty Images:** Bloomberg (br); Underwood Archives (cla). **102 Alamy Stock Photo:** Studio Octavio (br). **Getty Images:** Javier Larrea (r). **103 Getty Images:** Keystone (b); VCG (tr). **104 Alamy Stock Photo:** Dudley Wood (tr). **Getty Images:** Bettmann (clb); Science & Society Picture Library (c). **104–105 © ORACLE TEAM USA:** Photo Sander van der Borch (b). **105 BURGESS YACHTS:** Rupert Peace (cr). **106 Alamy Stock Photo:** Lordprice Collection (clb). **Getty Images:** Science & Society Picture Library (cla). **106–107 Alamy Stock Photo:** ITAR-TASS News Agency (c). **107 Alamy Stock Photo:** Loop Images Ltd (cra). **iStockphoto.com:** crokogen (tl). **108 Dorling Kindersley:** Science Museum, London (cb). **108–109 SD Model Makers:** (b). **109 Alamy Stock Photo:** Chronicle (tl); dpa picture alliance archive (cb). **Getty Images:** Rainer Schimpf (cra). **Yara International:** (br). **110 Getty Images:** Imagno (clb); Science & Society Picture Library (cl). **110–111 Alamy Stock Photo:** Granger Historical Picture Archive (c). **111 Getty Images:** Todd Gipstein (br). **112 Dorling Kindersley:** The Royal Navy Submarine Museum (tl). **Getty Images:** Universal History Archive (c). **112–113 Getty Images:** Education Images / UIG (b). **113 123RF.com:** Roy Pedersen (bl). **Rex Shutterstock:** Sipa USA. **116–117 Copyright The Boeing Company. 116 Dorling Kindersley:** Real Aeroplane Company (bl). **Getty Images:** Science & Society Picture Library (tl). **117 123RF.com:** Shutterbas (tr). **Alamy Stock Photo:** Robert Harding (cla). **118 Getty Images:** Apic / RETIRED (tl). **118–119 Library of Congress, Washington, D.C.:** (b). **119 Alamy Stock Photo:** American Photo Archive (bc); Science History Images (tl). **Getty Images:** Universal History Archive (cra). **120 Bridgeman Images:** Avion de chasse Heinkel He 178 / © SZ Photo (tr). **Maurits Eisenblätter:** (b). **121 Alamy Stock Photo:** RGB Ventures (cl). **DARPA Outreach:** (br). **Getty Images:** NASA (tr); Jean Revillard-Handout (cr). **122 Alamy Stock Photo:** imageBROKER (cra). **Getty Images:** Barcroft Media (bl); Science & Society Picture Library

(cla). **123 Lilium GmbH:** (b). **Volocopter:** Nikolay Kazakov (tl). **124–125 Getty Images:** Bloomberg. **126 Alamy Stock Photo:** Chronicle (tr). **Getty Images:** Science & Society Picture Library (b). **127 Dorling Kindersley:** The National Railway Museum, York / Science Museum Group (b). **iStockphoto.com:** Daseaford (r). **128 Alamy Stock Photo:** Archive PL (tr). **Dorling Kindersley:** National Railway Museum, York (bl). **Getty Images:** Science & Society Picture Library (ca, clb). **129 Getty Images:** Paul Almasy (cla); Gavin Hellier / robertharding (tr); VCG (b). **130–131 Alamy Stock Photo:** blickwinkel. **132 Getty Images:** Science & Society Picture Library (crb). **Science Photo Library:** Royal Institution Of Great Britain (cl). **133 Getty Images:** Science & Society Picture Library (bc). **134–135 Alamy Stock Photo:** Jochen Tack. **135 Alamy Stock Photo:** Sean Pavone (cla); Ahmet Yarali (cra). **Getty Images:** Ullstein Bild (ca/sea). **136 Dorling Kindersley:** The Science Museum, London (b). **Getty Images:** Print Collector (tr); DEA / A. DAGLI ORTI (ca). **137 Getty Images:** Science & Society Picture Library (tl); Universal History Archive (tr). **138 Alamy Stock Photo:** National Geographic Creative (cla). **Dreamstime.com:** Drimi (bl). **Getty Images:** FPG (br). **139 Alamy Stock Photo:** Greg Balfour Evans (cr); Lander Loeckx (t). **Getty Images:** Science & Society Picture Library (b). **140 Alamy Stock Photo:** DPA picture alliance (bc). **Dorling Kindersley:** The Science Museum, London (cr). **Getty Images:** SSPL (cl). **141 Cottone Auctions:** (tr). **Getty Images:** J. B. Spector / Museum of Science and Industry, Chicago (tl); SSPL (c); Neil Godwin / T3 Magazine (crb). **Seiko U.K Limited:** (bc). **142 Getty Images:** Stefano Bianchetti / Corbis (cla); SSPL (r). **143 123RF.com:** Antonio Diaz (bl). **Getty Images:** SSPL (cra); Welgos / Hulton Archive (tl). **Rex Shutterstock:** J. L. Cereijido / Epa (cb). **144 Getty Images:** Nicholas Eveleigh (bl). **145 Dreamstime.com:** Norman Chan (bl); Krystyna Wojciechowska - Czarnik (cl); Boris Fojtik (br). **Getty Images:** Heuser / Ullstein Bild (tr); SSPL (tc). **146 Alamy Stock Photo:** Deezee / iPhone® is a trademark of Apple Inc., registered in the U.S. and other countries. (c). **Ericsson:** (tr). **147 123RF.com:** Shao-Chun Wang (bl). **Alamy Stock Photo:** Cristian M. Vela (tl). **Depositphotos Inc:** Prykhodov (br). **iStockphoto.com:** MarKord (cl). **Rex Shutterstock:** AP (tr). **148–149 Alamy Stock Photo:** Xinhua. **150 Dorling Kindersley:** The Science Museum, London (cla). **Getty Images:** Science & Society Picture Library (c). **Science Photo Library:** Miriam And Ira D. Wallach Division Of Art, Prints And Photographs / New York Public Library (clb). **150–151 Bridgeman Images:** Granger (b). **151 Alamy Stock Photo:** Ahmet Yarali (crb). **Science Photo Library:** Emmeline Watkins (tr). **152 Getty Images:** Science & Society Picture Library (r). **Mary Evans Picture Library:** Interfoto / Hermann Historica GmbH (bl). **153 akg-images:** Interfoto (c). **Alamy Stock Photo:** Jeffrey Blackler (bl). **Dreamstime.com:** Mphoto2 (crb). **Joe Haupt:** (cr). **154–155 Getty Images:** Ullstein Bild. **156 from Camera Obscura & World of Illusions, Edinburgh:** (bl). **Getty Images:** Science & Society Picture Library (r, cb). **157 akg-images:** Interfoto (c). **Alamy Stock Photo:** imageBROKER (cr). **Getty Images:** Royal Photographic Society (tc); Science & Society Picture Library (bl, br). **158 Alamy Stock Photo:** Sergio Azenha (cr). **Getty Images:** CBS Photo Archive (cb); Science & Society Picture Library (cl, bl). **159 Dreamstime.com:** Bagwold (tl). **Getty Images:** Digital Camera Magazine (bl); George Rose (tr); Hulton Archive (c); T3 Magazine (crb, br). **160 Alamy Stock Photo:** World History Archive (clb). **Getty Images:**

Science & Society Picture Library (cl). **160–161 Getty Images:** Science & Society Picture Library (c). **161 Alamy Stock Photo:** David Cook / blueshiftstudios (cr); Mike V (br). **Getty Images:** Science & Society Picture Library (tl). **Toshiba Corporation:** (cra). **162 Alamy Stock Photo:** Darkened Studio (crb). **Dorling Kindersley:** Glasgow City Council (Museums) (bl). **Getty Images:** Fox Photos / Hulton Archive (cla); Thomas J Peterson (cra). **163 Alamy Stock Photo:** Goran Mihajlovski (clb); Hugh Threlfall (cra). **Getty Images:** Thomas Trutschel / Photothek (br); SSPL (tl). **164 Alamy Stock Photo:** Interfoto (bl, br). **Getty Images:** Steven Taylor (c). **165 123RF.com:** Sergey Kohl (clb); Andriy Popov (br). **Alamy Stock Photo:** Interfoto (cla); Vitaliy Krivosheev (tr). **166 123RF.com:** Carolina K. Smith, M.D. (cr). **akg-images:** (bl). **Getty Images:** Science & Society Picture Library (c). **167 Alamy Stock Photo:** imageBROKER (b). **"Courtesy of Perkins School for the Blind Archives, Watertown, MA":** (tr). **168–169 Alamy Stock Photo:** Sean Pavone. **170 Dorling Kindersley:** The Science Museum, London (cl). **Getty Images:** Joe McNally (cr). **170–171 Alamy Stock Photo:** Mike Stone (b). **171 Alamy Stock Photo:** Science History Images (tl). **Dreamstime.com:** Leung Cho Pan / Leungchopan (ca). **Getty Images:** Apic (cra); Mark Madeo / Future Publishing (t). **172 Alamy Stock Photo:** Agencja Fotograficzna Caro (clb). **Getty Images:** Future Publishing (cla); Mark Madeo / Future Publishing (cr, br). **173 Alamy Stock Photo:** DJG Technology (c); Sergey Peterman (crb). **Dreamstime.com:** Alexander Kirch / Audioundwerbung (b); Jovani Carlo Gorospe / iPad® is a trademark of Apple Inc., registered in the U.S. and other countries. (bc). **Getty Images:** SSPL (tl). **174 Alamy Stock Photo:** ukartpics (c). **Science Photo Library:** CERN (b). **175 Alamy Stock Photo:** Ian Dagnall (b). **© CERN:** (tr). **Depositphotos Inc:** simpson33 (cr). **Getty Images:** AFP (cla). **176 Getty Images:** De Agostini Picture Library (cl); Science & Society Picture Library (br). **176–177 Getty Images:** Print Collector (c). **177 Bridgeman Images:** British Library, London, UK / © British Library Board. (cra). **Fotolia:** Sai Chan / Zoe (br). **Science Photo Library:** European Space Agency / Cnes / Arianespace, Service Optique (cr). **178–179 Alamy Stock Photo:** Jerónimo Alba. **179 123RF.com:** Leo Lintang (cb). **Alamy Stock Photo:** Christina Peters (cb/mixer). **180 Alamy Stock Photo:** Artokoloro Quint Lox Limited (tr); Science History Images (c). **Getty Images:** Science & Society Picture Library (bl). **181 Dorling Kindersley:** The Science Museum, London (l). **© Philips:** Philips Hue Lights / Philips Lighting (tr). **182 Getty Images:** Tim Graham (cla). **182–183 Candice Gawne:** (b). **183 123RF.com:** swavo (br). **Alamy Stock Photo:** Hemis (tc); Jason Lindsey (cla). **Dreamstime.com:** Tamas Bedecs (cra). **184–185 Getty Images:** China News Service. **186 Alamy Stock Photo:** Pictorial Press Ltd (tl). **Getty Images:** Science & Society Picture Library (cl). **186–187 Getty Images:** Chris Hunter (t). **187 Alamy Stock Photo:** Falkensteinfoto (cra). **Getty Images:** Bettmann (bc). **Rex Shutterstock:** Ernest K. Bennett / AP (crb). **188–189 Getty Images:** Bettmann. **190 Science Photo Library:** Science Source (cl). **190–191 Reuters:** David Gray (b). **191 Depositphotos Inc:** Studioarz (ca). **Dorling Kindersley:** The Science Museum, London (t). **192 Getty Images:** Bettmann (cla). **192–193 123RF.com:** Stefano Sansavini (b). **Getty Images:** Science & Society Picture Library (c). **193 123RF.com:** Ivanna Grigorova (bc); Andriy Popov (cr). **Getty Images:** Science & Society Picture Library (tc). **194 The Advertising Archives:** (cl). **iStockphoto.com:** Blacklionder

ACKNOWLEDGMENTS

(tl). **Rex Shutterstock:** Alex Lentati / Evening Standard (c). **195 Alamy Stock Photo:** Cultura Creative (clb); Science photos (tl); Rasoul Ahadi Borna (bc). **Getty Images:** Pictorial Parade / Archive Photos (c). **196 Getty Images:** Science & Society Picture Library (r). **197 Alamy Stock Photo:** Bamboofox (cra). **Getty Images:** DAJ (tl); Ryan McVay (clb). **Samsung Electronics:** (br). **198 Alamy Stock Photo:** Martin Lee (tr). **Getty Images:** Bert Hardy Advertising Archive (b). **199 123RF.com:** Anurak Ponapatimet (bc). **Alamy Stock Photo:** Felix Choo (c). **Depositphotos Inc:** Mrsiraphol (cla). **iStockphoto.com:** Dbhanu (cra). **200 Science & Society Picture Library:** Science Museum (c). **200–201 Bridgeman Images:** Private Collection / © Look and Learn (b). **201 Alamy Stock Photo:** Korn Vitthayanukarun (cb). **Getty Images:** Science & Society Picture Library (cl, tr). **202 Tony Buckingham:** (cl). **Rex Shutterstock:** (crb). **TopFoto.co.uk:** (tl). **203 Alamy Stock Photo:** Randy Duchaine (br). **Dyson Ltd. 204 Getty Images:** Science & Society Picture Library (tr). **Mary Evans Picture Library:** (b). **205 Alamy Stock Photo:** Julian Ingram (cl); Pillyphotos (cra). **Rex Shutterstock:** Gavin Roberts / Future Publishing / iPad® is a trademark of Apple Inc., registered in the U.S. and other countries. (br). **206 Alamy Stock Photo:** Lynden Pioneer Museum (tl); Yakoniva (br). **Getty Images:** Science & Society Picture Library (c). **207 Alamy Stock Photo:** Design Pics Inc (br); Granger Historical Picture Archive (tc); D. Hurst (cl). **iStockphoto.com:** Gratomlin (tr). **208 Alamy Stock Photo:** Heritage Image Partnership Ltd (c); Science History Images (bl). **Getty Images:** Yasuhide Fumoto (tr). **209 Alamy Stock Photo:** Tracey Lane (bl). **Dreamstime.com:** Bazruh (cb). **Getty Images:** STR (br). © 2019 The LEGO Group: (t). **210 Alamy Stock Photo:** Chris Willson (ca, bc). **Getty Images:** GamesMaster Magazine (cr). **National Museum of American History / Smithsonian Institution:** (clb). **211 Alamy Stock Photo:** B Christopher (cra); Mouse in the House (tc); Oredia (b). **212 Alamy Stock Photo:** ART Collection (cla). **Getty Images:** Otto Herschan (bl); Science & Society Picture Library (cr). **212–213 Mary Evans Picture Library:** INTERFOTO / Sammlung Rauch (c). **213 123RF.com:** Alexghidan89 (c). **Ningbo JT Intelligent Sanitary Ware Technology Co., Ltd.:** (br). **214 Alamy Stock Photo:** Neil Baylis (cl); John Frost Newspapers (br). **Getty Images:** Science & Society Picture Library (bl). **215 Alamy Stock Photo:** XiXinXing (br). **Getty Images:** Lambert (tr); Science & Society Picture Library (bc). **Mary Evans Picture Library:** Illustrated London News Ltd (cl). **216–217 Science Photo Library:** US PATENT AND TRADEMARK OFFICE. **218 123RF.com:** vitalily73 (tr). **Dreamstime.com:** Raja Rc (crb). **Getty Images:** Topical Press Agency (c). **Mary Evans Picture Library:** Illustrated London News Ltd (clb). **219 Bridgeman Images:** Peter Newark American Pictures (tr). **Dreamstime.com:** Ilja Mašík (c). **220 Depositphotos Inc:** pp_scout (tr). **Getty Images:** H. Armstrong Roberts / ClassicStock (cb). **iStockphoto.com:** Kyoshino (crb). **Science Photo Library:** (clb). **The Metropolitan Museum of Art:** Gift of J. Pierpont Morgan, 1917 (c). **221 123RF.com:** Ellirra (tl). **Alamy Stock Photo:** Igor Kardasov (cr). **Getty Images:** POWER AND SYRED / SCIENCE PHOTO LIBRARY (cb). **222–223 Getty Images:** Science Photo Library - SCIEPRO. **223 Alamy Stock Photo:** Phanie (cb/eye); Kumar Sriskandan (cb). **iStockphoto.com:** Annebaek (clb). **224 Dorling Kindersley:** Science Museum, London (crb). **Getty Images:** Petershort (cl); Ariel Skelley (bl). **Wellcome Images http://creativecommons. org/licenses/by/4.0/:** (tr). **225 Getty Images:** Hero Images (tl); Alfred Pasieka / SCIENCE PHOTO LIBRARY (r). **226 Alamy Stock Photo:** Science History Images (c). **Getty Images:** Paul Popper / Popperfoto (bc). **227 Dorling Kindersley:** RGB Research Limited (tr). **Science Photo Library:** Library Of Congress (clb). **Wellcome Images http://creativecommons. org/licenses/by/4.0/:** (c). **228 Getty Images:** Science & Society Picture Library (ca, bl). **228–229 Getty Images:** Universal Images Group (b). **229 Depositphotos Inc:** Simpson33 (crb). **Getty Images:** Science & Society Picture Library (tl). **iStockphoto.com:** Annebaek (tr). **230 Alamy Stock Photo:** Heritage Image Partnership Ltd (clb). **Wellcome Images http:// creativecommons.org/licenses/by/4.0/:** Science Museum, London (ca). **230–231 Wellcome Images http://creativecommons. org/licenses/by/4.0/:** Science Museum, London (c). **231 Getty Images:** BSIP (tr); Echo (cr). **Wellcome Images http://creativecommons. org/licenses/by/4.0/:** Science Museum, London (tl). **232 Alamy Stock Photo:** Everett Collection Inc (bl). **Getty Images:** Denver Post (tl); Science & Society Picture Library (cr). **233 Alamy Stock Photo:** Joe Loncraine (br); Kumar Sriskandan (bl). **Getty Images:** Business Wire (tr). **Wellcome Images http://creativecommons. org/licenses/by/4.0/:** Science Museum, London (tl). **234 Alamy Stock Photo:** Pictorial Press Ltd (clb). **Dorling Kindersley:** The Science Museum, London (r). **Wellcome Images http:// creativecommons.org/licenses/by/4.0/:** Science Museum, London (tl). **235 Alamy Stock Photo:** The Granger Collection (clb). **Science Photo Library:** Custom Medical Stock Photo (tl); Dr Tony Brain & David Parker (br). **236 Depositphotos Inc:** Monkeybusiness (tr). **Getty Images:** Bettmann (b). **237 123RF.com:** Evgeniya Kramar (c); Tyler Olson (br). **Alamy Stock Photo:** Lowefoto (cla). **Wellcome Images http://creativecommons.org/licenses/by/4.0/:** Science Museum, London (tr). **238 Alamy Stock Photo:** Granger Historical Picture Archive (cl). **National Museum of American History / Smithsonian Institution:** (crb). **Science & Society Picture Library:** Science Museum (bl). **239 Alamy Stock Photo:** Phanie (cla). **Science Photo Library:** Peter Menzel (b). **240–241 Wellcome Images http://creativecommons. org/licenses/by/4.0/:** David Gregory & Debbie Marshall. **242 Getty Images:** Culture Club (bl); Science & Society Picture Library (c). **Wellcome Images http://creativecommons.org/licenses/ by/4.0/:** Wellcome Collection (tl). **243 Reuters:** Khaled Abdullah (br). **Science Photo Library:** TSGT. DOUGLAS K. LINGEFELT, US AIR FORCE (tr); NIBSC (cl). **244 Getty Images:** Douglas Miller (cla); Science & Society Picture Library (crb, bc). **244–245 Getty Images:** Heritage Images (c). **245 Alamy Stock Photo:** The Granger Collection (cr). **246 Getty Images:** Science & Society Picture Library (tr). **Wellcome Images http://creativecommons.org/licenses/ by/4.0/:** Wellcome Collection (clb). **246–247 Wellcome Images http://creativecommons. org/licenses/by/4.0/:** Science Museum, London (b). **247 Getty Images:** Barcin (cl); Science Photo Library - PASIEKA (tl). **Science Photo Library:** British Dental Association Museum (r). **248 Alamy Stock Photo:** Interfoto (cla). **Getty Images:** Science & Society Picture Library (cb); Thomas Trutschel (br). **Science Photo Library:** (cra). **249 Alamy Stock Photo:** WENN Ltd (bc). **Getty Images:** Martin Hunter (r). **Science Photo Library:** Hank Morgan (cl). **250–251 NASA:** NASA / JPL-Caltech. **251 NASA:** (ca, ca/ISS). **Science Photo Library:** Babak Tafreshi (cla). **252 ESO:** ESO / J. Emerson / VISTA. (cra). **Getty Images:** SSPL (cla). **Science & Society Picture Library:** Science Museum (ca). **252–253 ESO:** ESO / F. Kamphues (c). **253 Alamy Stock Photo:** Archive PL (tr). **Getty Images:** Science & Society Picture Library (cra). **NASA:** (crb). **254 Alamy Stock Photo:** The Granger Collection (c); ZUMA Press, Inc. (br). **Getty Images:** Science & Society Picture Library (bc). **SuperStock:** Iberfoto (tl). **255 Alamy Stock Photo:** NG Images (cl). **ESO:** (bc). **NASA:** (tr). **256–257 ESO:** ESO / B. Tafreshi (twanight.org). **258 Getty Images:** Alinari Archives (br); Print Collector (cl); Stocktrek Images (cr). **258–259 Wellcome Images http://creativecommons.org/licenses/ by/4.0/:** (c). **259 Depositphotos Inc:** Prill (cra). **260 Alamy Stock Photo:** SPUTNIK (crb). **ESA:** ESA / CNES / ARIANESPACE-Optique Video du CSG, P. Baudon (bl). **Science Photo Library:** Detlev Van Ravenswaay (t). **261 ESA:** ESA / ATG medialab (t). **NASA:** (clb). **262 Getty Images:** Science & Society Picture Library (cla). **Science Photo Library:** US GEOLOGICAL SURVEY (crb); US AIR FORCE (clb). **263 DLR (CC-BY 3.0):** (b). **NASA:** (tr). **Science Photo Library:** NASA (cl). **264 Getty Images:** SSPL (crb). **NASA:** (cl). **National Air and Space Museum, Smithsonian Institution:** (bc). **265 Alamy Stock Photo:** Everett Collection Inc (tl); imageBROKER (b). **266–267 ESA. 268 Getty Images:** SSPL (cl); Sovfoto / UIG (bl). **Rex Shutterstock:** Sovfoto / Universal Images Group (tr). **269 Alamy Stock Photo:** Newscom (2/ca); SpaceX (ca); PJF Military Collection (cra). **NASA:** (l). **270 Alamy Stock Photo:** RGB Ventures / SuperStock (cr). **Getty Images:** Hulton-Deutsch Collection / CORBIS (l). **271 Alamy Stock Photo:** NG Images (b). **Getty Images:** Stephane Corvaja / ESA (l). **NASA:** JPL / Martha Heil (tc). **Rex Shutterstock:** Scaled Composites (cr). **272 Getty Images:** SSPL (cla). **National Air and Space Museum, Smithsonian Institution:** (r). **273 Getty Images:** Scott Andrews (c). **NASA:** (clb, crb). **Science Photo Library:** Detlev Van Ravenswaay (tl). **274 ESA:** ESA / NASA (bc). **NASA:** (cr). **Science Photo Library:** SPUTNIK (cl). **275 Getty Images:** AFP (bl). **NASA:** (t). **Science Photo Library:** SPUTNIK (br). **276 Getty Images:** SVF2 (tr). **NASA:** (bl). **Rex Shutterstock:** Sovfoto / Universal Images Group (c). **276–277 NASA:** (b). **277 NASA:** (ca, tr). **278 NASA:** (l, crb, bl). **279 NASA:** (tl, cra). **Rex Shutterstock:** George Frey (b). **280 ESA:** ESA–Pierre Carril (cla). **NASA:** (br); NASA / MSFC / David Higginbotham (cb). **281 NASA:** Bill Stafford (c). **282 123RF.com:** Valentin Valkov (clb). **Alamy Stock Photo:** Jurate Buiviene (tr); sportpoint (bc). **282–283 Getty Images:** Shaunl (b). **283 Alamy Stock Photo:** Björn Wylezich (ca). **284 Alamy Stock Photo:** Granger Historical Picture Archive (c). **NASA:** ARC (crb). **Science Photo Library:** GIPhotoStock (tl). **285 NASA:** (cl); JPL-Caltech / University of Arizona (tl); JPL-Caltech / MSSS (r). **286 ESA:** (tr). **NASA:** NSSDCA / COSPAR (c, bc). **286–287 NASA:** JPL-Caltech / SwRI / MSSS / Kevin M. Gill (b). **287 Getty Images:** ESA (tc). **NASA:** Johns Hopkins University Applied Physics Laboratory / Southwest Research Institute (JHUAPL / SwRI) (cr); NASA / JPL (cl). **292 Getty Images:** Science & Society Picture Library (bc). **293 Getty Images:** Chris Hunter (tc). **294 Alamy Stock Photo:** Granger Historical Picture Archive (bl). **Dreamstime.com:** Tamas Bedecs (tc). **295 ESO:** ESO / F. Kamphues (br). **296 Dreamstime.com:** Alexander Kirch / Audioundwerbung (tr). **297 Getty Images:** Alfred Pasieka / SCIENCE PHOTO LIBRARY (br). **298 Alamy Stock Photo:** Mouse in the House (bc). **299 Dreamstime.com:** Anurak Anachai (tl); Mphoto2 (cr). **300 Dorling Kindersley:** Ernie Eagle (br). **301 Depositphotos Inc:** Mimadeo (br)

All other images © Dorling Kindersley
For further information see:
www.dkimages.com